P9-BIO-334

The COMPLETE IDIOT'S GUIDE TO FrontPage

by Jennifer Fulton and Nat Gertler

que®

A Division of Macmillan Publishing
201 West 103rd Street, Indianapolis, IN 46290 USA

For my Dad, whom I miss very much. *Jennifer Fulton*

To caffeine, without which my portion of this book would not have been possible.
Nat Gertler

©1995 Que™ Corporation

All rights reserved. No part of this book shall be reproduced, stored in a retrieval system, or transmitted by any means, electronic, mechanical, photocopying, recording, or otherwise, without written permission from the publisher. No patent liability is assumed with respect to the use of the information contained herein. Although every precaution has been taken in the preparation of this book, the publisher and authors assume no responsibility for errors or omissions. Neither is any liability assumed for damages resulting from the use of the information contained herein. For information, address Que corporation, 201 W. 103rd Street, Indianapolis, IN 46290. You may reach Que's direct sales line by calling 1-800-428-5331.

International Standard Book Number: 0-7897-0928-7
Library of Congress Catalog Card Number: 96-69947

98 97 96   8 7 6 5 4 3 2 1

Interpretation of the printing code: the rightmost number of the first series of numbers is the year of the book's printing; the rightmost number of the second series of numbers is the number of the book's printing. For example, a printing code of 96-1 shows that the first printing of the book occurred in 1996.

Screen reproductions in this book were created by means of the program Collage Complete from Inner Media, Inc., Hollis, NH.

Printed in the United States of America.

Publisher
Roland Elgey

Editorial Services Director
Elizabeth Keaffaber

Publishing Director
Lynn E. Zingraf

Managing Editor
Michael Cunningham

Acquistions Coordinator
Martha O'Sullivan

Senior Product Development Specialist
Lorna Gentry

Production Editor
Mark Enochs

Director of Marketing
Lynn E. Zingraf

Cover Designers
Dan Armstrong
Barbara Kordesh

Designer
Barbara Kordesh

Illustrations
Judd Winick

Technical Specialist
Nadeem Muhammed

Indexer
Cheryl Dietsch

Production Team
Angela Calvert
Kim Cofer
Tricia Flodder
Beth Rago
Megan Wade

Special thanks to Kyle Bryant for ensuring the technical accuracy of this book.

We'd Like to Hear from You!

As part of our continuing effort to produce books of the highest possible quality, Que would like to hear your comments. To stay competitive, we *really* want you, as a computer book reader and user, to let us know what you like or dislike most about this book or other Que products.

You can mail comments, ideas, or suggestions for improving future editions to the address below, or send us a fax at (317) 581-4663. For the online inclined, Macmillan Computer Publishing has a forum on CompuServe (type **GO QUEBOOKS** at any prompt) through which our staff and authors are available for questions and comments. The address of our Internet site is **http://www.mcp.com** (World Wide Web).

In addition to exploring our forum, please feel free to contact me personally to discuss your opinions of this book: on CompuServe, I'm at 75703, 3251, and on the Internet, I'm **lgentry@que.mcp.com**.

Thanks in advance—your comments will help us to continue publishing the best books available on computer topics in today's market.

Lorna Gentry
Senior Product Development Specialist
Que Corporation
201 W. 103rd Street
Indianapolis, Indiana 46290
USA

Contents at a Glance

Contents

Introduction

You know you're a pretty intelligent computer user. It's nothing to whip out a memo with your word processor or crunch some numbers in your spreadsheet. You can even surf the Net without breaking into too much of a sweat.

But somehow, looking at other people's sites on the Internet isn't as thrilling as it once was, is it? Nope, you're ready to have your own say. You want to get into this web publishing thing.

At least, that's what you thought until you started asking around and discovered a mess of techno babble about HTML, JavaScript, gateways, proxy servers, and such. You may have even been close to chucking the whole idea of web page publishing until someone recommended FrontPage.

FrontPage is simple and easy to use. Exactly how *simple* and how *easy* depends on your own level of experience with word processors and the Internet in general, but in any case, *The Complete Idiot's Guide to FrontPage* makes the whole experience as painless as possible.

The Ten-Minute, Hassle-Free, Low-Fat Introduction to FrontPage

FrontPage takes the hassle out of programming your web pages by letting you create them, on-screen, in about the same way you might create a report using a word processor. FrontPage also takes the grief-factor out of managing and maintaining your site once you create it. All-in-all, it's the non-nerds answer to web publishing.

As you can see in the figure, FrontPage has almost as many personalities as Sybil: FrontPage Explorer, FrontPage Editor, the Personal Web Server, and the To Do List. Before you start creating your own web, let's get the intros over with, so you'll know what you're going to do with the four faces of FrontPage.

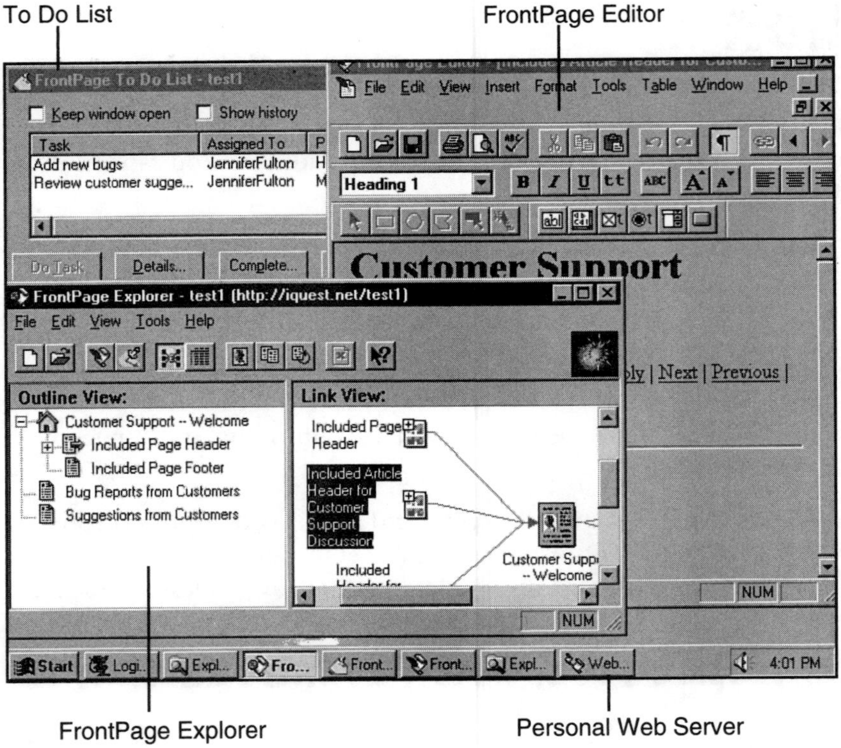

The four faces of FrontPage.

Construct Your Web with FrontPage Explorer

You start out by creating your web site using FrontPage Explorer. You use the Explorer to set up and view the structure of your web—what hierarchy the pages fall in, how the pages relate to each other, and what links to what. As you move into the next chapter of this book, you'll see that FrontPage Explorer bears an uncanny resemblance to its cousin, Windows Explorer, which you may have met before.

FrontPage Explorer has different views, which will need some explaining later on. But in the beginning, you won't be spending a lot of time in FP Explorer, so we can put off that lecture for awhile. If you're overly curious, you can jump over to Chapter 21.

Create Your Web Pages in FrontPage Editor

To create your web pages, you use FrontPage Editor. The Editor looks and acts a lot like an ordinary word processor, such as Microsoft Word. (Microsoft did that on purpose, to make creating web pages easier for those people who don't type text for a living.) With the Editor, you can easily add text, graphics, and other cool stuff to a web page.

Test Drive Your Web on the Personal Web Server

The Personal Web Server is like your Internet flight simulator. It lets you see your web work in actual Internet conditions, so you can test some of your links and such, without actually logging onto the Internet.

You won't mess around with the Personal Web Server much, since it starts up automatically, whenever you start working on your web. It then minimizes itself, remaining in the background while you work.

However, if you plan on publishing your web site on an *intranet* (a kind of private company-wide internetwork) you can later use the Personal Web Server to "run" your web site locally.

What's an Intranet?

You already know what the Internet is. An *intranet*, on the other hand, is a private (company-type) network that uses internet technology to enable companies to make vast amounts of information available to their employees in an easy-to-access, linked format.

Keep Your Web Shipshape with the To Do List

With the To Do List, you can keep track of maintenance tasks for your web and set priorities. A central list of tasks is especially handy if you're creating a web site with the help of a number of "cooks." With the To Do List, you can list your tasks and assign a particular "cook" to complete each one. (Then, you'll know who to yell at when something isn't done on time.)

What Makes FrontPage So Special

Now that you know what FrontPage is, you may want to know why it's so wonderful. Take a look at these FrontPage features:

- **No Messy codes to learn.** First, and probably most importantly, you don't have to learn bizarre HTML codes to create web pages with FrontPage. Nope, you simply type in your text, format it, and insert graphics—following the same process you might use to create a report in Microsoft Word—and FrontPage takes care of all the HTML nonsense for you. (You learn more about HTML in Chapter 1.)
- **Templates and wizards give you a jump-start to your web.** With FrontPage, you don't have to design your web site from scratch. FrontPage provides several

templates—prefab web sites in which you just fill in the blanks. Select a template, pop in the text and graphics for each web page, and you're basically done: FrontPage supplies the links between pages, the basic web structure, and all sorts of other cool elements.

If you want a slightly less assembly-line look to your site, you can use a wizard. FrontPage Wizards walk you through a series of dialog boxes in which you can choose individual options for your site. You place the order, and FrontPage delivers the goods.

- **End form fear and table terror forever.** You want to put a form on a web page that allows your readers to tell you what they think of your site? No problem! Currently, FrontPage is the only web page creation program that lets you add forms and process information your readers send back to you. No programming, no fuss, no muss. Tables are a snap to add in FrontPage, too, so you don't have to worry about going through a messy HTML process to add them to your pages.
- **Leave the difficult business for the WebBots.** WebBots (the name stands for "web robots," by the way) take care of the nasty chores you might have to do if you want to create a certain web page using another editor. This includes tasks such as creating a program to take the information entered onto a form and process it. With FrontPage, you hand the form over to a WebBot, and it takes care of the messy details. You'll learn more about WebBots in Chapter 17.

And there's more! With FrontPage and the amazing tricks you learn in *The Complete Guide to FrontPage*, you can:

- Snarf the best pages, graphic images, and entire sites from the web and use them as your guides to greatness.
- Add text, graphics, and sound to your web pages.
- Add lines, lists, and other cool stuff.
- Link multiple web pages together.
- Add pizzazz with forms, tables, frames, and so on.
- Publish your creation on the Web.
- Reorganize your web site as your needs change.

If FrontPage Is So Easy, Why Do I Need This Book?

Well, FrontPage *is* the simplest web site creation tool on the market, but there's still a lot you can learn about creating the perfect web site.

Even so, you don't want to waste time learning all that web publishing techno-crud, or you wouldn't have picked FrontPage as your editor in the first place.

What you need is a simple, easy-to-read guide that helps you get your web up and running quickly. You can learn the fancy stuff as you go along.

And that's where *The Complete Idiot's Guide to FrontPage* comes in.

The Complete Idiot's Guide to Skipping Chapters

You'll probably want to read this book all the way through, but don't feel that you necessarily have to read every chapter *in order*. If there's something you should have read that was explained in some previous chapter, I'll tell you about it so you can review that chapter if you want to.

But for now, here's what's coming up so you can skip the things you don't want to deal with right now.

Part 1: Up and Running with Front Page

This part's full of need-to-knows, including basic skills such as creating your first web. Don't skip this one!

Part 2: Creating Your First Web Page

Here's where you get into some real nitty-gritty: adding text and text formatting to your home page, creating lists, and drawing lines. And along the way, you can even add a fancy graphic or two.

You'll also learn how to add sound files to your home page and to import files into your web. To wrap things up, you'll learn how to spell check your creations (so you can avoid any embarrassments), add background images, and change text colors.

Part 3: Time to Start Planning Your Web Site

After fine-tuning your home page in Part 2, you'll be ready to add more pages to your web and to link them together. So in this part, that's exactly what you'll learn.

In addition, you'll learn some techniques for designing the perfect web site.

Part 4: Adding "Wow" to Your Web Pages

In this part, you learn only fun things, such as how to link a graphic image to another web page by giving it a *hotspot*. You'll also learn how to set up some tables, add forms, and divide your web page with frames.

Later in Part 4, you'll learn all about WebBots, and how you can use them to add fancies to your web site, such as toolbars and forms.

Part 5: Creating Templates and Specialty Pages

Here, you learn how to design your own templates that you can use to create webs. You'll also learn how to create some special interest web pages, such as a discussion page and a table of contents.

Part 6: Publishing and Maintaining Your Web Site

What's the use of creating great web pages if no one gets to see them? Well, in Part 6, you'll learn how to publish your masterpiece on the Web. You'll also learn how to maintain your web site and to make changes as needed (or as required by your boss-with-too-much-time-on-his-hands).

And, if you share responsibilities for the web with several co-workers, you'll find a chapter here on how to share the workload without losing your hair.

Conventions Are Not Just for Politicians

Politicians, carpet salesmen, and Amway dealers aren't the only ones with conventions: book publishers have them, too. So, as you read this book, keep these things in mind:

- Things you should type or menu options you should select appear in **bold**. For example, you might be reading along, and run into the following sentence: Open the **File** menu and select **Open Location**. Just do as it says, and nobody will get hurt.
- There's more than one way to do just about everything. For example, to open a file, you could select the File, Open command, or click a button. I typically use the simplest way to do anything, so clicking a button (if there is one for that command) is probably what I'll tell you to do. The name of the button, by the way, will also appear in **bold**, as in: "Click the **Open** button."
- If you have to press two keys together to get something to work, the keys will appear with a plus sign between them, for example, **Ctrl+C**. Of course, since the keys are something you have to press, they'll appear in bold, too.

Check This Out

In these boxes, you'll find a hodgepodge of information, including easy-to-understand definitions, time-saving tips, hints for staying out of trouble, and amusing anecdotes from your authors.

Technical Twaddle

These boxes contain technical background fodder; feel free to skip these boxes unless you're truly interested in nerdy details.

Acknowledgments

I want to thank the great people at Que for allowing me to write a computer book for you. Special thanks to Martha O'Sullivan for her support during the writing of this book, which occurred during the hectic (but joyous) move to our new home.
Jennifer Fulton.

Thanks to Martha O'Sullivan, Lorna Gentry, and San Dee Phillips for dragging me into this and seeing me through it.
Nat Gertler

Common Trademark Courtesies

As a courtesy to computer and program manufacturers who complicate our lives but otherwise cause no serious harm, we have decided to list their trademarks here (so you'll know who's responsible). In addition, terms that we suspect are trademarks or service marks have been appropriately capitalized. Of course, we at Que Corporation cannot attest to the accuracy of this information, so don't stake your life's fortune on it.

Microsoft Windows 95 and Microsoft FrontPage are registered trademarks of Microsoft Corporation.

Netscape and Netscape Navigator are trademarks of Netscape Communications.

Part 1
Up and Running with FrontPage

You've traveled up and down the cyberhighway, chatting with complete strangers until well past midnight. You've jumped through links, zipped out e-mail, and even taken home a file or two. The Internet is your universe, and you are fluent in Internet-ese.

Web publishing is a whole other planet, and you are a publishing newbie. In this part, you'll wave good-bye to newbie status as you learn how to create your first web site. And along the way, you'll learn something about FrontPage, the World Wide Web, and HTML, too.

Chapter 1

From Desktop to Webtop with FrontPage

By the End of This Chapter, You'll Be Able To...

- Understand what FrontPage does
- Understand what FrontPage doesn't
- Figure out the basic steps for creating your first Web

As you learned in the Introduction (assuming you didn't skip it in your haste to jump into the web publishing business), FrontPage consists of four parts:

With **FrontPage Explorer** (a fancy version of Windows Explorer), you create and manage your web site.

With **FrontPage Editor**, you create and edit your web pages just as you might use a word processor to create and edit documents.

With the **To Do List**, you keep track of all the things you want to do to your web—which you may or may not be able to actually find the time to complete.

And finally, with **Personal Web Server** running in the background, you can use your Web browser to see *exactly* how your new web pages will look out on the Web *without actually getting on the Net to do it.* (More on this in a minute.)

In the grand and complex world of web publishing, where exactly does FrontPage fit in?

How Does FrontPage Protect Me from HTML, CGI, and Other Awful Internet Acronyms?

Web pages are simply text documents that happen to look real good on-screen, thanks to HTML.

HTML (short for HyperText Markup Language) is the method with which text documents are coded so that a Web browser can display them on-screen in a graphical way—like a magazine: with graphic images, varying sizes of text, and dynamic use of colors. Learning and entering HTML codes can be a real pain. But thanks to Microsoft FrontPage, you don't have to bother learning funky HTML codes to create your Web pages.

How Does HTML Work?

The HTML commands mark each element on a web page (such as a headline, a bulleted list, or a graphic image). The Web browser, after reading these marks, knows how to display each element. It's easy for your Web browser to identify HTML commands (commonly called *tags*) within a Web document, because each command (tag) appears neatly in-between the < and > characters, as in the tag, <H1>, which designates a level one heading.

With Windows point-and-click technology, you can easily develop your web site—graphically, right on-screen. As you place information on your web page (a heading for example), FrontPage converts your choices into the proper HTML codes, which work just like any other web page.

Room to Grow

Of course, as you grow into your role as a big-time Web publisher, you may encounter some unusual HTML codes which you'd like to add to your Web pages. No problem; FrontPage lets you add such codes easily, as you'll learn in Chapter 15.

HTML is cool, but web page designers soon learned its limitations. In order to design an *interactive* Web site capable of accepting user input, such as someone's name and mailing address, the designer not only had to mess around with nasty HTML codes, but something called the Common Gateway Interface (CGI to its friends). For example, if you wanted to get feedback from your users through some kind of online form, you'd need CGI to do it.

CGI commands are complex and difficult to get right; lucky for you, FrontPage takes care of this nonsense for you. Whenever you need to gather input from a user, you simply create a *form*, which will look kind of like a dialog box pasted to the screen—complete with option buttons, list boxes, text boxes, or whatever you need.

To process the information from your form, you select one of the WebBots (preconstructed CGI programs) supplied with FrontPage to handle its particular type of data. The WebBot then uses the form data to perform a related task. You can have it save the data for you in a separate HTML page that can be viewed by you or by other users (if needed), in a web page linked to your web site.

Is There Anything FrontPage Can't Do?

Uh, although FrontPage is a ten in the ease-of-use department, it's only fair that you know *what it can't do*.

For instance, FrontPage does not include a Web browser—and without one, you cannot see your web page exactly as it will appear to your users. Without a Web browser, you cannot test your links and your forms.

No, the FrontPage Editor *does not* display your pages exactly as your viewers will see them—close, but no cigar. So, the bottom line: you'll need to keep your own Web browser handy—it doesn't have to be Internet Explorer (Microsoft's Web browser), though it can be. Netscape Navigator or NCSA Mosaic will work just fine, thank-you very much. (This shouldn't be much of a problem, since I'm sure you already have a browser and that you know how to use it, or you wouldn't be about to embark on the web publishing business.)

Also, you may have heard that FrontPage contains something called a Personal Web Server. As you've already learned, the Personal Web Server allows FrontPage to fool your Web browser into thinking it's connected to the Internet, so that you can view your own web pages *as they will appear to your users* without actually connecting to the Internet and running up a big bill. So, contrary to what the name implies, the Personal Web Server will *not* allow you to create your own private web server with which you can gain dominance over the World Wide Web. (However, you can use it to gain dominance over your company's intranet, if you like, by publishing your web site there, and not out on the WWW.)

There are some additional things that you should be aware of:

- You can't create web sites with more than about 1,000 web pages or so, because FrontPage won't handle sites that large. (And you were going to create the next www.microsoft.com., right?) You can, however, create multiple web sites and split up your information between all of them.
- You can't edit your graphic images with FrontPage. No real problem here, since there are plenty of good graphic editors (if you're into that sort of thing, that is) that you might use instead, such as LView Pro and Paint Shop Pro.

- FrontPage doesn't support the use of Java applets or JavaScripts in its web pages, although chances are, with as popular as Java is, FrontPage is sure to support it soon.

A Game Plan for Creating a Web Site

Now that you have some idea where FrontPage fits into the whole web publishing scheme, you're prepared to use FrontPage for creating a web site.

Here are the basic steps:

1. First, you use FrontPage Explorer to create an almost-empty web. An *almost-empty web?* Well, you see, when you create a web with FrontPage Explorer, you don't actually start from scratch. That's because Microsoft has thoughtfully provided you with *templates* (think of them as partially completed webs) and *wizards* (web creation guides) to help you through the birthing process. After you use FrontPage Explorer, you'll end up with a nice (but basically empty) web *structure*. (You'll learn more about these templates and wizards in the Chapter 2.)
2. Next, you use FrontPage Editor to fill in the blank web pages with text, graphics, and other neat stuff. You can also use the Editor to add more pages to your web as needed.
3. As you create new web pages, you add links to connect them to the other pages in your web. Now, when you create your web site using a template or a wizard, FrontPage not only creates the empty pages you requested, but it adds the proper links so your users can move back and forth between them. At this stage of the game, you're adding links to the pages you create manually, as well as links to pages out on the Web (or to other web goodies such as sound or graphics files).
4. When you're ready, test your web by viewing it with your Web browser, testing each link, each form, and so on. You'll learn more about this in Part 6.
5. Finally, you *publish* your web. Publishing is the process with which you copy your web site onto a host's computer. (You'll learn how to locate a host and copy your files in Chapter 21.)

Enough explanations—let's get to it! Now, because you should have some structure before you can add any content to your web, the next chapter begins by introducing you to FrontPage Explorer (Not to be confused with Windows Explorer, or the Ford Explorer for that matter. It seems that Microsoft has more explorers than Spain did in the 15th Century).

The Least You Need to Know

Where does FrontPage fit into the world of web publishing? Here are a few ways:

- FrontPage does not require you to mess around with HTML codes like many editors do.
- After you design a web page and save it, FrontPage converts your selections into HTML so that the resulting file looks just as if you did all that hard work yourself!
- FrontPage also takes the burden of CGI programming chores off your shoulders, with its automated WebBots.
- With its toolbars and graphical environment, FrontPage makes it easy to design great-looking web pages.

Chapter 2

Creating Your Web Site with FrontPage Explorer

By the End of This Chapter, You'll Be Able To...

- Create a web site so you can start making web pages
- Worry about web structure after you feel comfortable with FrontPage
- Open, close, and save your web site
- Get your web feet wet

In this chapter, start thinking of yourself as a web designer, since it's here that you begin the creation process for your first web site.

Yep, I know that all you *really* want to do is to create your first web *page*, so you'll be glad to know that, in creating your web site, FrontPage creates a home page for you. (A *home page* is the front door to your web; typically, all your users will pass through the home page to connect to the other pages in your web.) Of course, the home page is pretty blank, but you'll soon learn how to fill it with all those cool things you find out on the Web.

So, let's get this web site creation nonsense out of the way, so you can start the real work.

Meet FrontPage Explorer

Before You Start You should install FrontPage on your computer; if you haven't, check out the "Installing FrontPage" appendix in the back of the book.

To create your web, use FrontPage Explorer. You may have started FrontPage Explorer immediately following setup. If not, start FrontPage Explorer now by clicking the **Start** menu, selecting **Programs**, **Microsoft FrontPage**, and **FrontPage Explorer**. Soon, the FrontPage Explorer window shown here appears.

You won't see much at this point, since you don't actually have a web. You'll take care of that little matter in just a minute.

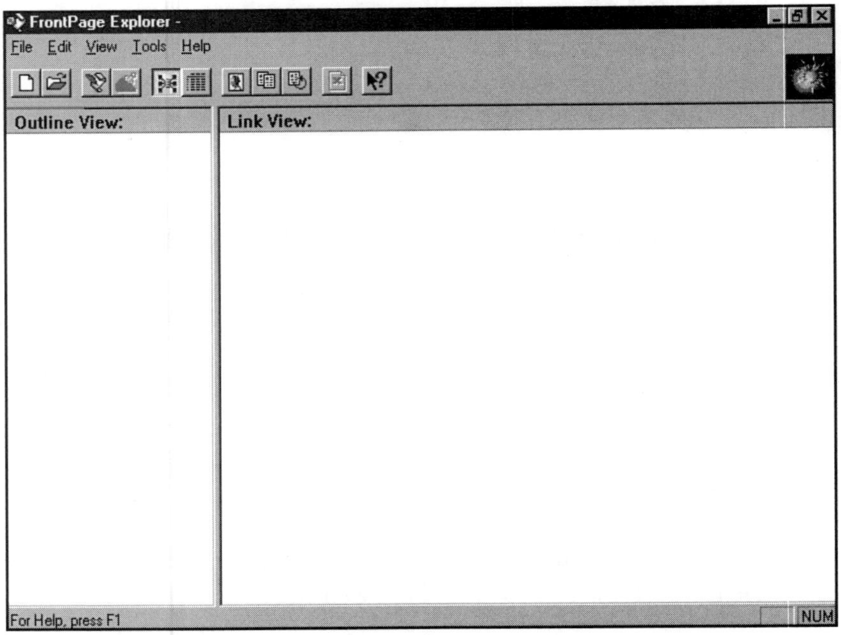

May I introduce the great Explorer?

Ready, Set, Go, Create!

Yes, it's true, FrontPage provides many web site *templates* (fill-in-the-blank web sites) and *wizards* (web creation guides) with which you can base your own web site. But to make the most of them, you have to have some idea about how you want your web site to look—*and to do that,* you have to spend some time organizing your information and planning a good strategy.

Eventually, you will, at some point, have to deal with the mountains of data you want to throw onto the Internet. But, if all you want to do *now* is to create a measly little home page so you can feel like a big-time web publisher, well, dat don't take no plannin' at all.

But What About My Web Site?

It doesn't take any planning to create a web site with just one page, your home page. But, when you get to the point where you want to add more pages to your web, well, that's when you need to think long and hard about how you want to structure and organize your information. If you want to deal with all of that stuff *right now*, great; just skip over to Part 3 first, before you continue with this chapter.

However, if you're like most people, then you'd rather deal with the problem of organization later —after your new-guy-on-the-block jitters disappear. If so, then hang on, 'cause you're gonna create your first web site!

Creating Your First Web Site

While following the steps here, you'll notice that FrontPage provides many *templates and wizards* for your web creating soul. *Templates* (in case you've been asleep through most of the text so far) are blank, preconstructed web sites that you can select if they fit your need. A *wizard* is a guide that steps you through the process of creating a particular web, while allowing you to make certain creative selections.

Here's the problem: how can you select one of these puppies if you don't really know that much about web publishing yet? As mentioned earlier, you can easily put off the nasty problem of organizing and planning a big web site until you're ready. So to avoid thinking about all this web structure stuff, create your site using the Normal template, which creates your Web directory and an empty home page.

Here's how:

1. First, start FrontPage Explorer.
2. Open the **File** menu and select **New Web; or** you can click the **New Web** button.
3. Choose the **Normal Web** template and click **OK**.

Why Doesn't This Work?

You have to start Personal Web Server to create a web site, so make sure that it's running before you try to create one. I know, I said earlier that Personal Web Server starts up automatically—but in case there's a glitch, simply start it manually.

4. At this point, you'll be asked to supply a name for your web. You can name it anything you want, as long as the name doesn't include any nasty spaces. Click **OK**.

What's in a Name?

When naming your web, even though you may be using Windows 95, it's a good idea to maintain the old DOS naming conventions, since this name is used to create the directory in which your web files are stored. Just limit your name to no more than eight characters, with no spaces, and make your first character alphabetic. The name you create will be used as the name for a subdirectory of **\FrontPage Webs\Content** directory.

Congratulations; it's a web.

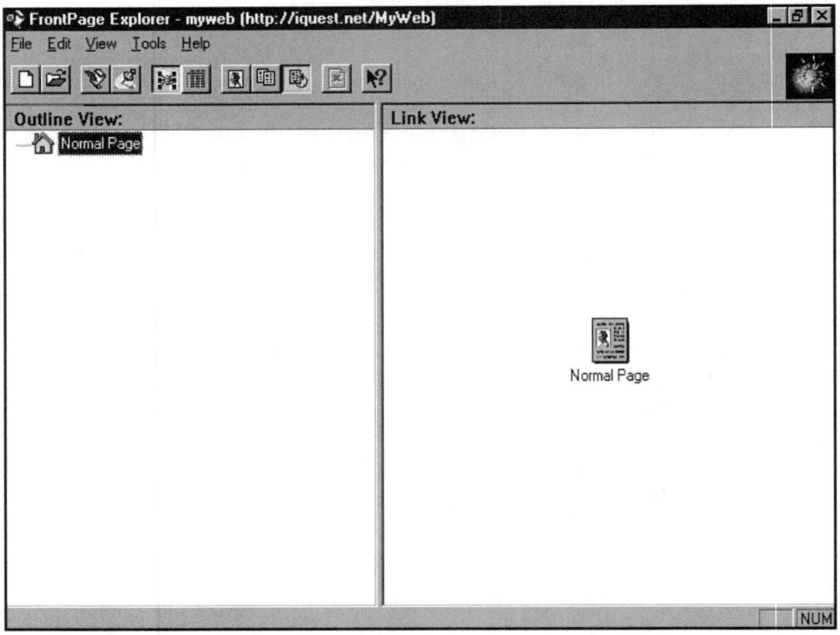

As your web evolves and grows, keep in mind that FrontPage allows you to create several different web sites. Simply repeat the steps. You can even link these various web sites together if you want.

Switching subjects: When you choose the **Normal** template, FrontPage creates a web with a single page: your home page. Now that you have an actual web site with a web page, you can start messing it up (uh, adding text, graphics, and so on), which you'll learn how to do in Chapter 3.

As you read Part 2, keep in mind that when you get to the point where you want to add more pages to your web, you should take a break and read Part 3, where you'll learn how to organize your baby web.

But before you get into all that, you need to know how to close and save your new web.

Safety First

As you begin working in FrontPage Editor to create and change your various web pages, it's important that you always begin by starting FrontPage Explorer first. This will start the Personal Web Server as well. With both of these programs running, you can save the changes you make with the FrontPage Editor *properly*. If you try to use FrontPage Editor alone, you may mess up your web site and lose some of your work.

Saving, Opening, and Closing a Web

Actually, there's no way to save a web *per se*. That's because, quite simply, you didn't actually create a file when you created your web—instead, you created a *directory* into which all your web pages are saved. So, when you add pages and other parts to your web, and you save those in FrontPage Editor, that saves your web content.

To close a web you're working on, from FrontPage Explorer's **File** menu, select **Close Web**. Don't expect to see the usual **Do you really want to save this thing?** dialog box. But, don't panic. *Your work is automatically saved*—that is, the directory changes you've been making in FrontPage Explorer are saved.

And when you want to open a previously saved web, here's what you do:

1. From FrontPage Explorer's **File** menu, select **Open Web**. FrontPage displays the Open Web dialog box. Notice that this isn't your usual list of Windows 95 files.

2. If there's more than one Web server to which you've been given access, then you have to select the server you want to use. (Usually, all you'll see listed here is the name of the server through which you connect to the Internet.) From the Web Server list, choose the name of a Web server.
3. Click the **List Webs** button. Don't panic if FrontPage takes a minute to wake up. Eventually, the names of the webs you've created will appear in the **Webs** list.
4. Choose your web from this list and click **OK**. If you recently started your FrontPage session, you might see a security dialog box.
5. Enter your password, and click **OK**. In a moment, FrontPage will bring up the web you selected.

Remember, the content of your web site is saved in each of your web pages, which you'll create and edit with FrontPage Editor.

Good thing that's what you'll learn in the next chapter.

The Least You Need to Know

FrontPage Explorer is the main control program for the FrontPage system. You don't edit any web pages here, though you do create the structure for your web. While doing so, keep these things in mind:

- To create a web, you use FrontPage Explorer. To create web pages, use FrontPage Editor.
- Create the web by opening the **File** menu, selecting **New Web**, and selecting the web template or wizard you want to use. Enter a name for your web and click **OK**.
- To open an existing web, open the **File** menu and select **Open Web**. Select the web you want to open from the list, and click **OK**. You'll probably have to enter a password; do so, and click **OK**.
- To close a web, open the **File** menu and select **Close**.

Part 2
Creating Your First Web Page

You learned how to create a one-page web site in Part 1, and that was a good start. In Part 2, you'll add some amazing talents to your repertoire: adding text to your home page and formatting it, slapping in a couple of lists, adding lines to divide text into sections, and dropping in some cool graphics and sound files.

At the end of Part 2, put the polish on your creation by playing around with text and background colors. All in all, a pretty fun part.

TED DIDN'T KNOW WHAT THE CHICKENS WERE DOING ON HIS COMPUTER... BUT HE KNEW IT COULDN'T BE GOOD.
WINICK©

Chapter 3

Introducing FrontPage Editor

By the End of This Chapter, You'll Be Able to...

- Open a page from your web
- Open HTML and RTF files saved on your hard disk
- Open pages from other people's web sites
- Open your sentences with the word "open"
- Save your changes and close web pages

Once you create a basic web structure (by following the steps *you shouldn't have skipped* in Chapter 2), you can add pages to it. If you created your web using the Normal template (as suggested), then FrontPage created a home page for you (albeit an empty one). In this chapter, you'll learn how to edit your home page and any other pages you eventually add to your web.

To create your web, you used FrontPage Explorer. To create and edit web pages, FrontPage provides a different tool: FrontPage Editor.

Starting FrontPage Editor

To begin editing your baby web, start FrontPage Explorer, and open your web first. Then select the page you want to edit by clicking it. Next, open the **Edit** menu and select **Open**. FrontPage Editor opens with the selected web page, nice as you please.

Other Ways

Another way to open the page you want quickly is to double-click its icon (in the Link View) within FrontPage Explorer.

You can also click the **Show FrontPage Editor** button to open the editor, but you'll still have to open a page to edit manually. To do that, open the **File** menu and select **Open From Web**. Then select the page you want and click on **OK**.

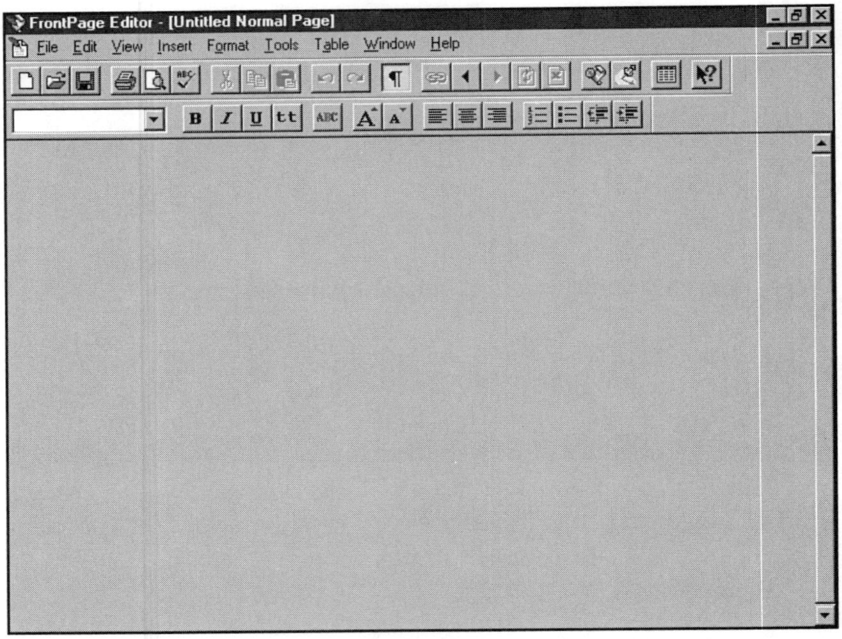

Web page ready to edit, sir!

Go ahead and open the home page for your web.

Feeling Homeless?

If you created your web using the Empty Web template, then at this point, you don't have a home page (or any page for that matter) to open. Skip to Chapter 12 for help in adding a page to your web.

What Are All Those Buttons?

FrontPage Editor is great because, like all my favorite toys, it has lots of *buttons*! The buttons appear on several Toolbars, as you can see in the next figure.

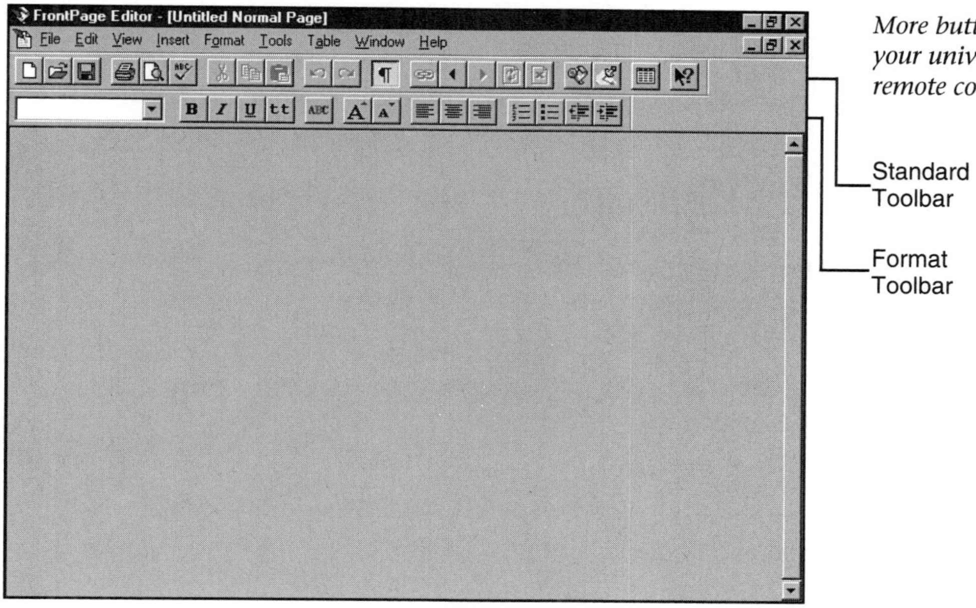

More buttons than your universal remote control.

You'll recognize most of the buttons if you've ever used a Microsoft product, such as Word or Excel. To figure out what a button is for, just point the mouse at it and you'll see an explanation of its purpose.

Get Rid of Those Unwanted Buttons Are there too many buttons, even for you? Well, you can remove unnecessary Toolbars by opening the **View** menu and selecting the one you want to get rid of. For example, since you won't be needing the Image or Forms Toolbars for awhile, you can get rid of them if you want.

Here's the short list of the buttons on the Standard Toolbar that you might not immediately recognize:

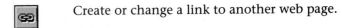

Create or change a link to another web page.

Move to the next page in the link history.

Move to a previous page in the link history.

Reload the current page.

Stop whatever is going on.

Start FrontPage Explorer.

Display the To Do List.

Insert a table at the cursor.

You'll probably recognize all the buttons on the Format Toolbar, but these guys:

Switch to a monospaced (typewriter) style font.

Change the color of text.

Make text bigger.

Make text smaller.

You'll learn about other toolbars, such as the Image and Forms Toolbars, as you move further into the creation of you web.

Saving Your Page and Closing It

After you learn to add text and other items to your home page in upcoming lessons, you'll want to save them (or risk losing the changes to the great beyond). Saving is the same as it is everywhere else in the universe: just click the **Save** button, or open the **File** menu and select **Save**. If you've never saved this particular page before, you'll have to give it a **Title** and a **URL.** The URL is basically the name of the page, relative to the directories on your web. For example, if you want to save this page to the root directory of the web, simply type in a name such as product1.htm. If you want to save it to another directory, enter that as part of the URL, like this: **/products/product1.htm**. This saves the current page in HTML format, to the indicated directory (in this example, the /JenWeb/ products directory) within the currently open web. The directory in which you want to save your page must already exist, because FrontPage can not create it. If you've added graphics to the page, you'll see additional dialog boxes asking if you want to save the graphics to your web or not.

Keeping It Secret

To hide your Web page from visitors, save it to the private directory. For example, you can type /_private/password.htm to keep a list of user passwords away from prying eyes. You might also want to save utility pages such as your banner and toolbar pages in the _private directory. (You'll learn more about banner and toolbar pages in Chapters 13 and 17.)

To save a page to the hard disk and not to your web (to *export* the file), in the Save As dialog box, click **As File**. To save the page as a template, click **As Template**. You'll want to know more than this before you try to create your own template; see Chapter 11 for more help.

Saving Time

You can save all open pages at one time by opening the **File** menu and selecting **Save All.**

To close a page once you're done with it, just click the **Close** button (in Windows 95, it's the X-thingie), or open the **File** menu and select **Close**. Have you made changes to this page that you haven't yet saved? That's okay because the File Fairy will appear, and ask if you want to correct your error and save your file. In addition, if you have any graphics that have been inserted into the page (and not yet saved), then the File Fairy will help you save them too.

Opening Your Page Later

How do you go back to some page you only *thought* you were through with? Well, there are several ways:

- *To open a page from one of your webs,* open the web site first, using FrontPage Explorer. Then, select the page you want to open, open the **Edit** menu, and select **Open**. If you already opened your web and you're working in FrontPage Editor, simply click the **Open** button to open the page.
- *To open a Web page from your hard disk,* open the **File** menu and select **Open File**. You'll see the usual File Open dialog box. Select your file and click **OK**. You can also open RTF (*rich text format*) or text files from this same dialog box by selecting the appropriate option from the list box.
- *To open somebody else's page on the WWW,* connect to the Internet first. Then open the **File** menu and select **Open Location**. Enter the URL address of the page you want, and FrontPage snarfs it from the Web, converting it as needed into FrontPage format for display. The page is not really copied to your web, however. If you try to save this page, FrontPage will comply, but what it's really doing is copying the file's location on the WWW. In other words, FP creates a link in your web to the page. To view the page while working in your web, you need to be connected to the Internet.

  If you want to copy a WWW page into your web, or copy an entire Web site to your hard disk, you can, but it's tricky. See Chapter 11 for the how-to's.

FrontPage Format? What's That?

Actually, FrontPage, like the rest of the Web, uses HTML format. But when you copy a file from the Web, FrontPage has to convert it slightly for its use. If FP discovers any HTML tags that it doesn't understand, it inserts an HTML bot and hands them over. See Chapter 17 for help with WebBots.

Quitting Time!

Gee, you absorbed a lot in this chapter! Time to come in for a landing. To exit FrontPage Editor, do what you do in any other program; return all tray tables to their upright and locked positions; then open the **File** menu and select **Exit**.

If you made some changes to open pages that you haven't saved yet, expect to see the File Fairy. You know what to do when she shows up.

Snarfing

You shouldn't try to steal (snarf) somebody's Web page, since it could be a copyright violation. Translation: if you're caught using copyrighted material to which you do not have a license, you face criminal charges, large fines, and the loss of your PC. Anything can be copyrighted, as long as it is original and in a "tangible medium of expression," legal-speak for recorded, printed, or photographed material. Get permission before you use anything you snarf.

You can use Web pages as inspirations, however. Use the **File, Copy Location** command to copy the Web page to your hard disk. Make changes to the page so that it reflects your thoughts rather than somebody else's. Just be careful not to copy original content, graphics, sound files, and so on, unless you're sure they're in the public domain.

By the way, you can use copyrighted material *without permission*, if you use it in the course of "criticism, parody, comment, news reporting, teaching, scholarship, or research." Of course, you can only use a smattering of the copyrighted material in such a case—just enough to make your point, but not enough to violate the owner's rights. Check out **http://lcweb.loc.gov/copyright/** (the Library of Congress home page) for more info.

The Least You Need to Know

A quick review of this chapter's top stories:

- Start FrontPage Editor within FP Explorer by simply clicking the **Show FrontPage Editor** button.
- Open the web page you want by opening the web site first, selecting the page in FP Explorer, and then using the **Edit, Open** command.
- Save changes to a web page by clicking the **Save** button. If you're saving a new page, enter a **Title** and an **URL**.
- You can also save a web page to your hard disk by clicking the **As File** button in the Save As dialog box. To create a template from the web page instead, click **As Template**.
- To open one of your web pages, open the web in FrontPage Explorer; then select the page and use the **Edit, Open** command. If the web is already open, just click the **Open** button in FrontPage Editor instead.

- Open a web page from your hard disk with the **File, Open File** command.
- To open a page on the WWW, use the **File, Open Location** command.

Chapter 4

Getting Your Text in There

By the End of This Chapter, You'll Be Able to...

- Add text to your web pages
- Master typing tips of the stars!
- Give your text a beauty makeover
- Break lines to your heart's content

Basically, FrontPage Editor is just a big word processor. So, if you've used Word, Word Pro, or WordPerfect, you'll have no problems entering text into your web pages. But, even if you're *familiar* with Word (or whatever), you're not *married* to it. In this chapter, you'll learn other ways for placing text onto your web pages (besides punching typewriter keys all day).

WYG Out

Yeah, just like a word processor, FrontPage Editor displays your text in WYSIWYG format (what-you-see-is-what-you-get). However, to truly see your pages as they will appear, you have to look at them through a Web browser. No, you won't have to pay for connect time while you check out your pages; the Personal Web Server allows you to view your pages in your Web browser without connecting to the Web. I'll show you how to view your pages later in this chapter.

EnterText—Stage Left

You enter text into a web page just like you're using a word processor: simply click someplace to set the insertion point; then type. If you select text (by dragging over it) and then type, whatever you type *replaces* the selection. (Same thing happens if you press the Insert key, but people only seem to do that by accident.)

Tips for the Typing Impaired

If you're reading this section, it's because you're not that familiar with word processors, and some of what I've already said doesn't make much sense. Not to worry; here's a list of the needs-to-knows:

Yech. Who Wants to Type Text?

If you have your text in another document, you can simply import that text, rather than retyping it. See Chapter 8 for more info.

- Again, to enter text, you click in the document where you want to start, and then you basically type what you want. When you click, you move the *cursor* (that blinking line). Text is always entered at the cursor point.
- If you make a mistake, press **Backspace** to back up over it. Delete one character at a time (the characters to the right of the cursor thing) by pressing **Delete.** To delete a lot of text, select it and press **Delete**.
- You can select text by pressing and holding the left mouse button while you drag over it. When it's highlighted, you can delete the text, copy it, or move it (more on that later).

- Once you select text, you can replace it with something else by simply typing something new.
- If you make a mistake, you can click the **Undo** button to undo it. In the case of typed text, you'll undo (remove) whatever you just typed.
- Don't press **Enter** at the end of a line, only at the end of a paragraph. When text hits the right-hand margin, it'll wrap onto the next line, automatically.
- Don't use the **Spacebar** to move the cursor; just click to move the cursor wherever you want it.

Adding Text to Your Home Page

Practice your typing skills on your home page, which you opened in Chapter 3. (Didn't open it? Well, jump back one space to Chapter 3 if you need a quick refresher.)

First, type the words, **Home Page**, and then press **Enter** a few times to leave some space. Next, type in your introduction. Keep it light but be clear as to the purpose of your web home page; remember that you'll probably only have a few minutes to grab your audience's attention.

Click to Select Text?

If you decide to create your web using one of the other templates or wizards (rather than using the Normal template), then you might see some filler text holding the place for your introduction. Normally, you simply select this text by dragging over it and replacing it with something else. But in the case of the text placed on a page by one of the templates, wizards, or WebBots, just click them to select them.

Don't worry about how the text looks at this point; you'll learn how to change your text later in this chapter.

You might want to add some sections to your home page, and add text for them, too. For example, the garden shop home page includes a Company Profile section and Contact Information.

Welcome to my home.

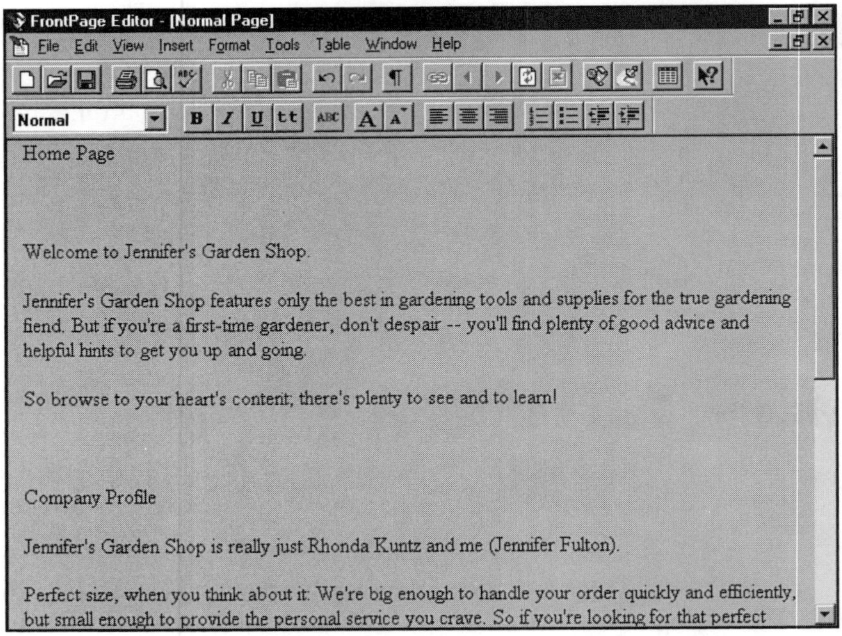

Dabbling with Special Characters

Sometimes, simple text isn't enough, and you have to add special characters as text, such as © (the copyright symbol), ™ (to denote a trademark), or “ and ” (double-closed quotes). Thankfully, FrontPage makes it easy for you to deal with these wacky characters.

First, click in the document where you want to add the character. Then, open the **Insert** menu and select **Special Character**. You'll see the following:

Select a character by clicking on it, and then click **Insert** to place it on the page. The dialog box remains open in case you need to add several characters (unlikely, to my way of thinking, but there you go). Anyway, when you're through, click **Close** to close the dialog box.

Quite a bunch of characters.

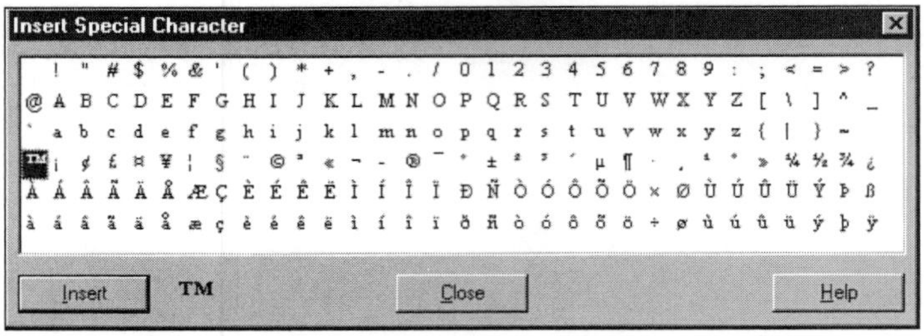

Inserting Line Breaks

Normally, text wraps between the margins of the page, until you press **Enter** to begin a new paragraph.

But what do you do
if you want to type
a poem,
an address,
or any small block of text
of short lines with no blank lines
between them?

If you type a line and press **Enter**, FrontPage thinks you've reached the end of a paragraph, so it inserts a blank line. You don't want all those blank lines cluttering up your addresses, or small blocks of text you type in a single cell of a table (or your poems).

Nope, so instead of pressing **Enter**, what you need to do here is insert a handy little item called a *line break*. A line break causes the user's Web browser to display the text after the break on the very next line.

For example, I wanted to include a phone number and address in the Contact Information section of my home page, so it would look like this:

E-mail:
jgs@indy.net

Snail mail:
Jennifer's Garden Shop
1201 East Garden Way
Cincinnati, Ohio 45678

Phone:
(513) 256-9090

To get it to look like this, I simply inserted a line break at the end of each line in the e-mail, address, and phone sections, so there wouldn't be any blank lines where I didn't want them. This is one reason for using line breaks. Another reason is to control how your graphics fit along side of your text. (Of course, we'll get to graphics later on.)

Here's how to insert a line break:

1. First, click at the point in the text *after* which you want the break to occur.
2. Then, open the **Insert** menu and select **Line Break**.
3. Choose the type of break you want and click **OK.**

Normal moves the text to the next line, but doesn't affect graphics on either side of that text.

Clear Left Margin moves text down so that it clears any graphics in the left margin.

Clear Right Margin does the same thing, but to the right.

Clear Both Margins does the same thing, but it moves the text down so that it clears any graphics on either the left or right margins.

You can also insert a line break by simply positioning the cursor at the end of a line, and pressing **Ctrl+Enter**, just like you would in any word processor.

Breaking tradition.

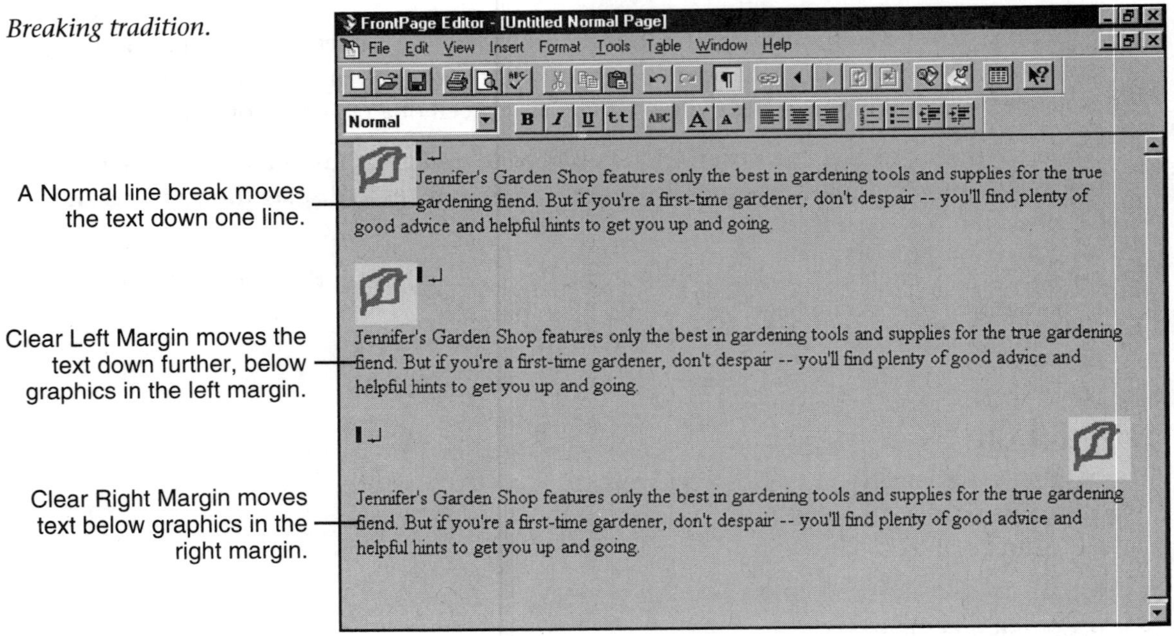

Extended Break

If, at some point in the future, the HTML code jockeys provide some kind of cute new attribute for line breaks (that is, other than breaking them to the left, the right, or normally), then you can add this new attribute to your web page simply by entering the proper HTML code for it. After locating the proper break code for whatever great break thing you want to do, return to the Break Properties dialog box. Click **Extended** and click **Add;** then add the name and value for the HTML attribute you want to enter. Boring stuff. Click **OK**.

Copying, Moving, and Getting Rid of Text

Copying, moving, and deleting text is often the key to "fine-tuning" a web page, so you'll probably use these skills quite often. Basically, you follow the same routine as you would in any other Windows program.

First, select what you want to copy, move, or delete by simply dragging over it. To copy the text, click the **Copy** button. To move it instead, click the **Cut** button. Then, click at the point on the page where you want the text copied or moved, and click **Paste**.

To delete text, select it and press **Delete**.

Drop That Thought!

Sorry, FrontPage doesn't support *drag-and-drop* so you can't use it to copy and move your text.

Making Your Text Look Nice

Earlier, you entered text into your home page as an introduction to your site. When you typed that text, it was entered in your basic 12-point size—no bold, no italics, no nothin'. In this section, you'll learn how to make individual sections of text stand out. This is called *character formatting*, since you're changing individual characters of text, and not whole paragraphs. If you want to change the appearance of an entire paragraph, such as aligning its text to the right, see Chapter 5.

Oops!

If you make some changes to a section of text which you hate, you can return that text to its normal look. Simply select it and press **Ctrl+Spacebar**. (This "normal look" is determined by the paragraph style of the text, explained in glorious detail in the next chapter.) You can perform this trick at any time during your web page creation. Of course, if you just *now* made the mistake, you can click **Undo**.

Well, now. Where to start?

On the Format Toolbar, you'll find lots of buttons to help you change text characters. Basically, you select the text you want to change (such as a word, a sentence, or even a few letters) and then you click the appropriate button. There's a button for making text bold, italic, or underlined. If you click the **Typewriter Font** button, text is changed from the proportional font (which looks like the font used in this book) to a monospaced font (which looks like it came off of a typewriter, because each letter takes up an equal amount of space.) Check this out!

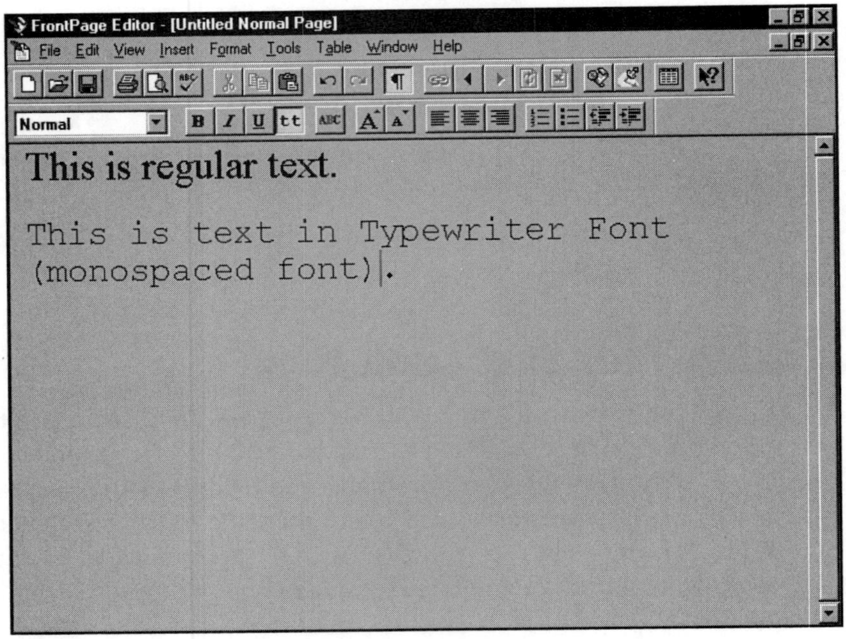

You can change text easily with the Format Toolbar.

To make text one font size bigger (or smaller) click the **Increase** or the **Decrease Text Size** buttons. Each time you click the button, your text changes two points.

Now that you know how to change your text, play around with your home page and make it look nice. For example, select the text **Home Page**, and click the **Increase Text Size** button a few times, to make your headline fairly large. If you added headings such as **Contact Information**, then change its size, too, and perhaps make it bold. (You'll learn how to center text in the next chapter.)

Changing the Color of Text

Changing the color of selected text is different than changing the text color of the entire page, which you will learn how to do in Chapter 9.

In any case, to change the color of *selected* text, click the **Text Color** button. You'll see a Color dialog box that looks like this.

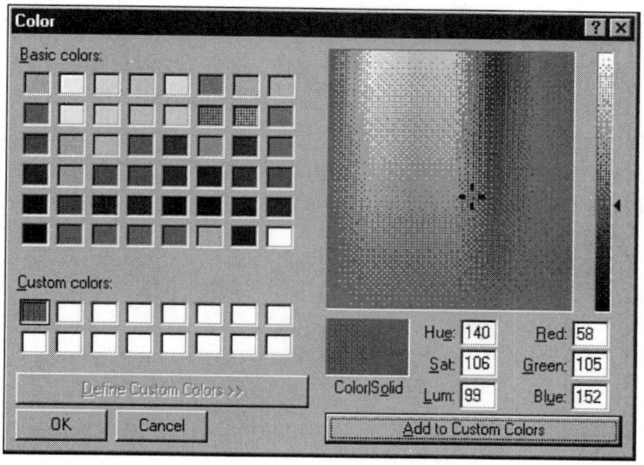

Color my world.

Color Wise

Keep in mind that, depending on the display settings your visitors are using, the background color you select may change from what you see during your testing, and that your text, if its close in color value, may fade from view. Choose a text color that contrasts well with your background color.

Click a color to select it. There are 48 colors to choose from; the actual colors you see depend on your current Windows display settings. If you feel like some hard work, you can create custom colors to increase the palette.

So, Show Me How!

You create custom colors in FrontPage the same way you would within Windows 95: First, in the Color dialog box, click **Define Custom Colors**. Click a blank square in the Custom colors area. Then, either click the color you want within the gradient box, or enter the proper hue, saturation, and luminescence, red, green, and blue values for it. Then click **Add to Custom Colors**.

But, how do you decide what settings to use for hue, saturation, and so on? First of all, you have to understand that screen colors are made up of varying amounts of blue, red, and green. So, to make a custom color, you simply mix different amounts of these three colors, ranging from a value of 0 to 255. A 0 indicates that none of that particular color is used in the final mix, whereas, a setting of 255 indicates that the color is used full-strength. By mixing varying amounts of these three colors, you can create just about any color.

Now, on to hue, saturation, and luminosity. What are they? Well, basically, you can ignore them, 'cause when you enter values under Red, Green, and Blue, they automatically change. But, if you must know, the *hue* of a color describes its place on the color wheel. Red has a hue value of 0, green has the value 80, and blue has the value 160. The saturation value tells you how much of the color is being applied to the final mix—a saturation of 240 gives you the brightest (or most intense) value of that color, while 120 will make the color appear less bright (intense). Luminosity tells you how much light (or white) is added to the color. Too much luminosity, and the color becomes almost white. Too little, and it becomes black.

So, what can you do with color? Well, on my home page, I selected the words **Jennifer's Garden Shop** wherever they appeared, and I made them green to create a kind of logo.

Changing Other Text Attributes

Yeah, changing the size, color, and boldness of text is not enough for some people. They want more. In the Characters dialog box, you can select as many attributes as you want, all from *one* convenient dialog box.

In the Characters dialog box (which you'll discover if you simply select some text, open the **Format** menu, and select **Characters**), you'll see some familiar friends: Bold, Italic, and Underlined, as well as Typewriter Font, Font Size, and Color. However, there are some other guys that you might not recognize:

Vertical Position This allows you to insert subscript and superscript characters, such as H_2O or 10^4.

Blink This causes the selected text to blink, a rather annoying trait, I think.

Watch That Blink

This is so annoying, in fact, that most Web browsers allow the user to turn off blinking text, which pretty much makes this attribute useless.

As for the rest of the attributes you see here, *don't use them*. Basically, those that aren't completely ignored by most Web browsers are used for doing boring things such as formatting programming code.

So, the Special Styles portion of this dialog box wins the "Complete Waste of a Section" award hands down.

Some Last Thoughts

After entering the text you want in your home page, you should save it by clicking the **Save** button.

The Least You Need to Know

Entering text can be a trying task, unless you know these things:

- Enter text into a web page the same way as you would enter text in a word processor. Just click to establish the insertion point, and then type.
- To replace the sample text in a web page created by a FrontPage Wizard or template, simply click the text and type what you want.
- To replace text you've typed, you must select it first by dragging over it.
- You can insert special characters and line breaks as needed in your web page text.
- Copy text with the **Copy** button. Move text with the **Cut** button. Then, place the copied or moved text where you want it with the **Paste** button.
- Format your text by selecting it and clicking the appropriate button on the Format Toolbar, such as the **Bold** button.

Chapter 5

Playing with Paragraphs

By the End of This Chapter, You'll Be Able to...

- Select the right style for a paragraph
- Align paragraphs to the left, right, or center
- Add indents and take them away

You'll probably want to change how your paragraphs look for many reasons—for example, to create indented paragraphs, centered headings, a right-aligned address, and so on. In this chapter, you'll learn how to do that, and more.

What Exactly Is a Paragraph?

A paragraph, don't ya know, is a section of text that ends where you've pressed the **Enter** key. So, a paragraph can be a long block of sentences, a line in a bulleted or numbered list, or a single-line heading. When you press **Enter**, you create a paragraph.

If you want to see the paragraph marks in your page, click the **Show/Hide Formats** button on the Standard Toolbar. Click it again to make the paragraph marks "disappear."

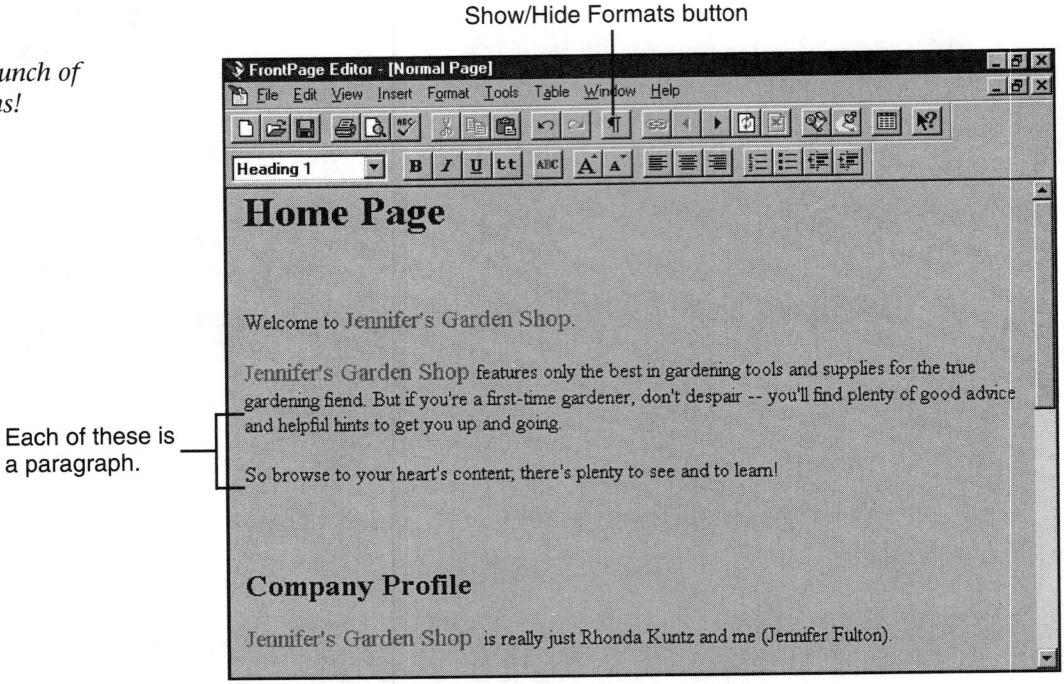

What a bunch of paragraphs!

Getting a Sense of Style

You might be familiar with styles if you've ever used them in your word processor. However, since most people get along perfectly fine while using a word processor without ever venturing into the mysterious land of styles, there's an equally good chance that you have no idea what a style is.

Working from that assumption, let me explain: basically, a *style* is a set of characteristics—point size, alignment, font, and so on—that are saved together and given a name.

Now, you might feel that you don't want to mess around with this style nonsense. That's okay, but you should know that (regardless of whether or not you want to use them) every paragraph has a style assigned to it.

Style Basics

When you assign a style to a paragraph, it takes on all the characteristics in that style set: for example, up until now, every paragraph you've added to your home page has been in the Normal style. Not surprisingly, the Normal style results in a very normal-looking paragraph, with 12-point text that's aligned along the left margin. A Normal paragraph is not centered, bulleted, or anything special. I guess that's why they're considered *normal*.

To make one paragraph look exactly like another, you simply give the second paragraph the same style. In fact, when you press **Enter** to create a new paragraph, the old paragraph style comes along for the ride. You get the same style until you change it (which you learn how to do in the next section).

How can you tell what style a paragraph is using? Just click inside the paragraph; the style name is listed in the Change Style window in the Formatting Toolbar, like you see in the following figure.

What's That Line?

Since you've entered some text into your web pages, you might have noticed that when you press **Enter** to begin a new paragraph, your cursor *is not* placed on the next line. Instead, your cursor is placed *two lines down.* That blank line that follows each paragraph is part of every paragraph style.

If you don't want a blank line to follow a paragraph for some reason, then insert a line break. (You can read all about those in Chapter 4.)

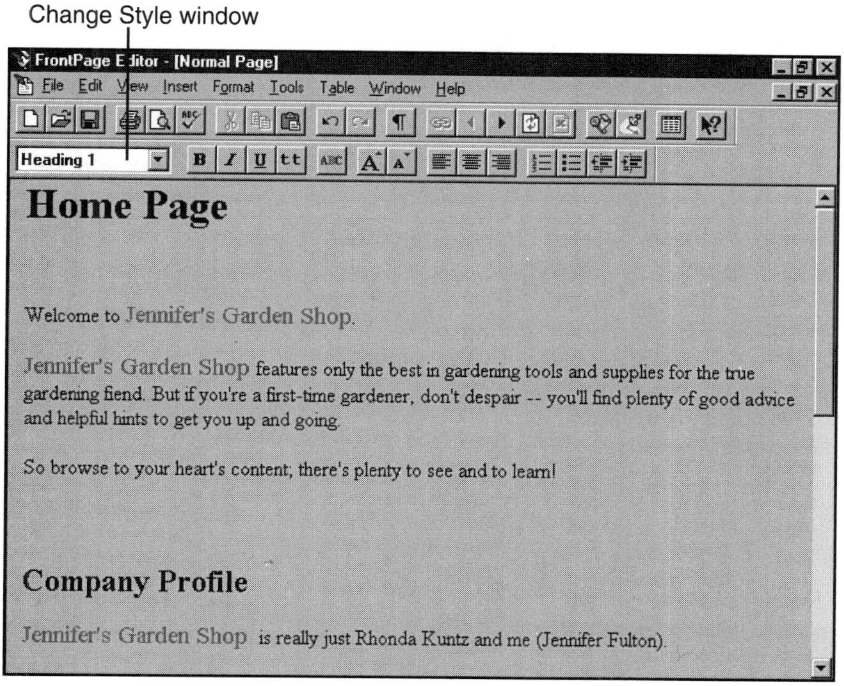

Getting a sense of a paragraph's style.

Selecting Your Style

You can apply a style to an existing paragraph. Or you can press **Enter** to begin a new paragraph, and select a style before you begin typing the paragraph's text.

Mirror, Mirror

In case you were wondering, the styles (Heading 1, Normal, and all the others) are basically the same within each template or wizard.

Just remember that when you create one paragraph after another, the paragraph style doesn't change *unless you change it manually*. To change to a different style, open the **Change Style** list and click a style name. Text you type, from that point on, will be in the new style.

To change the style of an existing paragraph, simply click in it and then select the style you want to use from the **Change Style** list. (You don't have to select the entire paragraph to change styles.)

What's with This Formatted Style?

The Formatted style changes you to monospaced (typewriter) font, which allows you to enter your text exactly as you want it to appear—FrontPage doesn't mess with it.

Unfortunately, this means that the text doesn't wrap as it normally might. While using the Formatted style, you must press **Enter** to begin each new line, or your text will run out the right margin into infinity. (Yeah, I know, the text appears to wrap when looking at it within FrontPage, but this is Windows' doing. When your user views the page on the Web, the text will not wrap at all and will run out to the right.)

Why bother with the Formatted style? Well, you might use Formatted style to enter lines of programming code, or other such things that require specific placement on the page.

Accessorize that Style!

Don't let the "sameness" of a style stifle your creativity. You can, if you like, add character (text) formatting such as bold, underline, italics, and color to any or all of the text within a paragraph, to make that paragraph a bit different from the others.

Keep in mind that any character formatting you add to text is like adding a tie or a flashy pin to a suit. If you decide you don't like it, just take it off. To remove all the character formatting in a paragraph, select the paragraph first, and then press **Ctrl+Spacebar**. The text returns to whatever look is dictated by the paragraph's style.

Can't I Just Change the Style to Suit My Tastes?

Not really. Unlike word processors, FrontPage doesn't allow you to change a style's definition. Basically, whatever FrontPage has decided a Heading 1 style should look like, that's what you have to work with. Bummer.

Aligning Paragraphs

The alignment of a paragraph controls how its text is placed between the left and right margins. FrontPage gives you three alignment flavors:

Left alignment (you get this by default) causes all the text in a paragraph to line up evenly with the left margin. In such a paragraph, text along the right margin is *ragged,* which means that it doesn't form an even line along the right edge.

Right alignment causes all the text in a paragraph to line up along the right margin. In this kind of paragraph, text along the left margin is ragged.

Center alignment causes all the text in a paragraph to be centered between the left and right margins. This makes both the left and right edges of the paragraph ragged. Although you may use center alignment on your headings, it is rarely used on regular paragraphs, since it makes the text more difficult to read.

Where's Full Alignment?

If you've used a word processor before, you're probably wondering where full alignment is. Well, it's just not supported by HTML, so FrontPage can't offer an option for it. Full alignment gives you straight margins on both sides; it uses extra spaces between words to make that happen.

To align a paragraph, click in it, and then click one of the appropriate buttons that you'll find close by on the Format Toolbar: **Align Left**, **Center**, or **Align Right**. For example, if you want to center your heading, **Home Page**, then select it and click the **Center** button.

Adding Indents

Paragraphs in FrontPage normally don't come with 'dents in them. But, you can add indents easily. An *indent,* by the way, is an extra amount of space placed between the margin and the edge of a particular paragraph.

Indenting a paragraph makes its text stand apart from your regular paragraphs; use indented paragraphs for important information you don't want the reader to miss.

When you change margins in a document, they affect all paragraphs. Adding an indent allows you to change only selected paragraphs instead.

When you add an indent, FrontPage moves *all the lines* of the paragraph an extra distance away from the margins (both the left and the right margins, in this case.). (See the following figure.) This is different from a word processor, which allows you to add an indent to the left or right margin only.

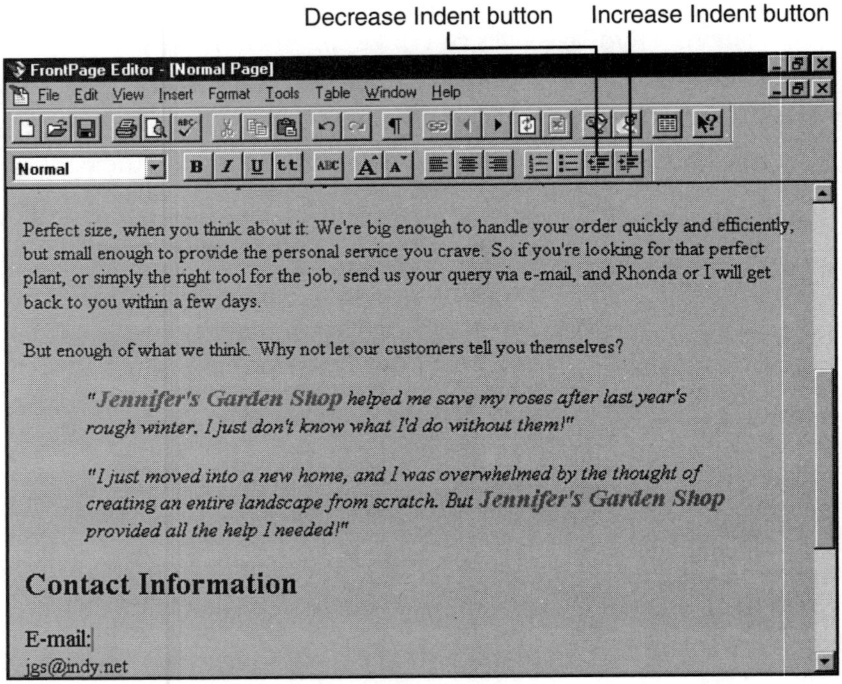

An indent adds extra space along the left and right edges of a paragraph.

Can I Indent Just the First Line of a Paragraph?

Unlike ordinary word processors, FrontPage can't indent just the first line of a paragraph. The problem isn't the fault of FrontPage; it's because the current HTML specification doesn't allow for that particular paragraph format. However, a bird told me that HTML 3.0 will soon offer a solution with its <TAB> tag.

To indent a paragraph, click in it and then click the **Increase Indent** button, which you'll find on the Format Toolbar. This will move each side of the paragraph a bit further away from both the left and right margins. Click more than once to add additional indents.

To move the edges of the paragraph closer to the margins, click the **Decrease Indent** button. By the way, no matter how many times you click the **Decrease Indent** button, you can't *outdent* a paragraph (that is, push its left edge *outside* the margins).

The Least You Need to Know

You'll have perfect paragraphs if you remember these things:

- A style is a set of characteristics that are saved together and given a name. When you assign a style to a paragraph, it takes on all the characteristics in that style set.
- As you enter paragraphs, they all have the Normal style, unless you change to a different style. Once you change to a different style, all your new paragraphs are entered in that style, until you switch back.
- Select any style you want to use from the Change Style list.
- You can change the style of an existing paragraph by clicking in it first, then selecting a style from the Change Style list. (You don't have to select the entire paragraph.) Or you can change from one style to another after beginning a new paragraph, as you enter text.
- To left-, right-, or center-align a paragraph, click in it and then click the **Align Left**, **Align Right**, or **Center** button.
- An indent is additional space placed between the margins and the left and right edges of a paragraph. Add indents by clicking the **Increase Indent** button. Remove indents by clicking the **Decrease Indent** button.

Chapter 6

Slapping in a Couple of Lists

By the End of This Chapter, You'll Be Able to...

- Put lists of items into your web page
- Tell a directory list apart from a menu list
- Build lists that automatically number themselves
- Create tiered lists such as outlines within a web page
- Format a list of definitions such as a glossary page

Uh, What's a List?

Throughout history, authors such as myself have used lists for basically three reasons:

1. To present a listing of related items

B. To list complex steps in order

iii. To make the author seem somewhat more intelligent by letting the reader know the author can count

A *list* is text that you can divide into individual items. In HTML (and therefore, in FrontPage) there are five different types of lists.

Miss That Mess

Before you add lists to your web pages, you should take a moment to feel smug about buying and using FrontPage. Creating lists using HTML codes is no picnic, but thanks to FrontPage, you don't have to mess with that task.

Popular list types.

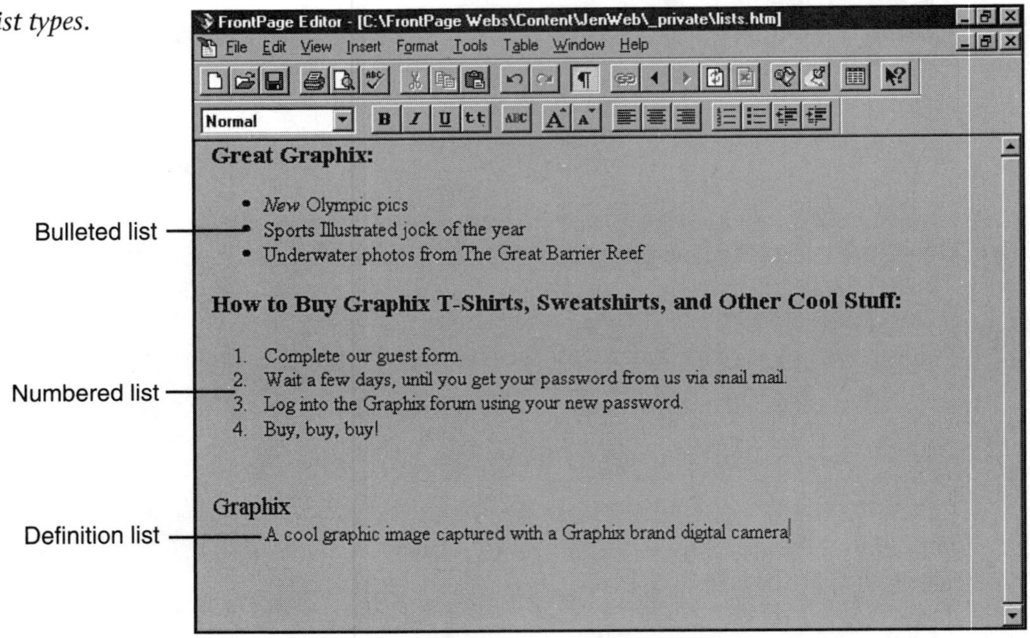

Bulleted Lists

At the beginning of this chapter, you'll find an example of a bulleted list. In front of each item in a bulleted list are *bullets*—those little dots that say "Hey, I'm an item!" A bulleted list contains items that are related, but that do not have to be presented in any particular order, such as a list of items sold at your web site:

- Miracle Garden Hoe
- Compact Composter
- Gardener's Knee Saver

Numbered Lists

You can use numbered lists to show items that occur in a specific order such as steps in a procedure:

1. Get lots of money.
2. Buy many things.
3. Get more money.

Unordered List By the way, a bulleted list is sometimes known as an unordered list, since its items do not have to be presented in any particular order.

Definition Lists

A definition list is (and please forgive me) *a listing of definitions*, such as you might find in a glossary. A definition list is made up of two parts: a term and its definition:

Gravity The thing that keeps me from falling off the planet.

Now, don't go skipping this section just because you have no plans for adding a glossary to one of your web pages. You can use a definition list for other things as well. Say, you have a list of people's names and some information about each person that you want to include. You can enter a person's name and his bio, followed by the next person and his bio, and so on. Each name would act as a *term*, and each person's bio would act as its corresponding *definition*.

Or perhaps, you want to include your résumé in a web page. In your employment history, you can list intervals of time, with each interval corresponding to an employer's name, or to some noteworthy event. Each time interval would be your *term*, and each description its *definition*. This way, you can create a, shall we say, "definitive" résumé.

Ordered List Numbered lists are also known as ordered lists, since the items in a numbered list must be presented *in order*, or some poor guy using the list might end up with a ceiling fan that's hanging crooked and has a couple of spare parts.

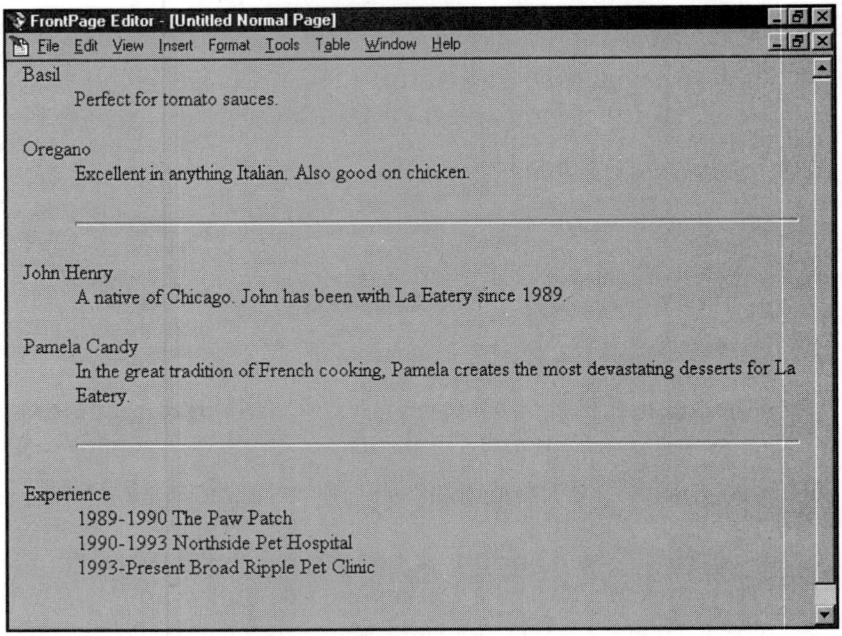

Several uses for the definition list.

Directory and Menu Lists

Bulleted, numbered, and definition lists—that's three. The last two list types are not well-defined, kinda leaving me to suspect that the list committee was on their way to the annual Christmas party when somebody realized that they only created three list types, and they had to rush back and come up with two more.

Anyway, here they are:

A *directory list* is similar to a directory listing such as you might get when you type **DIR** at the DOS prompt (or **ld** at the UNIX prompt):

email/
programs/
private/

A menu list looks like a menu—again, a listing without numbers or bullets.

Level 1: The Dark Passage
Level 2: Deadman's Land
Level 3: Fortune's Forest

Unfortunately, most Web browsers do not display a directory list any differently than a menu list (which in a lot of Web browsers, looks just like a bulleted list), so you should probably not bother with these two list types.

What a Web Browser Does with a List

Unlike a word processor—which sees a list as separate list items, each beginning with a tab, followed by a number or a bullet, another tab, and finally the item itself—a Web browser sees a list as one massive *list element*, containing a series of unnumbered, unindented items.

It's up to the Web browser to add the proper indentations, bullets, numbers, and blank lines, based solely on the list's designated *type*. In other words, how your list looks is determined by how the user's Web browser chooses to display it.

Most Web browsers support bulleted and numbered lists, so those lists look about the same from browser to browser. Yet, only a few Web browsers support those funky menu and directory lists. So, a menu list on one browser might appear with bullets, but it won't have bullets on another browser. Are you getting the picture about how valuable those menu and directory list types are?

So, How Can I Control How My Lists Look?

Well, you can't. On the one hand, with predefined list types, you don't have to bother with setting the tabs or the number of spaces between the bullet and the list item—you simply type the list.

On the other hand, there's the problem that you can't really do too much to stylize the appearance of your lists; you have to live with the style as it's dictated by HTML and interpreted by various Web browsers.

Entering Lists: 101

The important thing to remember is that to FrontPage, every item in a list is its own paragraph. So, at the end of every list item you type, you press the **Enter** key to start a new list item. How do you put a stop to this nonsense? Easy! When you finish typing all your list items, press **Enter** twice. FrontPage gets out of the list business and returns you to the paragraph format of your choice.

Enough generalities; let's get down to specifics.

Creating a Numbered List

You might want to add a numbered list to your web page to list a series of steps, or perhaps, to designate some order of importance, as in *The Top Ten List of Things I Absolutely Intend Not to Do Today*.

To place a numbered list in your Web page, here's what you do—presented here in a wonderfully numbered list of your very own, suitable for framing in your home or office:

1. Click a blank line where you want your list to begin. The cursor will move to this spot.
2. Click the **Numbered List** button. FrontPage Editor will automatically enter the "**1.**" for you.

A Different Way

If you're really stuck on using menu commands, you can also insert a numbered list by opening the **Insert** menu, selecting **List**, and selecting **Numbered**. But, if you do that, FrontPage moves the cursor *to the next line* in your page, and begins numbering. So, if you use the menu command, be sure that your cursor is at the end of the line *above* where you want your list to begin. Does it really seem worth it? Just click the button!

3. Type the first list item, just like you type any other text.
4. When you're ready to start the next list item, press **Enter**. FrontPage automatically inserts the next number in the list, which in this case, is number 2.
5. Repeat steps 3 and 4 until you reach the end of the list.
6. Press **Enter**. FrontPage will insert the next number. That's okay; simply ignore this silliness and press **Enter** *again*. This tells FrontPage that you mean business, and it will remove the extra number accordingly and return you to normal typing.

Inserting an Item into a Numbered List

One of the splendid things about working with computers is their unflinching tenacity for counting. Computers can count things automatically—even things as high as ten or twelve! So, when you need to add an item to the *middle* of an already numbered list—say, between items 3 and 4—FrontPage figures out what you're doing, fixes the numbering, and gives the new item its proper designation. No, not as item 3 1/2, but as item 4, making the old item 4 into item 5, and so on.

To add an item to the middle of a numbered list while preserving its natural order, as well as the precious balance of nature itself, follow these steps:

1. Place the cursor at the end of the list item *above* which you want your new item to go. In this case, place the cursor at the end of item number 3.
2. Press **Enter**. The cursor is moved to the next line, and the number 4 is inserted. The old item number 4 is automatically renumbered to 5, and so on, as you see here.

Move to the place where you want to insert an item, and press Enter…

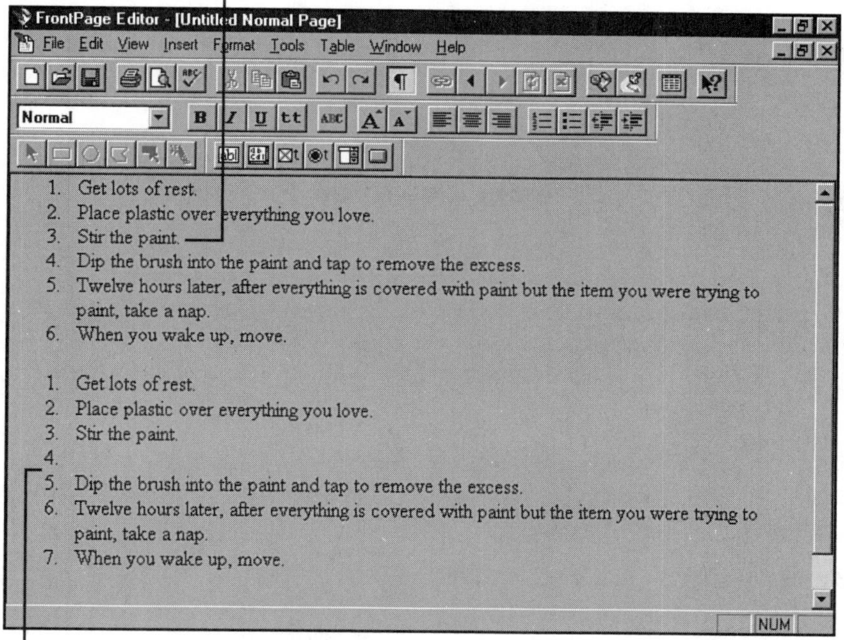

…and the list automatically renumbers.

Adding an entry to the middle of a numbered list.

3. You can press **Enter** at the end of your new list item, to insert more than one line into the list. If you do this, the newly renumbered item 5 will be renumbered *again* to item number 6. Likewise, all the other items that follow item 6 will be renumbered as well.

Dodging Bullets

If you're trying to list a bunch of related items, you don't need any numbers to make your list a list. You can use bullets instead! Unlike most word processors, in FrontPage, there's only one type of little dot you can use for your bulleted lists, and that is, well, a little dot.

Here's how to insert a bulleted list:

1. Click a blank line where you want your list to begin. The cursor will move to this spot.
2. Click the **Bulleted List** button. FrontPage Editor will enter the bullet (uh, a dot) for you.

Again, There's a Different Way to Do Just About Everything

All you menu aficionados should remember that if you want to use the **Insert** command to insert a list, make sure your cursor's at the end of the line *above* where you want your list to begin.

3. Type the first list item.
4. When you're ready to start the next list item, press **Enter**. FrontPage automatically inserts another bullet.
5. Repeat steps 3 and 4 until you reach the end of the list.
6. Press **Enter** twice to end the list.

Inserting Items into a Bulleted List

Just do it! Place your cursor at the end of one list item and press **Enter**. A fresh bullet appears. Type whatever item you want to insert. Enter as many items as you want, but press **Enter** at the end of each one.

Hey, How Can I Add My Own Dingbats?

As of today, you can't. When HTML 3.0 is finally (officially) released, you'll be able to add the HTML attribute, SRC, to a bulleted list to indicate a graphic bullet you want to use. The attribute will look something like this: SRC="cooldot.gif".

To add an HTML attribute to your bulleted list, just right-click an item in the list and select **List Properties**. Click **Extended**, then click **Add**. Type SRC as the Attribute, and enter the name of your file as the Value. Click **OK**. But, don't expect the thing to show up in FrontPage; you'll have to use your Web browser to see it.

Also, make sure that you import the graphic into your web, following the steps you'll find in Chapter 8, or the whole thing won't work.

An alternative method for adding your own bullets is to *not* use the bulleted list style. Instead, use the Normal style to create your items; then insert the bullet graphic at the front of each item (see Chapter 8 again). Want a space between the bullet and your item? If so, include extra space around the bullet within the graphic file, or create a graphic that is the same color as your background, and insert it as a "spacer."

Adding Definitions to a Web Page

If you look at the glossary at the back of this book, it's easy to tell that a glossary is simply a list of terms and their definitions; in other words, it's a definition list. What isn't obvious at first glance is that a definition list is a two-part affair: one part term, the second part definition. Entering a definition list is like typing two lists at one time, although the two lists are definitely related.

Here's how to insert a definition list:

1. Place the cursor *on the line above* where you want the list to appear.
2. Start by entering the first term. From the **Insert** menu, select **Definition** and then **Term**. The cursor moves to the next line, ready for you to enter your term.
3. Type your term. *Don't press Enter after typing the term, unless you want a blank row to appear between the term and its definition.*
4. From the **Insert** menu, select **Definition** and then **Definition** again. The cursor moves to the next line just below the term, with a little extra indentation on the left.
5. Type your definition.
6. To begin the next term, select **Insert/Definition/Term** again; otherwise, to end the list, press **Ctrl+Enter**.

What Gives?

Now, if you look in the **Help** section of FrontPage, it'll tell you to end your Definition list by pressing **Enter**. When I tried that, I ended my list all right, but my cursor was left indented. This left me with an urge to give FrontPage a dent or two—that is, until I figured out the **Ctrl+Enter** trick.

Creating a Menu or a Directory List

What are you doing here? I've worked hard to warn you about using Menu and Directory lists, haven't I? Okay, if you want to use one of these list types, even though about 90% of the Web browsers on the market won't display them as anything other than bulleted lists, I'll tell you how. Uh, actually, I've already told you how. Just follow the same basic steps as before: place the cursor *on the line above* where you want the list to appear; open the **Insert** menu and select **List**; then, select either **Menu** or **Directory**. Type your list, pressing **Enter** after each item. Press **Enter** twice to end your list.

Making a List After the Fact

Suppose you have several rows of text already typed in the middle of your web page. You want to make them into a numbered or bulleted list, but you don't want to type them over again. No problem.

Simply select the rows of text by dragging over them, and then click the appropriate button: **Numbered List** or **Bulleted List**. The rows of text that you select will change into a numbered or bulleted list, complete with the proper numbers or bullets.

And what about the other list types? Yes, you can also create a definition, menu, or directory list after the fact, but, you'll soon discover that there's no button for them. Don't worry; in this case, you simply select your rows of text, and then select the appropriate style (**Definition**, **Menu List**, or **Directory List**) from the **Change Style** list box.

Adding a List Within a List

When trying to come up with a reason to put a list within another list, you're probably left scratching your head. But, if you've ever looked at a formal outline, or a table of contents, you've seen at least a few examples of a list inside a list.

You *can*, quite easily, embed a bulleted list inside a numbered list, or vice versa. Truth be told, you can embed any kind of list inside another, although you might not like the result. Let me explain: when you embed a numbered list into the middle of another numbered list, you're probably looking for a result like this:

1. The Fantastic Life of a Fly
    a. Birth
    b. Blood sucking activity
    c. Death by swatting
2. The Equally Fantastic Life of a Beetle

Now, such a list is easy to create just about anywhere else, but not in FrontPage. When you insert a numbered list into another, you get this:

1. The Fantastic Life of a Fly
    1. Birth
    2. Blood sucking activity
    3. Death by swatting
2. The Equally Fantastic Life of a Beetle

The result is not only confusing, but it's funny as well. Your sense of humor aside, you'd probably like the result of inserting a bulleted list into a numbered list much better:

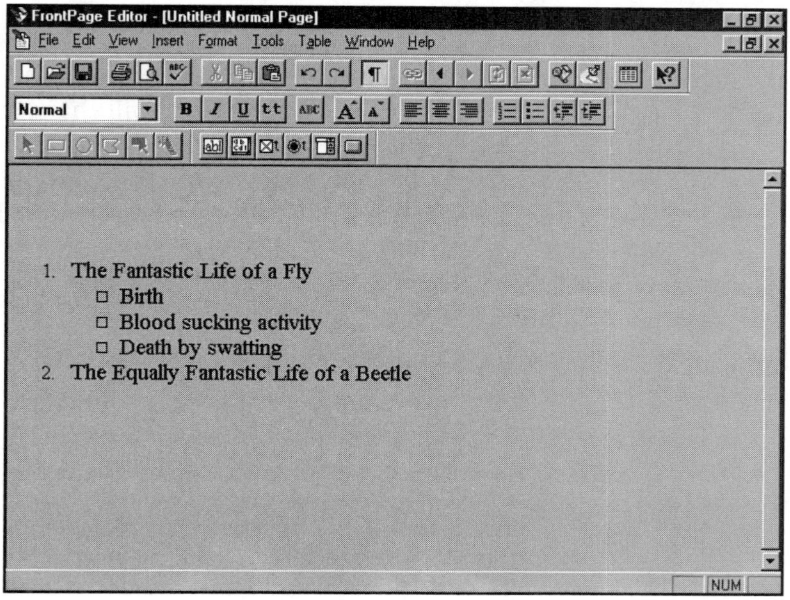

Making sense out of insensibility.

Here's how to embed one list inside another:

1. Create the first list—all of it.
2. Then move the cursor at the *end of the line above* where you want your embedded list to begin.
3. Open the **Insert** menu, select **List**, and then select the type of list you want to insert. FrontPage will move the cursor to the next line, slightly indented inside the other list.
4. Type the first item in your list, and then press **Enter**. Repeat for all items in the embedded list.
5. When you're done entering items into the embedded list, simply move the cursor to the next place where you want to enter text.

The Least You Need to Know

The Earth was formed after the primordial gases that formed our solar system cooled. After that, there evolved five different forms of web page lists:

- Although there are five list types, only three are of any use: numbered list, bulleted list, and definition list.
- The two other types, menu and directory lists, typically result in a list which looks exactly like a bulleted list, so using them is pretty pointless.
- When you type a bulleted or numbered list, FrontPage automatically enters the bullets or the numbers for you.
- A definition list (also called a glossary list) is made up of two parts: the term being defined and its definition. Each part is entered separately.
- To end a list, press **Enter** twice.
- Whenever you're feeling daring (or the need arises), you can embed one kind of list within another kind of list.

Chapter 7

Adding Lines

By the End of This Chapter, You'll Be Able to...

- Divide your web pages into sections using horizontal lines
- Give your pages a professional appearance with lines
- Stick bunches of lines in your page at random locations

Yes, this chapter is all about *lines*. You know, _______. Those geometric thingies you put together to make shapes. Why are lines so important? Why is there an entire chapter devoted to them in this book? Well, with horizontal rules, you can easily divide your information into relevant sections. This helps the user locate what she's looking for more quickly. Sections also help the reader change focus from one topic to another. In this book, I use headings to section off the material in each chapter; in your web pages, you could use headings and *rules*.

One place you may want rules is just above your headings, as shown in the following figure. Another place for rules is between a section of text and a long list.

Rules allow you to create sections within your web pages.

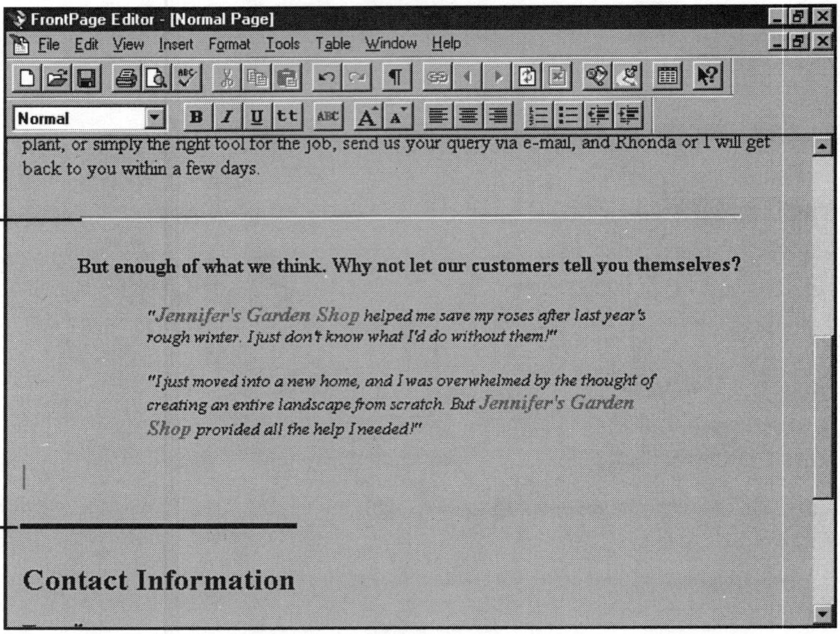
This line sets off the customer quotes.
This line signals the beginning of a new section.
FrontPage Editor - [Normal Page]
File Edit View Insert Format Tools Table Window Help
Normal
plant, or simply the right tool for the job, send us your query via e-mail, and Rhonda or I will get back to you within a few days.
But enough of what we think. Why not let our customers tell you themselves?
"Jennifer's Garden Shop helped me save my roses after last year's rough winter. I just don't know what I'd do without them!"
"I just moved into a new home, and I was overwhelmed by the thought of creating an entire landscape from scratch. But Jennifer's Garden Shop provided all the help I needed!"
Contact Information

One thing you shouldn't do with lines is use too many of them. A line between each item in a list would be too much. Likewise, a line between each paragraph on a page would divide the page so much that it would appear as a confusing jumble. So, use your lines wisely and sparingly—probably, no more than two lines per windowful of information.

Another thing you can do to make lines more useful is to vary their width and length, as you might vary the size of individual headings (see the next figure). You'll learn how to change the look of your lines later in this chapter.

Adding a Horizontal Line

Between the rooms of your house, you have walls; between you and your tax refund, you have infinite red tape; between sections of a long document, you should have *lines*.

Why? Because lines help the reader see the structure of your information—lines help him see where topics begin and end. So, using lines on a web page is important, provided you don't overdo them.

Getting a line in your web page isn't stressful. There are some things you might want to do to it later, but first, you have to get the line on your page. Here's how:

1. Place the cursor at the end of the row of text *above* where you want the horizontal line to appear.
2. Open the **Insert** menu and select **Horizontal Line**. FrontPage inserts a horizontal line just under the row of text in which you placed the cursor.

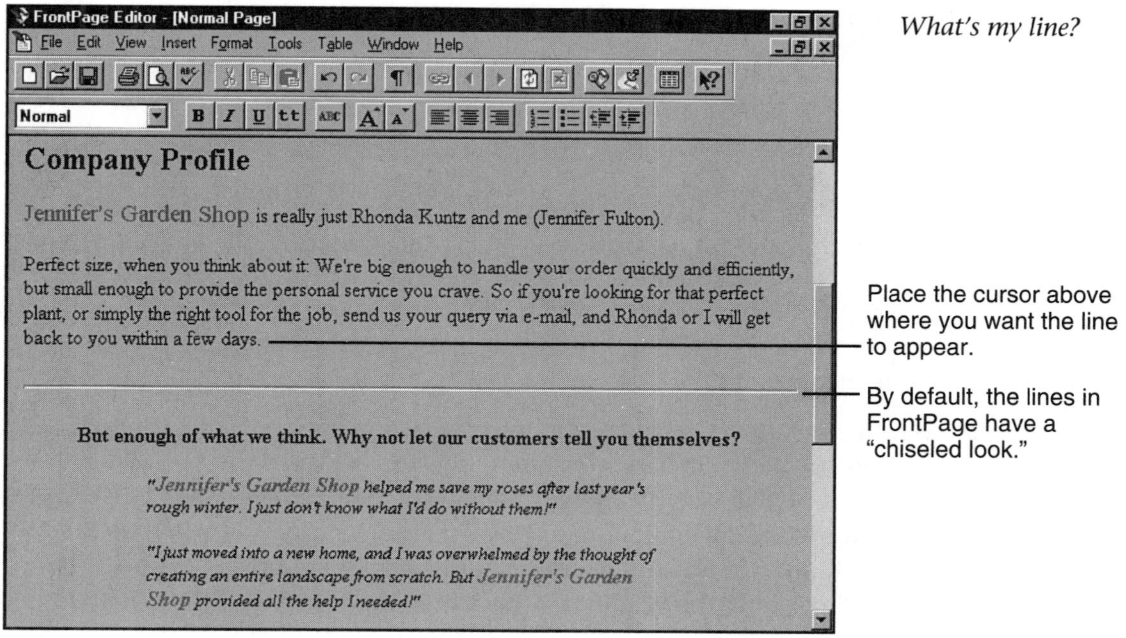
FrontPage Editor - [Normal Page]
File Edit View Insert Format Tools Table Window Help
Normal
Company Profile
Jennifer's Garden Shop is really just Rhonda Kuntz and me (Jennifer Fulton).
Perfect size, when you think about it: We're big enough to handle your order quickly and efficiently, but small enough to provide the personal service you crave. So if you're looking for that perfect plant, or simply the right tool for the job, send us your query via e-mail, and Rhonda or I will get back to you within a few days.
But enough of what we think. Why not let our customers tell you themselves?
"Jennifer's Garden Shop helped me save my roses after last year's rough winter. I just don't know what I'd do without them!"
"I just moved into a new home, and I was overwhelmed by the thought of creating an entire landscape from scratch. But Jennifer's Garden Shop provided all the help I needed!"
Place the cursor above where you want the line to appear.
By default, the lines in FrontPage have a "chiseled look."

What's my line?

Changing How a Line Looks

In FrontPage, you insert your line first, and change its appearance later. So, now that you inserted your line, you can change how it looks.

You can change the length and width of a line, as well as other popular attributes, such as the alignment on the page, and the shading. In this section, you'll learn how to do just that.

Techno Talk
blah blah

Why Change It? I Like the Way the Line Looks By default, a FrontPage horizontal line looks like a long, chiseled notch (see the previous figure). However, that may or may not be the way they'll appear to your viewers. You see, some older Web browsers interpret horizontal lines as plain, black lines, regardless of how they look in FrontPage. If this bothers you, you can change it so that your lines appear as plain black for all your users. Simply choose the **Solid line** option in the Horizontal Line Properties box.

To change the appearance of a line, follow these steps:

1. First, click the line you want to change.
2. Right-click and a pop-up menu appears.
3. From the pop-up menu, select **Properties**. You'll be treated to a viewing of the Horizontal Line Properties dialog box, shown here.

Pruning and trimming your new horizontal line.

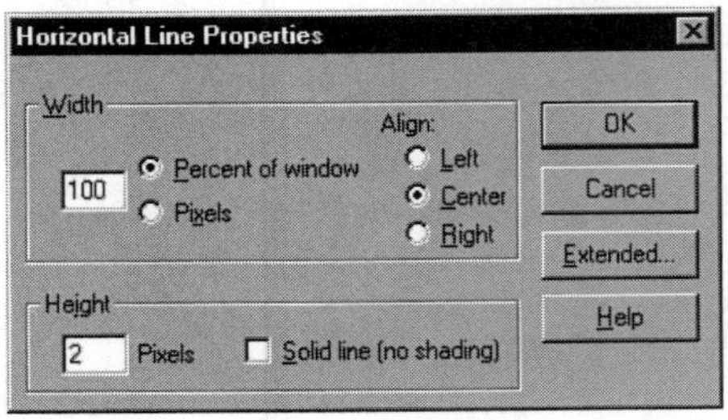

4. Make your changes and click **OK**:

   ➤ **Width** refers to the percentage of the page width being consumed by your line. So **100** means the line consumes the entire width of the page. To reduce the width of your line, change this number to something smaller. Leave the **Percent of window** option set to **ON**. For example, you can match the width of your line to the size of the heading just below it, as shown in the first figure. For the line above the heading **Contact Information**, I set my width to 35%.

   ➤ Under **Align**, you'll notice that, by default, a line is centered between the left and right margins. To align the line along the left or right margin, set the **Left** or **Right** option. For example, to create the line above the **Contact Information** heading in the first figure, I used the **Left align** option.

   ➤ With the **Height** option, you can set the height of the horizontal line in pixels. To make the line fatter, increase this number. By default, the line is set to 2 pixels. I wouldn't go over 10 pixels, unless you're looking for a very fat line. Also, if you use a fat line, consider using the Solid line option explained next, which will make a thick line look *thick*. In the first figure, I set the line above the **Contact Information** heading to 4 pixels.

   ➤ To eliminate the chiseled look of a FrontPage line, select the **Solid line (no shading)** option. This might be a good option to choose if you're trying to create a dark, thick line. If this helps you decide when you use this option, your line will have rounded endpoints.

I Want to Colorize My Line! Who do you think you are, Ted Turner? Well, in any case, you can't. This isn't a problem with FrontPage, but if you have to blame something, blame HTML, the language that defines each element on a web page. For some reason, HTML allows for adjustments to width, alignment, shading, and height, but not to *color*. Go figure.

For the most part, FrontPage provides options in the Line Properties dialog box for changing just about anything you might want to do to a horizontal line. Basically, you can just ignore the Extended button in the Line Properties dialog box—most sane people do. However, if you catch yourself reading those thick, boring books on HTML codes again, and you accidentally discover an HTML code for changing the look of a line, then in the Horizontal Line Properties dialog box, click **Extended**. In the next dialog box, click **Add**. Finally, in the Set Attribute Value dialog box, enter the **Name** and **Value** of the HTML code (tag) you want to use. Click **OK** twice and you're through.

Making the Most of Your Lines

When inserting lines into a web page, the key is to use *restraint*. A web page with too many lines divides the text so much that it becomes almost unreadable. Since you should use only a few lines in key places (such as between major sections of text), it makes sense to make the most of them. Here are some sample lines you might want to try.

Create the Look You Want One way to achieve the perfect look is to create your own line and to save it as a graphic. That way, no Web browser can come along and "interpret" it into something else.

Create a colorful line using a simple drawing program such as Windows Paint; then save your work—as GIF or JPEG, if possible, or BMP, PCX, or whatever. Then insert the graphic wherever you'd normally place a line—FrontPage takes care of converting the file to the proper format, GIF or JPEG. (See Chapter 8 for help.)

Want a sample?

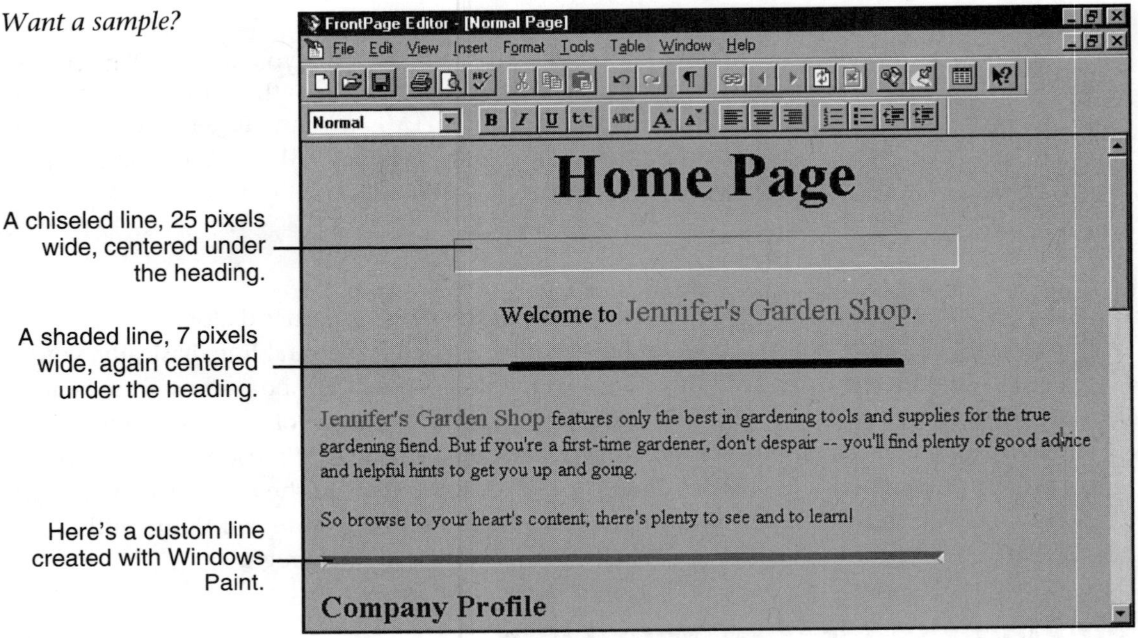

Deleting a Line

Removing a line is easy—almost as easy as inserting one in the first place. Simply click the line to select it, and press **Delete**.

The Least You Need to Know

Lines, as it turns out, aren't terribly difficult, as long as you remember these things:

- To create a line, click at the end of the text *above* where you want the line to appear. Then, open the **Insert** menu and select **Horizontal Line**.
- After inserting a line, you can change the way it looks.
- To change the look of a line, select it. Right-click and select **Properties** from the menu. Here, you can change the width, height, or alignment of your line.

Chapter 8

Importing Pictures, Text, and Sound

By the End of This Chapter, You'll Be Able to...

- Borrow material from existing text files
- Assemble a web page using pieces of other pages
- Import a foreign file into a web
- Place a graphic image exactly where you want it in your page
- Create separate "blow-up" pages for your images (without getting in trouble with the ATF)

Why Type When You Can Insert a Text File?

Microsoft has pretty much defined the way word processors work in the '90s. So, while entering text into a web page, if the FrontPage Editor environment seems familiar, you have Microsoft to thank. But, suppose you have electronic text stored somewhere, and you want to build a web based on those text files. There's no reason you have to be stuck typing in all that information from scratch—no matter how much you like doodling at the keyboard.

In the world of FrontPage, there are two distinctly different ways to bring text into your web pages: *inserting* and *importing*. Inserting deals with the process of taking the text in a document file and copying it into a web page. Importing is a different process that simply makes the contents of a file accessible to people using your web, so they can download it to their systems and then view it. I'll talk about both of these techniques later, but first, you have to get your text ready to travel.

Getting Text Ready to Travel

The key to success in copying text from a file into your web page is to get your information into some kind of format that FrontPage likes. Most word processors allow you to save your files in ASCII (pronounced: "AS-key") format, which is pretty much the Plain Jane of the word processing world. The up side to ASCII is that it's universal, meaning that chances are good you can get your data into ASCII format. The down side is that when you save a document in ASCII format, it is saved as simple text, without any of the formatting you've grown accustomed to, such as bold, italics, and underline. In addition, font size and selection is also lost in the translation to ASCII format. Bottom line: what you get is your words, nothing else, as you can see in the following figure.

How your file will look when inserted into a Web page.

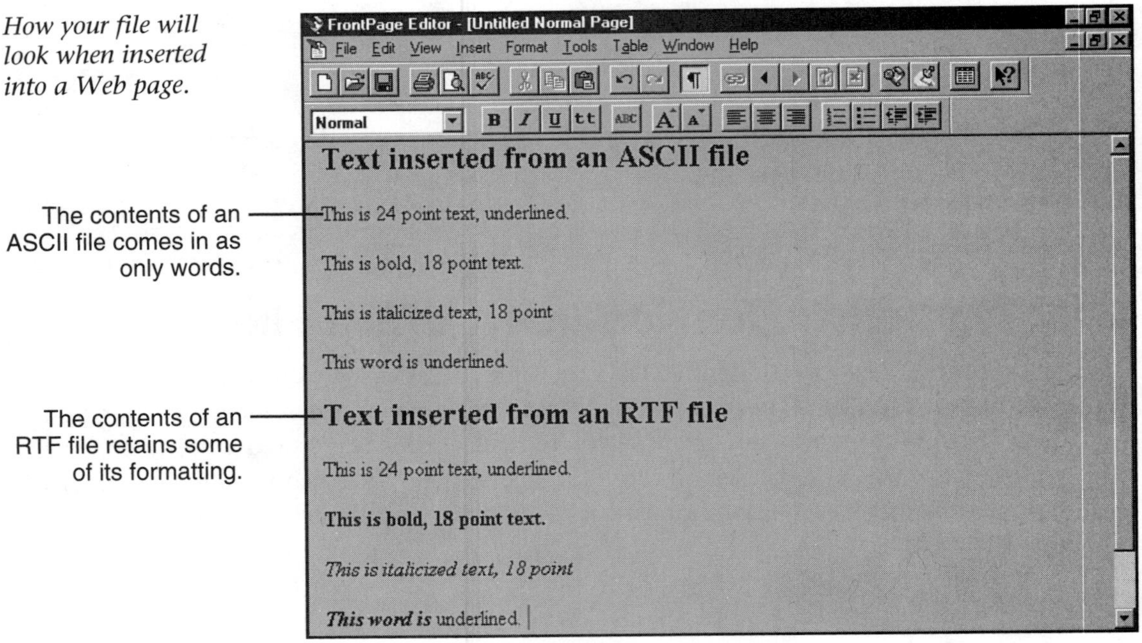

Don't despair. If you need those italics, you can save your files in Rich Text Format. RTF lets you save your text with some of its formatting intact. Specifically, when you save a file in RTF, you save any bold, underline, or italics. RTF format also saves other things that FrontPage ignores, such as font selection, point size, and tabs.

If your word processor can export your data to either of those formats, you can insert the text in these files into your web pages.

No Conversion Required

If you want to insert part of a document file, and you don't care about trying to save the formatting using RTF, then you can simply copy it into a web page using the Windows **Copy** and **Paste** buttons *without saving the file in ASCII format first*. See the "Inserting Part of Any File" section later in this chapter for help.

To save a document file in either ASCII or RTF format, first open the document in its native program, such as Microsoft Word. Then, open the **File** menu and select **Save As**. Under something such as **Save as type**, you'll see the various formats from which you can choose. Select either ASCII or RTF, depending on what's available, and then click **OK**.

Inserting Web Pages into Other Web Pages

If your text is saved in HTML format, you can insert it directly into any FrontPage web page, without converting it into ASCII or RTF format first.

Now that you have your text saved in a format that FrontPage can understand, you're ready to insert that text into a web page.

Inserting a Text File

To insert text from an ASCII file into a web page, FrontPage must first convert its contents into HTML format, so it can be used on the web. Basically, all this involves is adding little <p> tags to indicate where paragraphs begin and end. After you convert the contents of your ASCII file, the FrontPage places the text in the page, beginning at the point you select.

Inserting the entire contents of a text file into your page is a simple matter. Inserting only a section of a file is a bit more complex, but you can still do it. First, here's how to insert the entire contents of a file:

1. First, click in your web page where you want your text inserted.
2. Open the **Insert** menu and select **File**.
3. Under **Files of type**, select **Text Files.**
4. Now, change to the proper directory, select your file, and click **OK.**
5. FrontPage brings up the **Convert Text** dialog box. The choices here are a bit misleading—but are important. (If you hear sirens blaring, it's just a warning that this discussion is about to get a bit deep. Make sure you have your waders on; then, feel free to continue…)

To reformat or not to reformat, what was the question again?

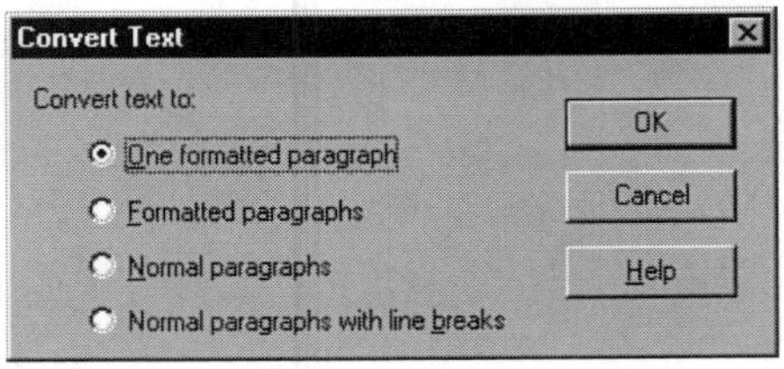

- **One formatted paragraph** If you select this, the text in the *entire file* will be inserted as one large paragraph in the Formatted style. The Formatted style, you may remember, uses a monospaced (typewriter-like) font, rather than proportional font (like the font used in this book). And, if that isn't enough, FrontPage will insert little line breaks at the end of each text line, where the text originally wrapped. The line breaks appear on-screen as little bent arrows. Use this option to insert lines of programming code, a poem, or any other text where you want the words placed in a specific spot on the page.

Why Are Line Breaks So Bad?

Well, they're not *really* bad, but that doesn't make them good. In Chapter 4, you learned that line breaks create separate lines of text with no blank lines in between (like the lines in an address).

Here's the problem: line breaks tell the system exactly where to break the line, instead of letting the text wrap as it normally would. If you insert text that has a lot of line breaks into your web page, the text won't wrap naturally. It'll be chopped up by all those little line breaks. This may or may not be the effect you want.

- **Formatted paragraphs** This option's the same as **One formatted paragraph**, except that your inserted text will still retain its separate paragraphs. A line break will still be inserted at the end of each line of text, but in addition, a blank line will be inserted at the end of each paragraph. Use this option to insert a long list of addresses, where you want to have a blank line between each address. You can also use this option to insert long sections of programming code.
- **Normal paragraphs** After you've been wrestling with the HTML concept of "formatted text," anything that introduces itself to you as "normal" should be an instant relief. If you choose this option, your text is inserted in Normal style, which (as you may recall) results in a proportional font, such as Times New Roman. The line breaks are *not* inserted, so that each line of text can wrap naturally. In most cases, this is the option you'll need.
- **Normal paragraphs with line breaks** This one is just like the **Normal paragraphs** option, except, in this case, the line breaks are inserted, and text is broken (cut off at the right-hand margin) at the points where it was broken in the original file. See the previous Techno Talk box for more comments about line breaks and their pluses and minuses. You can use this option to insert addresses using a proportional font, instead of the monospaced font you get with the Formatted option.

6. Select an option and click **OK**. FrontPage converts your text and inserts it into the current web page, beginning at the cursor.

Well, excluding the "snore-full" discussion of line breaks, that wasn't so bad. Now, see how to insert an HTML file.

Inserting an HTML File

HTML is the format in which all web pages are saved, so when I talk about inserting an HTML file into one of your FrontPage web pages, I'm talking about inserting one web page into another.

You might have gotten your HTML file from just about anywhere on the Internet, and that's okay, as long as you have permission to use its contents in your web pages. If you don't have specific permission, you should try to get it, unless you know that the file's text and images are in the public domain (meaning they are not copyrighted).

Forget how to snarf a file from the Internet? Well, let me remind you: turn your Web browser to the page you want to snarf. Then, open the **File** menu and select **Save As**. Select a directory in which to save the HTML file, and click **OK**. You have to save the graphics, too, if you want them. In Netscape, you right-click a graphic and select **Save Image as** to save each graphic.

What You See Isn't Necessarily What You'll Get

Each HTML file (files with either the .HTM or .HTML extension) has its own characteristics. And, when you try to insert the contents of another HTML file into your web page, an interesting thing happens: the characteristics of your web page win out—not those of the other file.

When you insert your HTML file into the middle of your FrontPage web page, don't expect a mirror image of the HTML file to appear, with all of its specially colored links and cool-looking background image. Expect, instead, just the basics: the main body of the text of the HTML file, along with its embedded image files at roughly the same location. The link colors and the background of the HTML file are overridden by the selections you made in your FrontPage web page.

The procedure for inserting an HTML file is a simple one:

1. First, place the cursor in the web page where you want the contents of the HTML file to appear.
2. Open the **Insert** menu and select **File**. You'll see the familiar file selector box.
3. Select your HTML file and click **OK**. Eventually, your HTML file will appear in your web page, beginning at the cursor.

What If I Don't Want to Insert the HTML File into a Web Page, but I Want to Import It Whole, into My Web?

Then, see the upcoming section on importing files. When you import an HTML file to the web (instead of inserting its contents into a web page), you import the file more or less as is, including embedded graphics and links to other pages out on the web.

Inserting an RTF File

RTF (Rich Text Format) allows you to save more of your formatting than with simple ASCII format, which saves only the words within a document. With RTF, you preserve formatting such as bold, italics, and underline, which you can't do with ASCII.

If you saved your file in RTF format, follow these steps to insert it into a web page:

1. In your web page, place the cursor where you want the contents of the HTML file to appear.
2. Open the **Insert** menu and select **File**.
3. Open the **Files of Type** list box and choose **RTF Files**.
4. Select your file and click **OK**. After a while, your HTML document appears in the web page, beginning at the cursor.

Inserting a Part of Any File

If you use a word processor, and you want to copy part of one file into another, it's a simple matter of having both documents open and doing a quick cut-and-paste operation. Well, you're not using a word processor now; but surprise, with Windows, it's still a simple cut-and-paste operation.

What You See Won't Be What You Get

Using the Copy and Paste buttons to insert text into a web page is the same as using the Insert command with the Normal option. In other words, when you insert text this way, it will be inserted as Normal text, *without* line breaks (except where they would normally fall between paragraphs).

1. First, open the file whose text you want to insert, in its native program. For example, open your file in Microsoft Word.
2. Select the text you want to insert into your web page.
3. Click the **Copy** button or choose the **Edit, Copy** command to copy the selection to the Windows Clipboard.
4. Switch to FrontPage Editor, and click within the web page at the point where you want your selection inserted.
5. Click the **Paste** button, and the text appears, beginning at the cursor. Again, your inserted text will appear in Normal format, and it will wrap naturally.

It's easy to copy information from another application and insert it in FrontPage.

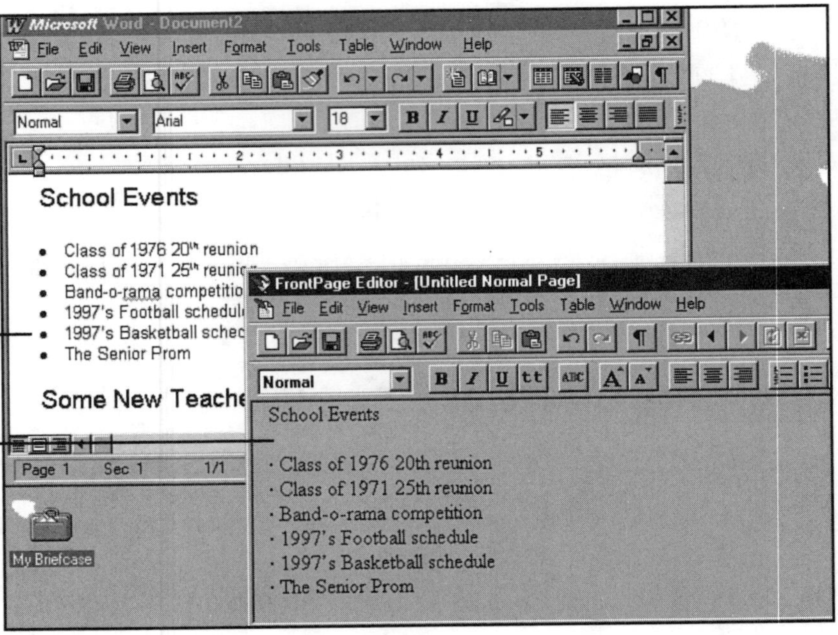

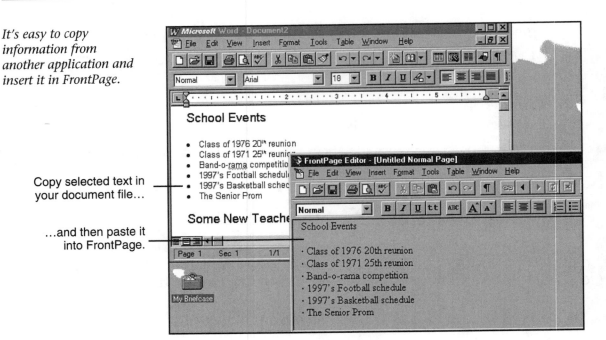

Copy selected text in your document file...

...and then paste it into FrontPage.

Importing a File into Your Web

Again, before you continue, I need to distinguish between the process of *inserting* a file (which you've just been doing) and *importing* a file. You insert a file to get its contents into your web page. You import a file to bring it into your web, not your web *page*. The imported file shows up in the FrontPage Explorer, and you can link to it from within one of your web pages, making the file available to your users through the link.

Now, what kind of files am I talking about here? Well, just about anything you might want to link to, which doesn't already exist out on the Net. In other words, files you store locally, on your own PC, which you now want to make available to the WWW. For example, you might want to import sound files, text files, HTML files (which you don't want to insert into an existing web page), or program files, and provide links to them in your web pages. You can import just about any kind of file (including files you want to make available for downloading), so simply use your imagination.

Why Do I Have to Import a File Just to Link to It?

You see, for a file to be able to be linked to, it has to be placed on the Web somewhere. So, just because you have a file on your hard disk, and you can get to that file from within FrontPage, that doesn't mean the file is accessible to the outside world of the Internet.

When you publish your web to a host Web server, you're simply copying all of your web pages to the server's hard disk. Once on the server, each of those pages will have its own URL (or Internet address) through which it can be accessed or linked, to another web page.

Now, you can create links to files you find on the Web, but what about files you have in your personal possession? How do you make those files accessible to the Internet? Simple. You add the files to your web, and "publish" them along with your web pages. In other words, you copy the files to your host server, at the same time you're copying your web pages.

Because the files are a part of your web, they will be assigned a similar URL address, making them accessible to your users through regular Web links.

What About Graphic Files?

Graphic files (um, .JPEG and .GIF files, that is) are typically not imported, but rather, they are inserted into a web page like you might insert text. You'll learn how to insert a graphics file a bit later in this chapter.

You might use the importing process to bring in other graphic file types to your Web if you like (such as .BMP files), but your users may not be able to *see them*, if they don't have a program that recognizes that particular graphic file format.

So What Happens When a User Clicks on One of These Links?

After you import a file and create a link to it within a web page, what happens then? As you know from using your own Web browser, what happens when you click a link depends on your file associations. A file association links a file type (such as .WAV, .RA, .ZIP, or .VRM) to a specific program on your system that handles (plays) that type of file. If your user has a sound player (or a Web browser with the sound function built-in) and he clicks a link to a sound file, then the sound should play. If he clicks a link to a file that his Web browser doesn't recognize (and doesn't have a file association for), then the browser typically brings up a download box, so the user can save the file to his hard disk for later use (that is, once he installs a program capable of using it.)

Here's how the importing process works:

1. Start up FrontPage Explorer. Open the **File** menu and select **Import**. FrontPage Explorer brings up the delightful and ever-charming **Import File to Web** dialog box.

2. Click **Add File**.

3. Choose the file you want to import to your web, and click **OK**.

Uh, The File I Want to Use Is on the WWW

That's alright; simply copy the file to your hard disk (using your Web browser) before you try to import it. For example, to copy a whole Web page to your hard disk, open the **File** menu and select **Save As**. Select a directory in which to save the HTML file, and click **OK**. To copy a graphic file using Netscape, just right-click a graphic and then select **Save Image as** to save each graphic. To copy a sound file to your hard disk using Netscape, simply right-click the link to the file, and select **Save Link As** from the pop-up menu. Then click **OK** to save the file. You follow a similar procedure to copy other files.

4. The file you chose now shows up as an entry in the Import File to Web dialog box. Notice it shows up as both a file name and a URL. You can repeat steps 2 and 3 to select additional files for importing, if you want.

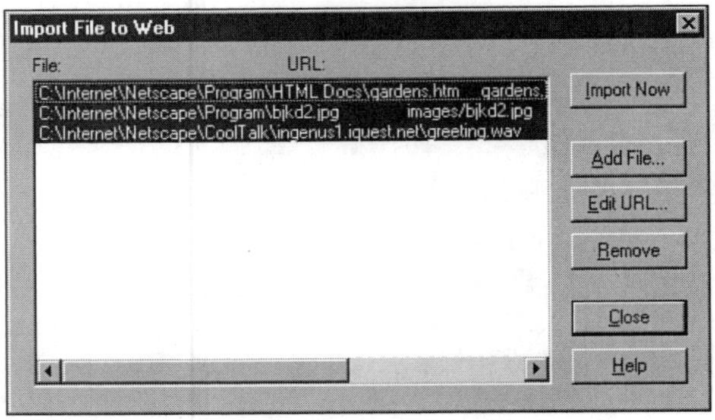

You can import many different types of files into your web.

5. Once you select all your files and they appear in the Import File to Web dialog box, make sure they are highlighted; then click **Import Now**.

6. Wait a while. Don't click **Stop**—just be patient. Nothing will happen for what seems like the length of a TV miniseries. Soon, the file you imported will show up in the Outline View of the FrontPage Explorer window.

7. Click **Close**.

Now that the file is a part of your web site, you can provide links to it through your FrontPage web pages. See Chapter 12 for help in that area.

Adding Sound to a Web Page

You already know the steps involved in adding sound to a web page, because they're similar to what you've already learned. Basically, you import the sound file first and then link it to the web page. But, how does the sound file get played?

First, import the sound file into your web, following the steps in the previous section. As you'll learn in just a moment, you'll increase the chances of your user being able to play your sound file if you use one which is in a common format such as .WAV, .AIFF, and .AU.

At this point, you can open your web page in FrontPage Editor and add a link to the sound file. (You'll learn the steps for adding a link in Chapter 12, so hold on a sec.)

Now that the sound file is linked to a web page, how does it get played? When your user clicks this link, his Web browser will copy the file to his system and hand it over to the appropriate program, which will play it. Exactly which program takes this honor depends on how the user's system is set up; it depends on what program is associated with that particular sound file type.

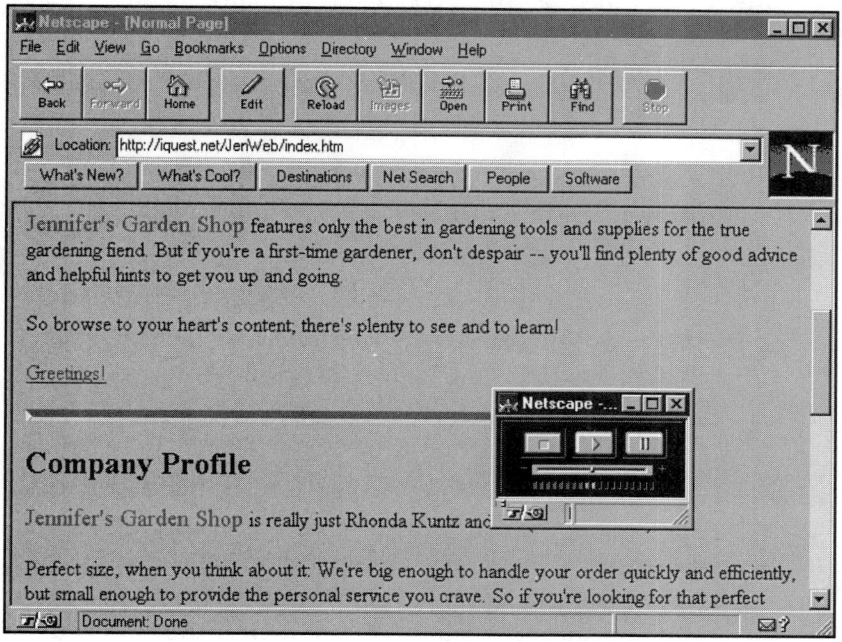

When a user clicks a link to a sound file, it plays on his system.

If there isn't any program associated with the sound file type, then the user won't hear any sound. He will, however, get the opportunity to download your file and play it later, although this isn't exactly the effect you were looking for, I'm sure.

Dropping Pictures onto a Web Page

Switching now to the subject of graphic embellishments: There isn't a World Wide Web page in existence worth its weight in pixels that doesn't have some sort of graphic image (a nerd word for "picture") in it. Chances are, you'll want to insert at least a few graphics into your web pages.

Don't Get Graphic Crazy

Don't go crazy here and insert tons of graphics into your web pages, in a pathetic effort to win "Coolest Site of the Year." When you load up on graphic files, you increase the amount of time it takes for an ordinary user to download (and view) your web pages. And, in that time, the user will probably give up and go somewhere else.

A nice rule of thumb is to limit the total size of any given web page (plus its embedded graphics) to about 100,000 bytes or so, in order that your user (who typically is receiving data at somewhere between 1,000 and 2,000 bytes a second) can view your page in something short of a year or so. Of course, you should still exercise some common sense, even using this rule of thumb: if you put 95K worth of graphics with 5K worth of text, you're still going to end up with a web page that takes too long to view.

Another useful trick is to reuse graphic images in lots of web pages. Since, typically an image only has to be downloaded to the user's system once during a session, reusing images speeds things up quite nicely.

Added Support The current version of Netscape provides its own support for several common sound file types, including .WAV, .AIFF, .MIDI, and .AU.

As you probably already know from using Windows (and all of its associated programs), there are way too many graphic file formats. Umpteen zillion. Thankfully, with the World Wide Web, you'll only be dealing with two: JPEG and GIF files.

Now, before you start getting too depressed, let me tell you that FrontPage allows you to insert just about any graphic file you can think of into your web pages, including Windows metafile, Paint, PostScript, TIFF, and automatically converts the image into a GIF or a JPEG file for you (if it can), so that it can be used over the Web.

Know Your Graphics!

There are only a few things you need to know about the two graphic image formats supported by the World Wide Web. The Graphics Interchange Format (GIF) compresses 256-color, high-resolution graphic images without any loss of picture quality. GIF files are the smallest graphic images you can use in which picture quality is not compromised for size.

The image format created by and named for the Joint Photographic Experts Group (JPEG) is capable of storing images with over *16 million colors!* Before you start sneering at a GIF, however, you should be aware that JPEG files are often quite large. In order to make them smaller (and thus, more manageable), they are compressed. The images in *highly* compressed JPEG files aren't nearly as sharp (or as full of detail) as their GIF cousins. However, using a graphics file editor, you can always adjust the JPEG compression level to whatever you consider is the best compromise between file size and image quality.

Because you often need to mess around with a JPEG image in order to finesse its quality down to a reasonable size, you may want to stick with GIF files *only*, at least at first. Then, when you're ready for the next level in geekiness, you can try your hand at messing with JPEG. To do that, get a nice graphics editor such as LView Pro, which you'll find at all the popular download sites on the Net. Open your JPEG file with LView Pro; then open the **Options** menu and select **Jpeg I/O.** Lower the **Compression quality** to decrease the size of the file while also decreasing the quality of the image. To increase quality (and file size), increase the Compression quality value. Click **OK** when you're done. Save the file, and then reload it with the **File**, **Reopen** command. You should notice a difference. Repeat these steps as needed until you get the results you are looking for: a smaller file size that is not too grainy.

Inserting a Graphic Image

When you insert your GIF or JPEG image file into your web page, you actually see it in the FrontPage Editor window, much the same way it will appear in a Web browser.

That's pretty cool. However, the process of getting an image into your web page exactly where you want it is a bit involved. Oh, well. At least you get some compensation for all this extra work by having the option of directly inserting a graphics file from your own hard disk, or from the World Wide Web.

Here's how to go about inserting a graphics file from your hard disk:

1. Open your web page and place the cursor at the point where you want the image to appear. Once the image is inserted, any text falling to the right of the cursor will be moved down.

2. Open the **Insert** menu and select **Image**. The Insert Image dialog box appears.

Inserting an image.

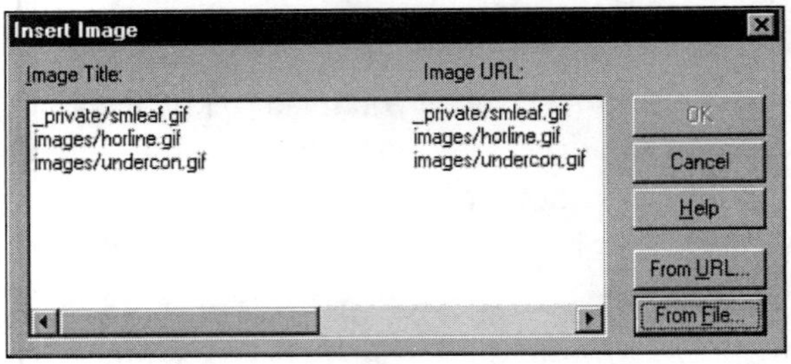

3. You'll see images already in your web listed in this dialog box—mostly FrontPage images. Click **From File**.
4. Select a file type from the **Files of Type** list.
5. Choose a file you want to insert, in whatever format, and click **OK**. If you didn't choose a GIF or a JPEG file, it may take some time for FrontPage to do the conversion.

The image may not appear exactly how you want it to. This is not a problem, since you can adjust the image as needed, as you'll see in the "Adjusting Your Image" section.

Inserting a Graphic from the Web

Instead of inserting a graphic located on your hard disk, you can insert a graphic file directly from the Web, if you like. However, if you use the Insert command, the file *will not be imported to your web*, which means that it won't be copied to your web directory.

If the graphic file isn't imported into your web, how will your users be able to see it?

Well, every time someone views your page, FrontPage will insert the graphic file into your page from its original location on the web. This is fine, except that, if sometime in the future the file is moved to a new location on the Web, you'll have a big gap in your web page, because FrontPage won't be able to insert the graphic.

If you want to be perfectly safe, you might want to *import* the graphic to your web (following the steps given in the "Importing a File into Your Web" section). Importing is a process that copies the file to your web, where it can stay, safe and sound. Once the graphic's imported, you can insert it using the technique in the previous section, "Inserting a Graphic Image."

Given all that, why would someone ever use this option? Well, suppose you wanted to insert the image that Microsoft features on its home page (the one that changes every day) into your home page. By following the steps here, the current image would be inserted automatically, each time someone views your page.

Like before, open your web page and place the cursor at the point where you want the image to appear. Then, open the **Insert** menu and select **Image**. Click **From URL**. Type the Internet address for the image and, *after connecting to the Internet*, click **OK**. For example, type **http://coolplace.com/graphics/image.gif** and click **OK**. Your image appears in the web page, just as normal. However, it is actually being temporarily downloaded from the Internet for viewing. When you close this page, the image will not remain on your hard disk. If you disconnect from the Internet and then reopen the page, you'll get an error telling you that FrontPage could not insert your image. That's annoying, but okay, provided that once you publish the page to the WWW, the graphic file can be located and inserted whenever someone tries to view the page.

How Do I Get the Address for a Graphic?

Sometimes, coming up with the exact location of an embedded graphic can be tricky. However, if you use Netscape, try this: simply connect to the web page that contains the graphic you want to insert; then right-click it. From the pop-up menu, select **Copy Image Location.** This copies the URL for the image to the Windows Clipboard. Switch over to FrontPage and follow the steps to insert the file. When you're asked to enter the URL for the image, click in the URL text box and press **Shift+Insert** to paste the address from the Clipboard.

Adjusting Your Image

Once you get the image into your web page, you can adjust it so that it's placed more exactly. Remember back in Chapter 7, when you were inserting horizontal lines, and you had to insert the line first and then use a Properties dialog box to adjust the line's length and width? The process is much the same here; once the image is loaded, you can tell FrontPage how you want it adjusted.

To begin, simply right-click your image, and from the pop-up menu, select **Properties**. You're presented with this magnificent Image Properties dialog box.

All the things you can do to an image packed in one neat box.

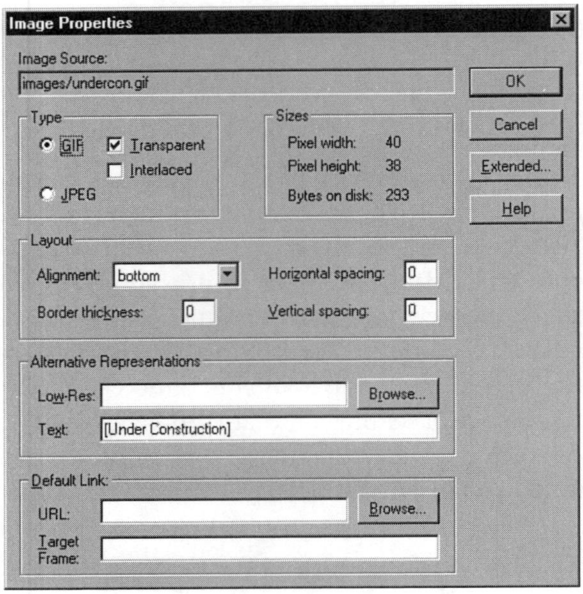

Looking at this dialog box, you should note that the only image attributes you can change are those that the current version of HTML supports. In other words, it's not everything you could hope for. The most obvious thing missing here is that *you cannot resize an image once it's inserted*—because that option is not supported by the current version of HTML.

What Do You Mean I Can't Resize an Image Once It's Inserted?

In HTML, a graphic image is not an elastic thing. You can't have a large image and tell the Web browser to make a smaller version of it. If you want it small, you have to somehow make it small *before* you insert it into your web page. "Somehow," in this case, means that, if you need an Image file of a particular size, you have to use a graphic editor program to resize the image. Then, save the smaller copy as a separate file, and insert it into your page.

If your image is too big or too small, click it to select it, and press **Delete** to remove it from your web page. Then, start from scratch with your graphics editor, resizing the file and reinserting the changed file into your web page.

There are plenty of options here, and this is what they all mean:

- The **Type** frame shows you the current format of your image. You can change the image format being used if you like. If you change from GIF to JPEG, the options under the Type section change to fit the format you selected.

Why Change?

If you choose GIF (as choosy mothers do), you can make the background part of the image **Transparent**. In such a case, the GIF's transparent background allows whatever's behind the image (for instance, the background color) to show through. The result is an image with a contoured outline, rather than a rectangular one.

You can also make the GIF file **Interlaced**, which makes your image appear full-sized but kind of rough at first—the image gets gradually clearer as more of it downloads to the user's system. This allows the user to get a sense of the picture fairly quickly.

However, if you choose **JPEG**, you can change its compression rating, thereby improving its **Quality.** Here, a 100 offers great quality, while increasing the file size. A setting of 75 is usually a nice compromise between quality and size.

- Under **Layout**, you can change your image's **Alignment**. There are many options here, so hang on. When you inserted your image, it was placed using bottom alignment, which aligns the *bottom* of the image with the *baseline* of your text (where the bottoms of o's and s's fall, but not y's or q's that fall below).

  Top alignment places the top of your image with the *ascent* line of the text (the top of capital letters). **Middle** places the middle of your image in line with the middle of your text.

  The really useful alignment choices here are **left** and **right**, and you may use them often. **Left** places the image on the left, with text running down its right. **Right** works the same way, but in the opposite direction.

Getting all your graphics in a-lign.

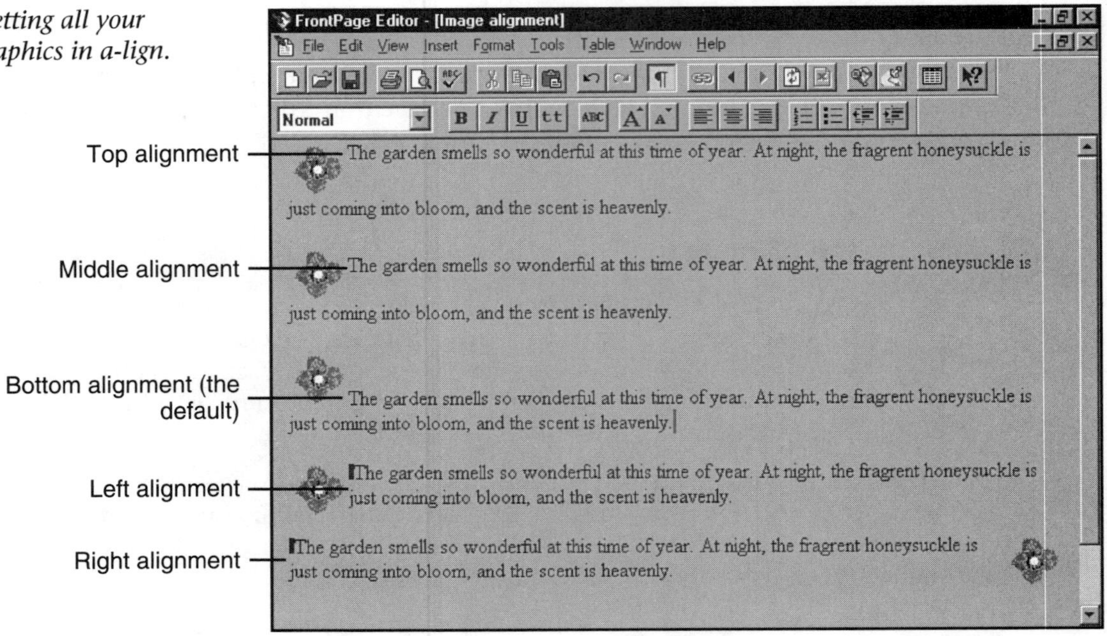

What About the Other Alignment Options?

You might as well skip the other alignment options: **absbottom** and **baseline** (which are the same as **bottom**), **absmiddle** (which is the same as **middle**), and **texttop** (which is the same as **top**). Some Web browsers (about 10% of them) will see these settings just a bit differently, but most of your viewers won't.

- You can add a border around your image with the **Border thickness** option.
- You can add extra spacing above and below (vertical), and to the right and left (horizontal) of the image, by setting **Horizontal spacing** and **Vertical spacing**.
- Under **Alternative Representations**, you can select a lower resolution image to display on user's systems when they're currently using a lower resolution display, such as 640 × 480. Under **Text**, you can enter a text line that appears in the image's place while it's downloading to the user's system.
- Under **Default Link**, you can specify a link for your image, or "hotspot" if you want. When users click the image, the link you specify connects them to some other web page, or some other point on this page. I'll be covering graphic links in detail in Chapter 13.

- By clicking **Extended**, you can add any miscellaneous HTML graphics codes that you may discover in your travels.

The Least You Need to Know

In this chapter, you learned about inserting and importing. Here's the gist of it:

- When you *import* a file, it becomes part of your web—the structure you're building that you'll publish later to a server.
- By contrast, when you *insert* a file, its content is copied into one of your web pages.
- You can insert all or part of a text file, HTML file, or RTF file into your page.
- The Web supports only two graphic formats: GIF and JPEG images.
- You'll find that you probably need to use some type of graphics editor program to spruce up and properly size each image you want to insert into your page, before you insert it, because FrontPage doesn't give you any picture editing tools.

Chapter 9

Putting the Polish on Your Page

By the End of This Chapter, You'll Be Able to...

- Buff out any unsightly spelling errors
- Set the background color for a page
- Change the text and link colors
- Place a graphics image in the background

You've done a lot so far to make your web pages interesting: formatting your text, applying styles to your paragraphs, adding lines and lists, and dropping in some graphics and sound files along the way. In this chapter, you'll learn how to add a final coat of polish that will make your pages really shine.

Spell Checking a Page

What did we all do before spell checkers? Even if you're a spelling bee champion, you're still apt to make a few typing errors, if nothing else. This is not a problem because FrontPage will find and correct any spelling errors for you.

The process is similar to spell checking a document in a word processor: simply open the page you want to check in FrontPage Editor. Then, click the **Check Spelling** button on the Standard Toolbar, or if you're a keyboard guru, press **F7**.

FrontPage starts checking the spelling of the page from the top—meaning that it ignores wherever your silly cursor is located. FrontPage, being the efficient know-it-all that it is, also checks for repeated words (you know that that means it may find words you intended to repeat, like "like"). However, FrontPage does not check the spelling of files whose contents you have inserted into this page through the Include WebBot, which you'll learn about in Chapter 17.

But, I Don't Want to Check the Whole Thing!

If you want to check only a section of text, you can. Just select it first, before clicking the **Check Spelling** button. To select text, you drag over it.

What You Should Do When FrontPage Finds a Mistake

If FrontPage sniffs out an error, you'll see this box.

Way too many choices.

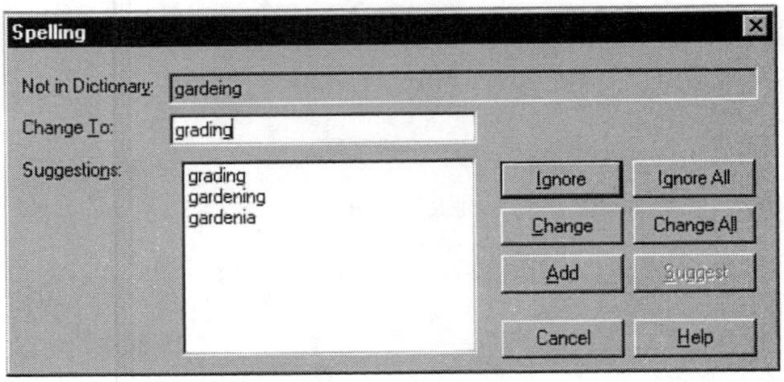

Here are your options:

Correct the mistake by clicking the **Change** button, that is, if the correct word is already in the Change To: box. To correct the same mistake throughout the page, click **Change All** instead. Be careful when using the Change All button; if you change all occurrences of "abel" to "able" but your text includes a reference to a Dr. Jane Abel, her name will be "corrected" to the wrong thing.

Spell Check Just Ruined Everything!

If you accidentally click **Change All**, and it changes some words to the wrong spelling, you're not completely without hope. Just click **Undo** to undo the spell check.

Make a suggestion by selecting one from the Suggestions: box, or by typing your own correction in the Change To: box. Then click **Change** or **Change All**. Again, be careful when using the Change All option.

Ignore the mistake by clicking **Ignore** (to ignore this mistake only) or **Ignore All** (to ignore the same mistake throughout the page).

Add the "mistake" to the dictionary by clicking **Add**.

Delete a repeated word by clicking **Delete**. (You won't actually see this button until FrontPage finds a repeated word.)

Forget the whole darn thing by clicking **Cancel**.

When FrontPage is done, it'll tell you so. Click **OK** to close the dialog box and return to your web page.

Changing the Background Color

You can create a tone for a web page through its background color. Choose **white** or **light gray**, and your page will look crisp and business-like. Choose **black**, and your page will look dark, brooding and oh so Generation-X. Whatever you choose, keep in mind that you'll probably need to change the text color, too, in order to maintain the "proper level of contrast" (fancy-schmancy way of reminding you to keep the text legible). Good timing, since you'll learn how to change your text color in just a minute.

Read This If You're Using a Page Created by a Wizard

When you use a wizard to create a web site, you make what seems like an endless series of selections, some of which affect the look of the page (that is, its background color or background image). The FrontPage wizard then generates a single page from your choices and calls it **Web Colors**. All the other pages in your web get their colors from the choices stored in this one web page.

To change the background color *for all the pages in your web*, make your changes to the Web Colors Web page. Start by opening the Web Colors page, then simply follow the steps here to change its background color. By changing the background color in the Web Colors page and then saving it, you'll automatically change the background of all the other pages in your web to the same color.

If you only want to change the background color for one page in the web, then ignore everything I've just said, and perform the following steps, using the page you want to change.

To change the background color of a particular web page, follow these steps:

1. First, open the web page you want to change in FrontPage Editor. Remember, to change all the background colors in a web created by a FrontPage wizard, open the **Web Colors** page.
2. Then open the **File** menu and select **Page Properties**.
3. Click the **Use Custom Background Color** option.
4. Click **Choose** to select your color. You'll see the Color dialog box.
5. This dialog box works just like the color boxes throughout Windows 95: simply click the color you want, and then click **OK** to select it.

Creating a Custom Color

If you don't see a color you like, you can create a custom color. Start in the Color dialog box and go from there:

1. Start by clicking an empty box in the Custom Colors section.
2. Click the **Define Custom Colors** button and the dialog box gets bigger.

Pick a color, any color.

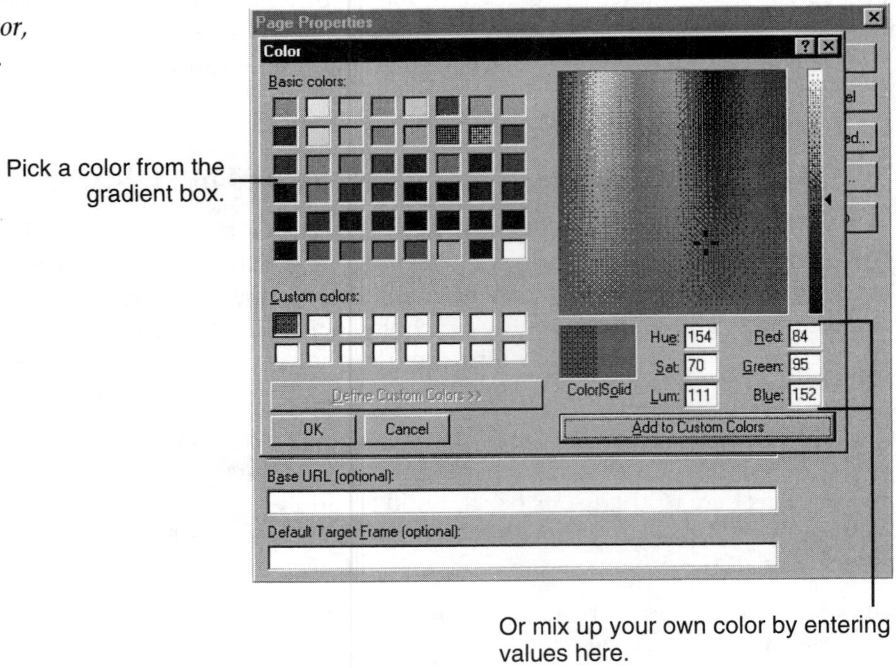

3. Click in the color gradient box or enter values in the Hue, Saturation, Luminescence, Red, Green, and Blue boxes to create a color.

Uh, Change the What?

Any on-screen color is made up of varying amounts of blue, red, and green. So, to make a custom color, you mix these three colors. Each color has a value, ranging from 0 to 255. A 0 means you get none of that color; 255 says it's that color to the max. By mixing varying amounts of these three colors, you can create just about any color you can dream of.

As for those odd (yet artsy-sounding) color values: The *hue* of a color describes its place on the color wheel—red is 0 on the color wheel, green is 80, and blue is 160. Other colors have hue values in between these values. The *saturation* value tells you how much of the color is being applied to the final mix—a saturation of 240 gives you the brightest value of that color, while 120 will make the color appear less bright. And *luminosity* tells you how much light (or white) is added to the color. Too much luminosity and the color becomes almost white. Too little and it becomes black.

Feel free to play Vincent Van Gogh by changing these values. The results of your color blending will show up in the Color/Solid box below the gradient box. Enjoy!

4. Click **Add to Custom Colors**.
5. Once you create your custom color, click it to select it. Click **OK** to choose it as your background color.
6. In the Page Properties dialog box, click **OK**, and the background of your page changes to the color you picked.

Changing Text Colors

Often when you change the background color for a page, you're forced to change the text color too, if for no other reason than to make the text legible against the new background color. What you're looking for is enough contrast to make your text distinguishable from the background.

Changing the text color is remarkably similar to changing the background color, so I won't bore you with too much of a repeat. Just make sure that you read that section first, since there are some warnings and such that you might find helpful.

Web Colors?

One warning I want to make sure you read in the previous section has to do with whether or not you created your web site using one of FrontPage's wizards.

If you did, you need to know that during the creation process, an extra web page called Web Colors was created. In this one web page are stored the common color choices (background, text, and link color) that all your web pages now share. So, if you want to change the text color *for all your web pages,* then you must make your change in the Web Colors page.

Anyway, to change the text color of a page, open your web page in FrontPage Editor. Next, open the **File** menu and select **Page Properties**.

Hey, this looks familiar.

Click the **Use Custom Text Color** option; then click **Choose** to select a color. If you need help with this dialog box, see the previous section. Basically, you click the color you want, and then click **OK** to select it. Once you're back at the Page Properties dialog, click **OK**, and your text color is applied to the current page.

Changing Link Colors

A *link* is a connection from one web page to something else, such as another web page, a sound file, or a data file available for downloading. As you visit each link on a page, the color of that link changes to let you know which links you've seen, and which ones you have not yet visited.

FrontPage lets you change the color of links as they appear on your web page when it's first viewed. You can also change the color of links that have been visited by the user, along with the active link color (the color the link changes to when it is first clicked by the mouse).

Will This Work?

Now, don't go hog wild changing your link colors, because they could be overridden by the user's Web browser—assuming that the user has made specific selections for his link colors in his Web browser's preferences screens.

The process of changing link colors is basically a repeat of the steps under the "Changing the Background Color" and "Changing the Text Color" sections, so I'll try not to bore you too much.

If You're Using a Web Created By a Wizard, Read This

If you created your web site using one of FrontPage's wizards, then you need to read the warning you'll find in the "Changing the Background Color" section. Go ahead; I'll wait.

Okay. To change the color of your links, open the page you want to change in FrontPage Editor. Then, open the **File** menu and select **Page Properties**.

Click the appropriate link color option (such as the Link, Visited Link, or Active Link Color). Click **Choose** to select the color you want to use.

You and the Color dialog box should be old friends by now, but if you need help using it, see the "Changing the Background Color" section. Without repeating all the details here, I can tell you that all you need to do is to simply click the color you want, and then click **OK**. At the Page Properties dialog, click **OK**, and your link color is set.

Adding a Background Image

You can replace the background color of a web page with a tiled image, which is similar to placing an image on the Windows desktop. *Tiled*, as you know, means that the image is repeated over the web page both horizontally and vertically until it completely fills the Web page.

Before you start, let me warn you that a lot of images will not make great backgrounds for text, because they are too detailed (uh, busy). For example, photos don't work very well, unless they are fuzzied up so much (using a graphics editor) that you can barely make out the image. To make an image more acceptable as a background, you may want to edit the image using a graphics editor such as Paint Shop Pro. With such a program, you can decrease the contrast level and, perhaps, make the image less bright (more gray) in order to make the image fade into the background where it belongs. In the process, you'll make your text stand out better on top of it.

When Speed Is the Issue

Adding graphics (such as a background image) to a web page makes it bigger, which in turn, makes that web page take longer to download. So, remember to keep the total file size of your web page and your images under 100,000 bytes in order to limit the user's download time to about 50 seconds or so. (Of course, if you reuse the same background image again and again, this usually saves on download time as the user moves from page to page—since the image typically has to be downloaded only once.)

Now, you can't just pick any graphics file and insert it as a background for your Web pages. On the Internet, there are only two supported graphic file formats: GIF (Graphics Interchange Format) and JPEG (Joint Photographic Experts Group format). Your graphics file should be in one of these two formats. If you import a .BMP file, it'll work but you'll be leaving the file conversion (to JPEG or GIF) up to FrontPage. (Wanna know more about these two file formats? Check out Chapter 8.)

How Tos

Enough background fodder; time to get down to business. Now, when it comes to selecting a graphics file for your background, you have several choices:

You can link to a file on the web somewhere. Risky, since the file isn't under your control, and if the file's deleted or moved from its original location, you may be left without a background for your web pages.

You can link to a file on your hard disk. Silly idea, since people on the Internet can't connect to your hard disk, and so they couldn't view the background image.

You can "import" an image file into your FrontPage web, and link to that. This is the only method that works well. What you do here is take an image on your hard disk (or the web) and *import* it so that it is copied to your web directory. Then, when you publish your web later on (put it out on the World Wide Web for all to see), the graphics image is copied to your host's hard disk along with all your web page files. Thus, the background file becomes available for use on your web pages.

Hey! Are You Using a Page Created by a Wizard?

At the risk of sounding like your mother screaming "Don't slam that screen door!" ten million times...to change the image that was used (or to replace the common background color with an image) *for all the pages in your web*, you have to make your changes to the Web Colors page. Open the page; then follow the steps here to import a graphics image to the web and to select that file as the background image.

And as always, if you only want to change one page in the web, then ignore all this gobbledy-gook and follow the next steps, using the page you want to change, and not the Web Colors page.

Here's how to include a graphics image as a background for a web page:

1. Open the **File** menu and select **Page Properties**. Lots of options, huh? Don't sweat it—you only have to deal with one of them.
2. Select the **Background Image** option and click **Browse**.

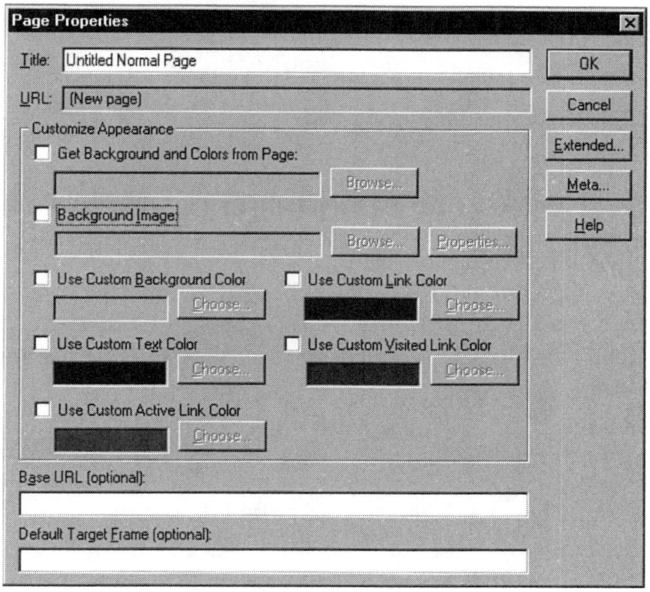

Welcome to Page Properties.

3. You'll see a list of image files in the web; since your graphic file has not yet been imported, it's not here. No problem. Simply click **From File** (to use an image file located on your hard disk) or **From URL** (to use an image file on the Internet—just keep in mind that this may be a bad idea).

4. When you click **From File**, you'll see the usual file selector box. Select your graphic file and click **OK**. If you click **From URL** instead, you need to connect to the Internet and then enter the exact address of the graphic file you want to snarf. (See Chapter 8 if you want more details.)
5. You'll land back at the Page Properties dialog box. Click **OK** and the graphic is tiled onto the page's background. If you selected a file in a format other than JPEG or GIF, then it will be "converted" to one of these two formats by FrontPage. If you want more control over how the final file will look, convert it using a nice graphics editor such as Paint Shop Pro.
6. When you save the page later, you'll be asked if you want to save the image file as well. Answer **Yes** to this, and the image file will be imported to your web (which, as I said earlier, makes the image available to users who view your page out on the Internet).

The Least You Need to Know

If you follow the steps in this chapter, your web pages will look like they were created by a professional Web master (as opposed to someone who actually has a life "offline").

- To check the spelling in a page, click the **Check Spelling** button.
- Remember that if you change the background color, text color, link color, or background image, you're changing it for the current web page only.
- If you create your web using a wizard and want to change the background, text, or link color or the background image *for all your web pages* at one time, make your changes to the **Web Colors** page.
- To change the background, text, or link color of a page, open the **File** menu and select **Page Properties**. Click the appropriate option (such as **Use Custom Background Color** if you're changing the background color) and then click **Choose**. Select your color and click **OK**. Click **OK** again and you're done.
- To add a background image to a page, start with a GIF or a JPEG file. Import the file into the web by starting FrontPage Explorer, opening the **File** menu, and selecting **Import**. Click **Add File**, select your graphic image, and click **Open**. Finally, click **Import Now** to import the image into the web. Click **Close** when you finish.
- After your image has been imported, open the **File** menu and select **Page Properties**. Click **Background Image** and then click **Browse**. Select your image file from the list, and click **OK**. Click **OK** again, and you're through.

Part 3
Time to Start Planning Your Web Site

You've come far: you've conquered your first-night jitters and have, by now, created a pretty cool-looking home page.

Now, it's time to relax, put your feet up, and take a good look at the information you want to publish on your web. Yep, it's decision time. Before you start adding pages to your web willy-nilly, use what you learn in this part to organize your web site and decide which pages you need. In this part, you get your act together (or at least, your web site).

Chapter 10

Designing the Perfect Web Site

By the End of This Chapter, You'll Be Able to...

- Plan out your web site
- Decide on your web's structure
- Present your information in the best way
- Understand what makes a site "good" or "bad"

Now that the creation of your Home page is well under way, it's time that you start thinking of adding more pages to your web. However, before you do that, take a moment or two to figure out what you want to publish on the web and how you want to organize it.

Yes, it's time to start thinking of yourself as a Web publisher. As a publisher, you should keep your audience (and its needs) in mind. No, you don't have to plan out every detail *right now*, but you should give the structure of your web at least a little thought before you start adding pages willy-nilly. And in this chapter, you'll learn how to design your perfect Web site.

Good Place to Start

The best place to learn about web design is on the World Wide Web. Visit various Web sites, and as you do, consider what makes one Web site easy to use, while others are difficult. When you connect to a site, do you immediately see what the site offers? Can you find what you need easily? Is the design of the site inviting? Logically organized? Fun? Frivolous?

A Quick Look at Your Options

A web's structure is defined by the organization of its pages. At this point, your web's structure is fairly simple.

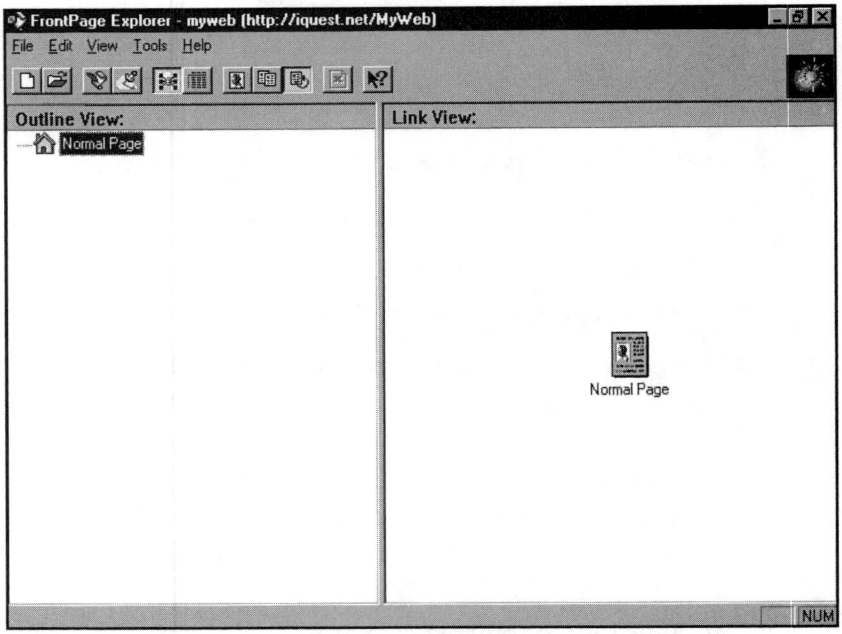

A pretty simple web, wouldn't you say?

Obviously, as you add more pages to your web and link them to other pages, the structure of your web will change and become more complex.

Say you have a web site with one page, your home page. You want more. Where do you go from here? Well, you have a few options:

- ➤ You can plan out the exact structure you want on paper. Then, by following your plan, you can add pages and links to your existing home page to recreate it. A little more work, maybe, but you end up with exactly what you want.
- ➤ You can use one of the FrontPage templates or wizards to create a new web with the structure you want; then you can copy your existing Home page into it. This isn't such a bad idea, since most of the work of structuring your web (and linking your pages together) is done for you. On the other hand, you're stuck changing (or deleting) the parts of the web you don't like.
- ➤ You can copy a web site off the Internet and use it as a basis for your web. (Uh, sorta. You can't copy the web directly, as you'll find out later in this chapter.) Once you copy the web to your hard disk and you make changes to it to suit your needs, you can copy your home page into it.

Before you can decide which of these to use, you need to have some idea about how you want your web site to look.

Some Thoughts About Web Structure

Don't frown. I'm not saying that you have to plan out your entire web *right now*, but getting a rough idea of your web's purpose, and the type and amount of information you want to organize in it will help you get off to the right start.

Identifying Your Web's Purpose

Identifying the purpose of your web is one way you can figure out how to organize it. For example, if the purpose of your web site is business-related, then you should provide quick access to *business-related activities*, such as sales and product information, background information on your company, press releases, and contact information. To feature your hottest new products, consider adding a What's New page, as shown in the next figure.

If you base your web on a personal interest, then *keep things personal*, and devote your main web pages to the things you like most about your interest. For example, if you base your web page on your love of golf, then devote your main pages to the things that interested you in the first place, such as a listing of your favorite courses, background information on your personal golf heroes, and tips and techniques for improving your game.

Make the things your users want to find easily accessible.

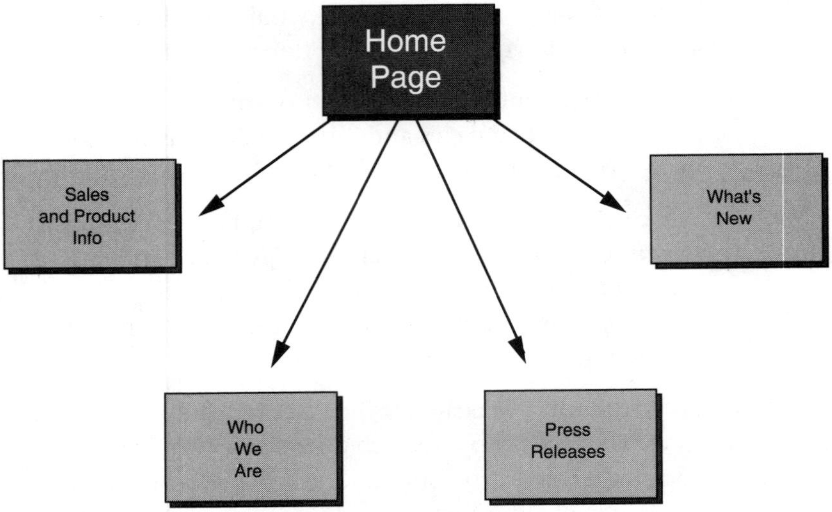

If you gear your web toward children (see next figure), then you might want to keep its organization simple, with only a few main pages. Of course, simplicity in your site's organization is always a plus, even if the site is geared toward adults.

This home page is set up for children—keeping things simple.

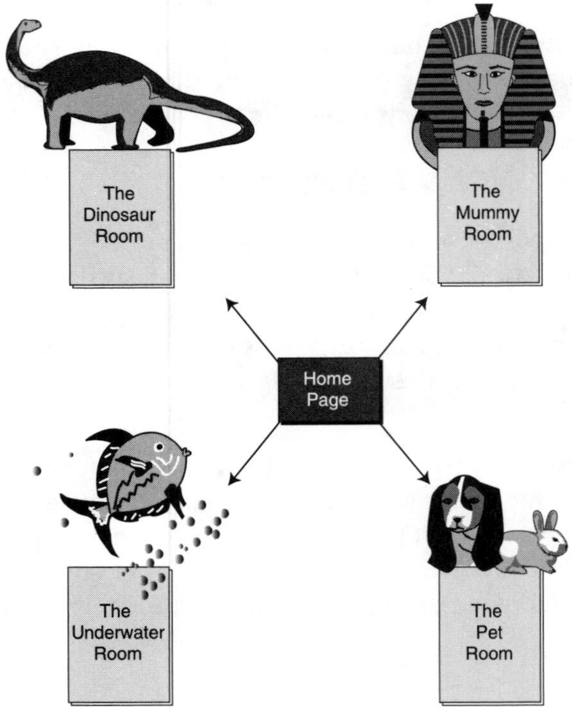

The use of *rooms* gives young users something to relate to. In addition, you can use pictures instead of words to represent your various links, making it easy for a child to recognize which room he wants to visit.

Examining Your Methods of Organization

Now that you understand your web's purpose, it's time to start taking a harder look at your proposed organization. For example, if you plan to devote the web to *both* fishing and scuba diving, then you should consider that, although these topics are *related*, they are quite *different*. In such a case, you might want to divide your home page into two sections.

One of the most important things you can do for your site's readers is to make sure they can find the information they need—quickly and easily. In a book, readers can thumb through the Index or the Table of Contents to locate a particular page. You need to build the same sort of "reference points" into your site. For example, in your home page, you add a *frame* that contains a miniature table of contents, with links to each of your main pages. (Chapter 19 gives you the scoop on creating a table of contents.) You might also can add a search page to your web and place a link to it on your home page.

Frames

Use frames to divide a web page into sections—like the separate panes of glass in a window. A framed window is actually just a set of instructions that tells the Web browser how to divide the window and what to display within each frame.

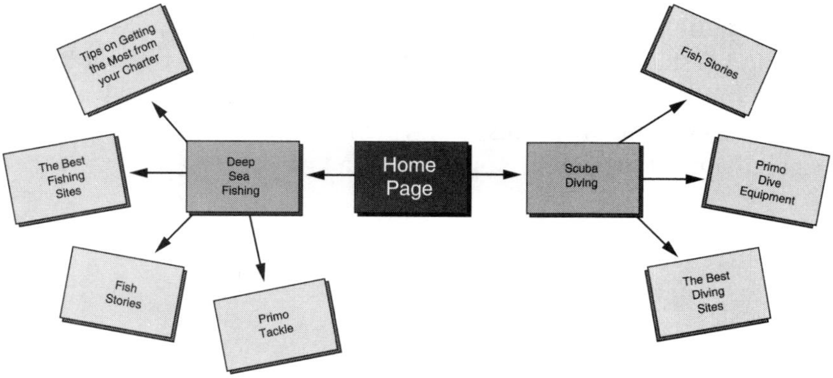

You can divide your Web into sections.

A TOC makes it easy to find information.

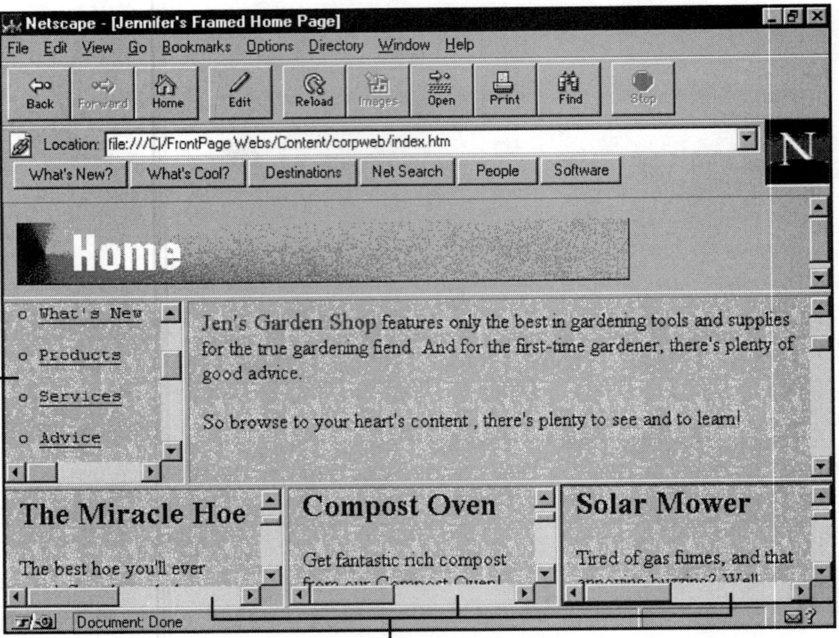

Frames allow a user to view several pages at once.

A great way to help your readers get where they want to go within your site is to give them access to many pages all at once. Frames are the heroes in this story; divide your home page with frames, each containing a different web page from your site. Readers can see several of your site's pages at once and click the page they want to visit.

Links, of course, are an important tool for helping the user locate information quickly. Provide links to pages within your web which are related to the topic on the current page. Also, make sure to provide a link to your home page on all your other pages, so that the reader can always return to his starting point. If you're looking to combine cool with convenience, then consider linking your main web pages through a *link bar (toolbar)*—a series of graphics (or one large graphic with hotspots) which, when clicked, jumps the user to a particular page. Chapter 13 explains how to create a link bar.

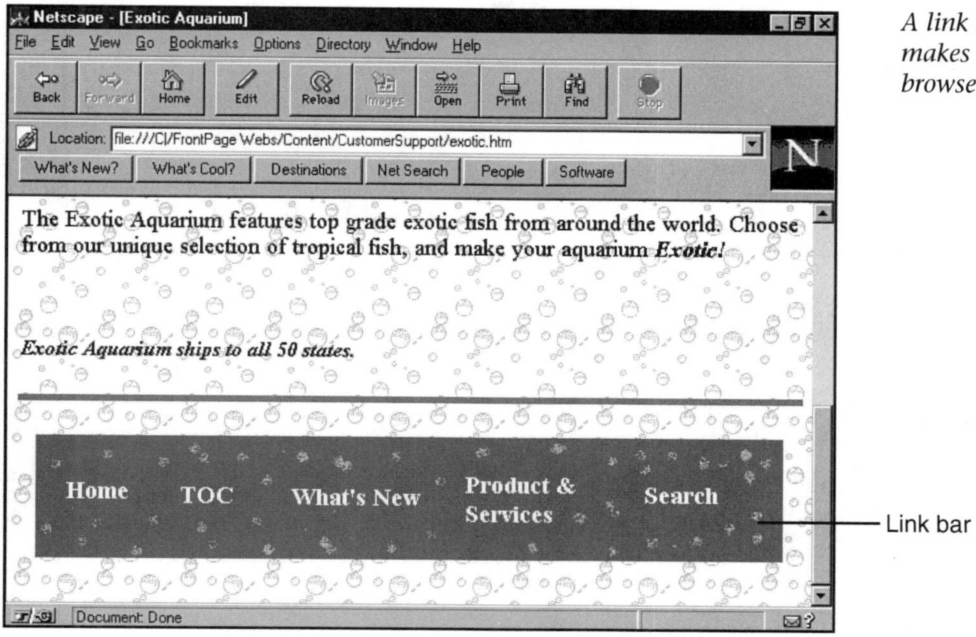

A link bar (toolbar) makes it easy to browse your web.

Learning by Design

After you have your web sketched out, how can you tell if it's any good? First of all, don't rely on the user to always follow a particular order. Walk through your web like you might walk through a museum, and see if the information flows from one topic to the next. Did you provide links to related pages? How easy is it to simply explore? How quickly can you locate specific information? Can you always get back to the home page, or to a key page in a particular section?

When touring your web, don't assume that the user will start at your home page. He might have clicked a link out on the WWW that brought him directly to one of your product pages, and now that he's interested, he may want to see what else you're selling. So, anticipating that, can the reader find what he needs quickly? In this example, you might consider placing a link to a complete product index (which is searchable through a form). Having come in the "backdoor," can the user still find his way around? A link to your home page within all your pages will at least assure that the user can find a good starting spot. But consider links to an index or a TOC as well. Will the reader *know* that your site contains more information than what's on the first page he sees? Will he know how to get to it? To solve this problem, consider inserting "ads" for related pages at the top of each page. I mean, why not? Everyone else has them!

Here are some other thoughts to chew on:

- First impressions are important. Most of us "channel-surf" the Net, using only a few seconds to say "yeah!" or "yech" to a web page. So, make sure that your home page is eye-grabbing.
- Don't fill up your pages with large graphics in an effort to look "cool." Most people have no patience with pages that take too long to load, and they'll jump onto something else. (Keep the total of your document and its graphics to less than 100k.) To entice your users to stay, make sure that each of your web pages has a descriptive title, with a nice paragraph, bulleted list, or other "content-revealing" element at the top to let people know what they'll get if they stay long enough.
- Try to keep each page to about one or two screenfuls. If your page is larger than that, consider breaking it into logical sections providing links to those sections. If you want to offer the document for viewing in its long form, then provide a link to the file for downloading.
- Along this same vein, put a few important links at the top of large pages so that the truly impatient (like me) can skip ahead if a page is loading too slowly. (Chapter 12 tells you how to create links.)
- Many people make the mistake of thinking that they can organize their web site like they might organize a pamphlet or a lecture, with one page following another in a specific order. Remember that on the Web, you can link any page to any other page. So just because page 1 of your brochure lists the benefits of lake-side living, and page 2 lists nearby conveniences, that doesn't mean you have to link these two pages *together*, or that they have to be linked *in a particular order*.
- If you feel that you must control exactly how a visitor views your site, you can link your first page to your second, your second page to your third, and so on. But, again, be aware that too much control turns people OFF. Typically, a user will prefer to browse the pages on the Web following his own path. If you have to present your pages in sequence, then you need to make sure that the content of each page is so *good* that a person will practically *beg* to read it before going onto the next page.
- Don't get so caught up in being different that you turn people off. A web site that uses strange icons, mysterious links, and dark graphics may turn away the people who came to your site expecting to find information quickly and easily.
- Design your web for your intended audience. If you expect only experienced Net users, then add many quick links, frames, and cool graphics. (See Chapter 8, "Importing Pictures, Text, and Sound," and Chapter 13, "Giving Your Graphics Hotspots," for information on how to add ultimate cool to your site.) If you expect a few newbies, then add help that *really* helps (hey, there's a novelty), and make it available from every page. Consider adding a good table of contents page as well

(with descriptions of each page), so the new user can find what he wants, even if he doesn't exactly know what to call it. Also, consider *not* using frames if you expect a lot of inexperienced users. For the newbie, frames (at least, more than two per screen) may be annoying.

- Since you're designing a site for other people (and not yourself) to use, why not include a page where your visitors can tell you what they think? (Don't worry; nobody says you have to actually *read* the comments.) What you need here is a form, and you can read all about those in Chapter 15.
- If you want to impress new customers (and keep your old ones), you need to cater to both. Remember, a newbie's needs are a lot different than somebody who has ordered from your company before. You might want to design a second way into your web site that skips the introduction stuff and jumps your existing customers to What's New. For example, you could design a simple home page with only two links: one for new customers which links them to a detailed introduction, and one for existing customers which takes them past the introduction junk. (You could provide a reminder to existing customers to add a bookmark to this "backdoor" so that they never have to come in through the home page if they don't want to.)

Learning by Disaster

Sometimes, the best way to figure out what's wrong with your web site plan is to look at a web that has problems. Here's a web site that needs some help.

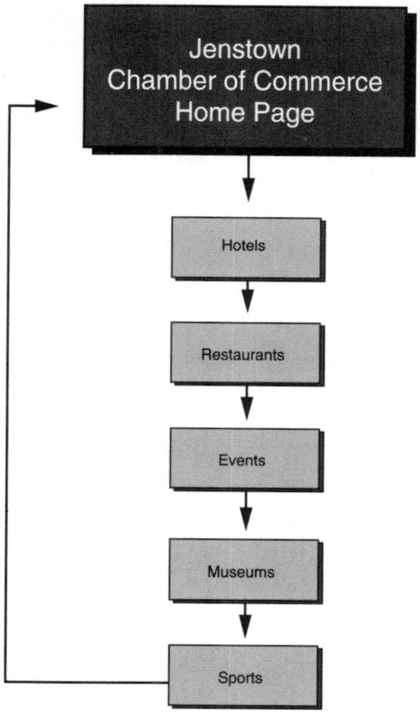

Designing the site as you might design a pamphlet is a mistake.

The arrows in the figure represent the links within the web. They also indicate the direction of the link.

Notice these things:

- ➤ The users' path through the site is predetermined, and most users don't like that.
- ➤ There's no easy way for users to return to a previous page, other than using their browser's **Back** button.
- ➤ There's no apparent comment page, so users can't leave any feedback on what they might want to know about this city.
- ➤ The site reads like a typical Chamber of Commerce pamphlet, and you know what people usually do with pamphlets.

Here's another bad egg!

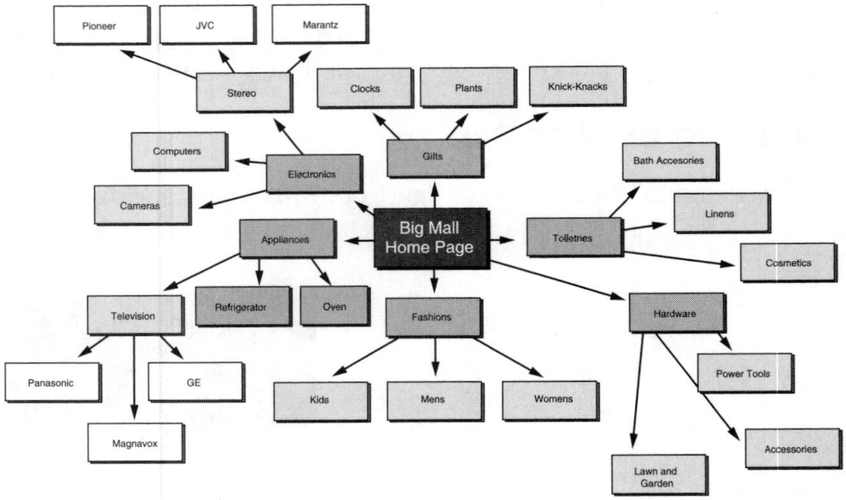

Do people really browse the malls like this?

Again, the arrows indicate links and their direction. Notice these things:

- ➤ Nobody shops the same way he changes from one directory to another on his hard drive (by backing in and out of them), but that's how this site is laid out.
- ➤ Often, an item will fit into more than one category, making it difficult for the user to know in advance which category to choose. For example, televisions might be listed under both appliances and electronics.
- ➤ This site more or less assumes that the user knows exactly what he wants, and what category it's in—there's no way to browse.

Ready to Put Your Plan in Action?

If you haven't already laid out your web site, you should be ready to do so now. You've seen what you like and don't like on the Web; you've carefully memorized all of the words of wisdom on Web design, and with a little time and a lot of thought, you can draw up your web master plan.

But now I hear you asking "Okay, so how do I make this lovely plan of mine a web?" FrontPage is flexible in its solution to that problem. As mentioned at the top of this chapter, using your plan as a guide, you have three options for creating your dream site:

- Build your web site from a template or wizard (very easy).
- Build your site based on another web site (pretty easy).
- Build your site from scratch (not too easy).

In the next chapter, you'll take a look at each of these options in detail. Don't forget your site plan!

The Least You Need to Know

When planning your web site, remember these things:

- Start by identifying the purpose of your web. Is it for business or pleasure?
- Don't include a myriad of unrelated topics in one site.
- Examine your organization. Are your main sections divided logically? Ask someone else to look at your site and offer an opinion.
- Can the user find what he needs?
- How are the pages linked together? Is it easy to jump to a related page? Is it easy to jump to an unrelated topic?
- Remember to "walk through your web."

Chapter 11

Your Blueprints Are Ready; So Build Your Web Site!

By the End of This Chapter, You'll Be Able to...

- ➤ Identify each of the FrontPage templates and wizards
- ➤ Make adjustments to the FrontPage templates or wizards so they fit what you want to do
- ➤ Copy web sites from the Internet
- ➤ Create your own web site from scratch, with the least amount of hassle

Using what you learned in the last chapter, you should have a good idea of how you'd like to organize your web.

So where do you go from here?

The first step is to compare your site plan with the templates and wizards that you'll find described in this chapter. If one of them is a good match, then you can use it to create your web site.

If you don't find a good match, I'll show you how to copy something off the Web, although, let me warn you, the process isn't exactly a walk in the park. If you can't find anything to match what you want to do, you can simply build your web from scratch, adding pages one at a time and building your links. To help you do this, I'll show you how to create your own page templates so that each page in your web will have the same "look."

In this chapter, you'll examine each of these options more closely, and, after you select an option, you can begin to build your web structure. You'll also learn how to reuse your existing pages in your new web.

Cheating with the FrontPage Templates and Wizards

By far, the best thing you can hope for is that one of the FrontPage templates or wizards contains a web structure that you can easily amend for your use.

In this section, you'll meet each template and wizard in turn, and hopefully, you'll hit it off with one of them.

What's the Difference?

A *template* is a predesigned web site; a *wizard* is a guide that steps you through the process of creating a web site, while allowing you to customize it.

As a result, the FrontPage templates don't offer a lot of *style*, although they do offer a lot of functionality. The wizards are more flashy and cool because they let you customize the web site they create.

Using the Corporate Presence Wizard

If you want to design a business-related web site, the Corporate Presence Wizard is probably your best bet. When you create a web site with the Corporate Presence Wizard, it will ask you about a bazillion questions, including these (answer them as best you can, and click **Next>** to move to the next dialog box).

You should give each of these questions some consideration before moving to the next dialog box. However, you can always delete unwanted pages from your web later on (and add the ones you forgot to choose), if you make a mistake.

- First, the Corporate Presence Wizard asks if you want certain pages added to your web, such as a What's New, a Product/Services, a Table of Contents, a Feedback, and a Search page.
- The wizard will want to know if you want certain headings on your home page, such as an Introduction, Mission Statement, Company Profile, and Contact Information. Since you'll most likely replace this page with the home page you've been working on, this is pretty much a moot question.

- Next, the wizard asks you what headings you want on your What's New page—that is, if you added one to the web. You can choose from such awe-inspiring topics as Web Changes, Press Releases, and Articles and Reviews.
- The Corporate Presence Wizard assumes that you're in business to sell *something*, so it'll ask you how many products and services you plan to feature. All of these end up on a separate page, so you probably don't want to enter something like 1,000,000.

Outer Limits

Actually, FrontPage Web can probably handle only about 1,000 pages total, so don't plan on making it larger than that.

If you need a large site, consider creating several webs and simply linking them together. You'll have a much better result.

Each web site, by the way, does not have to be based on the Corporate Presence Wizard. You can create multiple sites using any of the templates or wizards and then link them together as needed.

- The wizard has to know *everything*, it seems, and so it will ask you what amazing things you want on each of your product pages, such as a product image, pricing information, and information request form. For each service, you can add headings such as "Capabilities List," "Reference Accounts," and "Information Request Form."
- Will the questions never end? Next, the wizard asks you what kind of information you'd like the user to give you through your Feedback Form (that is, if you added one): Full Name, Job Title, Company Affiliation, Mailing Address, Telephone Number, FAX Number, and E-Mail Address. You'll need to select the format you want the results stored in: a web page format or a tabbed format that you can use in another program such as a database program.
- The wizard wants to know about your TOC. Would you like to keep it updated automatically? Would you like to include pages that aren't linked to any other page? Would you like to use bullets? Would you like fries with that?
- Next, you tell the wizard what you'd like to see at the top of each page on your web: a company logo, perhaps? Maybe the page title and the link bar? Or would you rather add the link bar (the graphic that links all your major pages) to the *bottom* of each page? Do you want to add your Web master's e-mail address, your copyright notice, and the date you last modified the page to the bottom of each page?

- The wizard is pretty accommodating; it even lets you choose how you want your pages to *look*. You can choose from several slick styles; you can modify each style slightly by choosing different colors.
- You can add an under construction sign to each page, so you can skip town for awhile and no one will notice (at least, not your web visitors). After answering all these questions, you deserve it. One thing, though: many users consider under cons to represent the height of lazy. If you want people to revisit your site, the general thinking is that you should only publish it when it's completely ready. You could add the under cons to your pages as a reminder to finish them before publishing, if you want.
- One last thing before you go: you have to tell the wizard the name of your company, its address, and phone number.

Lotsa Things to See, Lotsa People to Find

The wizard will add reminders to finish your web pages to the To Do list. If it could only add the people you'll need to get the work done, then it'd be perfect.

Depending on the options you select and the number of products and services you plan to offer, your web will end up looking like this.

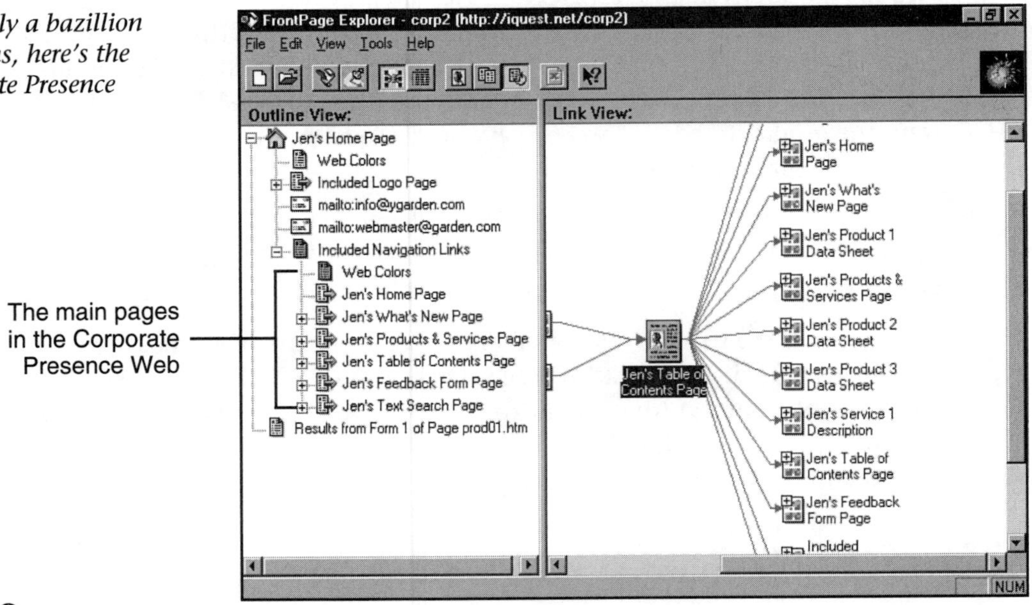

After only a bazillion questions, here's the Corporate Presence Web.

Notice that you get a basic home page that links (through the Included Navigation Links page) to all the other pages you selected from the wizard, including the What's New, Product & Services, TOC, Feedback, and Search pages. You can add or delete pages from this structure as needed—you'll learn how later.

When to Use the Customer Support Web Template

The next FrontPage Web is a template, designed for creating a customer support site. Wish I'd had one when I was in charge of technical support. If you like this one too, you can add it *onto any other existing web*, to create a customer support *section*. Or you can use it as a stand-alone site.

You can use this template even if your site isn't business related. For example, if the focus of your site is bird watching, you might easily adapt this template to that purpose, by simply changing the titles of some of the resulting pages. You can change the "Bugs" page to "Trials and Tribulations in Bird Watching," and use the Download page for downloading graphic images of birds, and so on. So don't let the assumed purpose of a template restrict your thinking. Use your imagination!

I Can Add This Web to My Existing Web?

Yep. You can add any of the FrontPage webs onto your existing web, creating a special *branch*. Or you can use the wizards and templates to create a new stand-alone web site.

However, because this thing's a template, you basically have to take it as is—no choices like you get with the Corporate Presence Wizard. But that doesn't mean that you have to leave it like that—oh, no, like all the other FrontPage Webs, you can change it to suit your needs once it's created.

The Customer Support template results in a web that looks like this.

Provide technical support for your customers with this web.

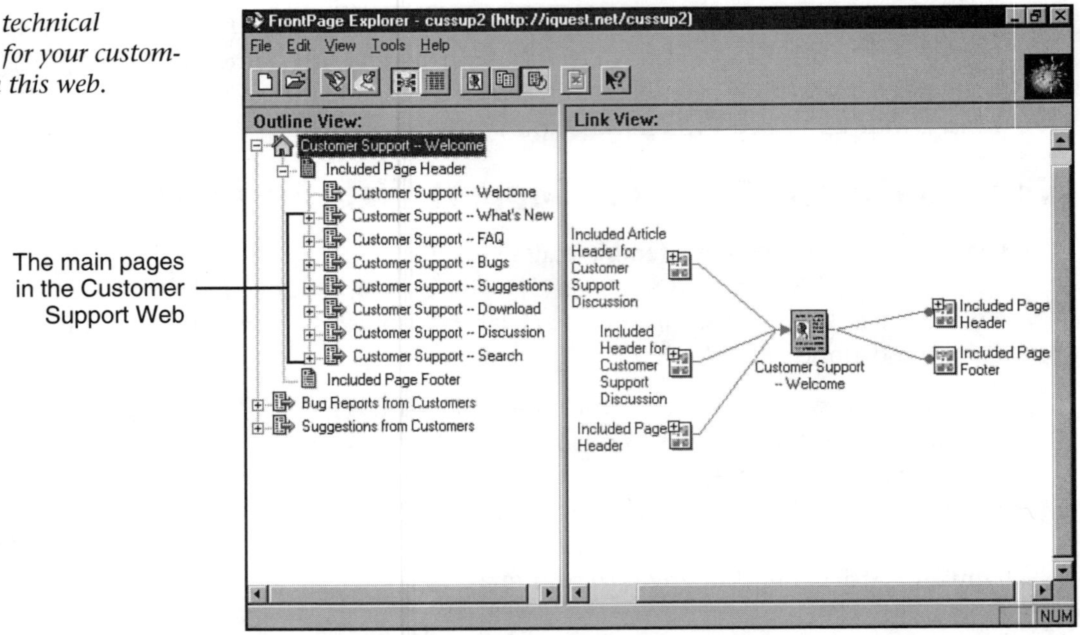

You'll notice that the web supplies you with necessary pages such as What's New, FAQ (frequently asked questions), Bugs (known problems), Suggestions, Discussion (a forum page where your customers can leave questions and get answers to problems), Download, and Search. But again, you can customize this web to suit your own support needs, as you'll learn later in this chapter.

Have Something to Discuss?

The Discussion Wizard helps you create a discussion *forum*. A forum here is similar (at least, in concept) to the newsgroup forums you find on the Internet. Once you create your web, a user can post an article (a comment or a question) and review previously posted articles and their replies. Since most people on the Net like to discuss just about anything, you can easily use this wizard for business- or pleasure-related webs. For example, in your company, a discussion web devoted to answering benefit and personnel questions might be very valuable, while a discussion web devoted to recent *Star Trek* episodes might be fun.

A few more things: You can restrict access to the Discussion Group Web if you want. And you can add the Discussion Group Web to any existing web, or you can create it as a stand-alone web site.

Since this is a wizard, you'll have some questions to answer, such as:

- ➤ Whether or not you want to include a TOC listing all articles, a Search form, and a Confirmation page. You can also choose to allow threaded replies, which in English means that your users can reply to the postings.
- ➤ The name of the topic you want to discuss.
- ➤ What particular information do you want to know about each article? For example, do you want your users to simply post a subject and their comments or questions? Or do you need them to list a category or product name? This is actually a little bogus, since you can easily change the Submission form later. See Chapter 15 for help with the form.
- ➤ Do you want to use security on this site, or not? (If you're insecure about your ability to answer this question, Chapter 23 gives you the full scoop on securing security.)

Registration Hassle

If you restrict your web, then you have to register your users to allow them access. After you create your web, you'll be escorted to a registration form web page, which you then need to modify before you can publish your web. This can get a bit messy, so you should check out Chapter 20 if you run into trouble.

- ➤ How do you want articles listed on the TOC (that is, if you added a table of contents)?
- ➤ The next question depends on *where* you're adding this web. If you want the TOC to act as the home page, it can, but it will *overwrite* any existing home page, so be careful.
- ➤ You're then asked how much information you want to display in response to a search: only the article name, or additional information such as article size, creation date, and a score indicating how close this article fits the user's actual query.
- ➤ Finally, something fun! Here, you get to choose the colors used in your site.
- ➤ Cast your vote for or against frames. If you're not sure what frames can do for your web site, see Chapter 16.

As you can see, structurally at least, the Discussion Web is not terribly complex.

Can we talk?

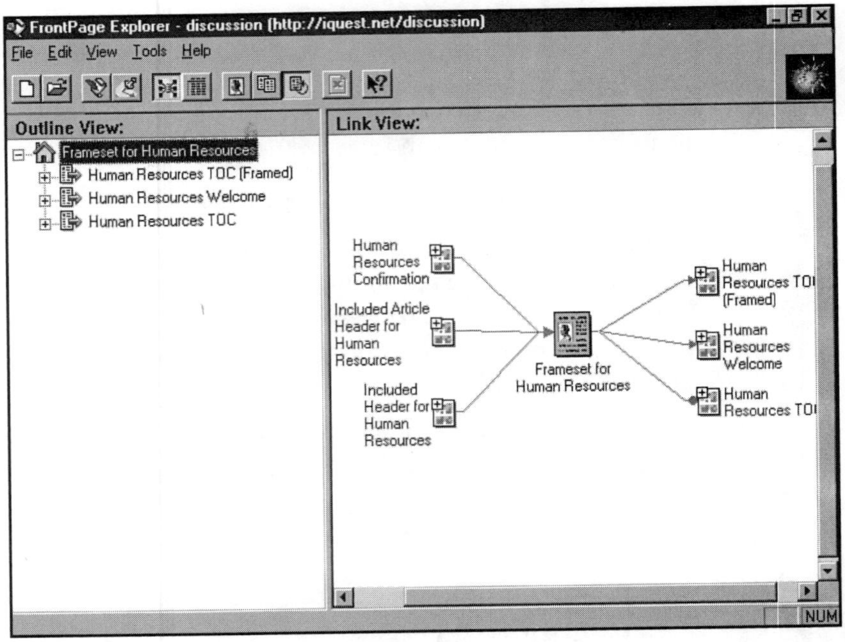

Basically, a discussion web consists of only a Welcome page and a TOC (if you added one). The Welcome page has links that allow the user to add a comment or question, view previous comments or questions, and search for a particular topic. For a more thorough discussion of discussion webs, see Chapter 20.

Get Personal with the Personal Web Template

You'd think that you could use the Personal Web template to create a web geared toward some personal interest such as skiing. Or you might think it'd be great to use in creating your personal web site. But no dice.

The Personal Web template does have some personal elements to it, but it's geared more for use on a company-wide *intranet*, as you'll soon see.

What's an Intranet?

An *intranet* is a private company-wide network that uses Internet standards and technologies (such as hyperlinks). Intranets allow companies to make vast amounts of information available to their employees in an easy-to-access, linked format, similar to what you find on the web.

Because you're using a template to create the Personal Web, you don't get to say a lot about how it turns out. Here's what one looks like.

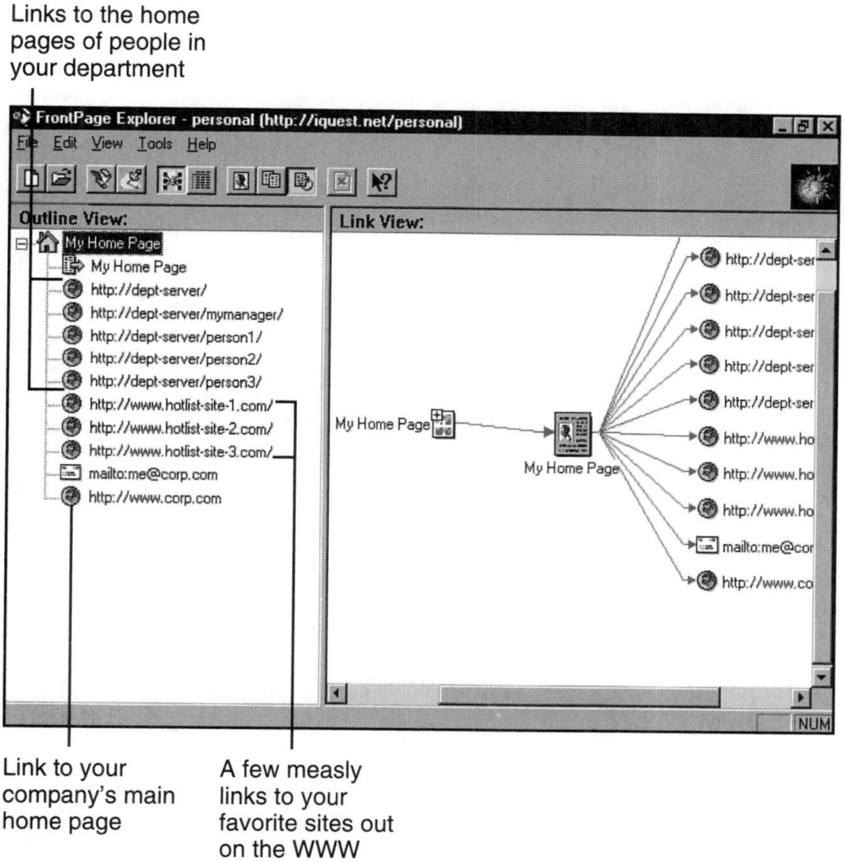

Get personal—uh, sort of.

As you can see, you get your basic home page and a bunch of links (represented by those tiny globes) to various work-related things, such as your company's and your department's home pages, your supervisor's home page, and coworkers' home pages.

The *personal* part of this web is, I guess, the links to your favorite places (a big three). If you're connected to your company's intranet, this web may be ideal for you. Otherwise, for a personal interest web, it's probably not too salvageable.

Keeping All Those Projects Organized

If you're in charge of a large engineering or programming group and you have to manage many projects, the Project Web may be a dream come true. This web site works well if your company has an intranet, or a direct Internet connection, so that everyone working on the project has quick, cheap access to the web site.

As before, since you create this web using a template, you don't get to select from any options. You basically end up with a web that looks like this.

Your projected Web.

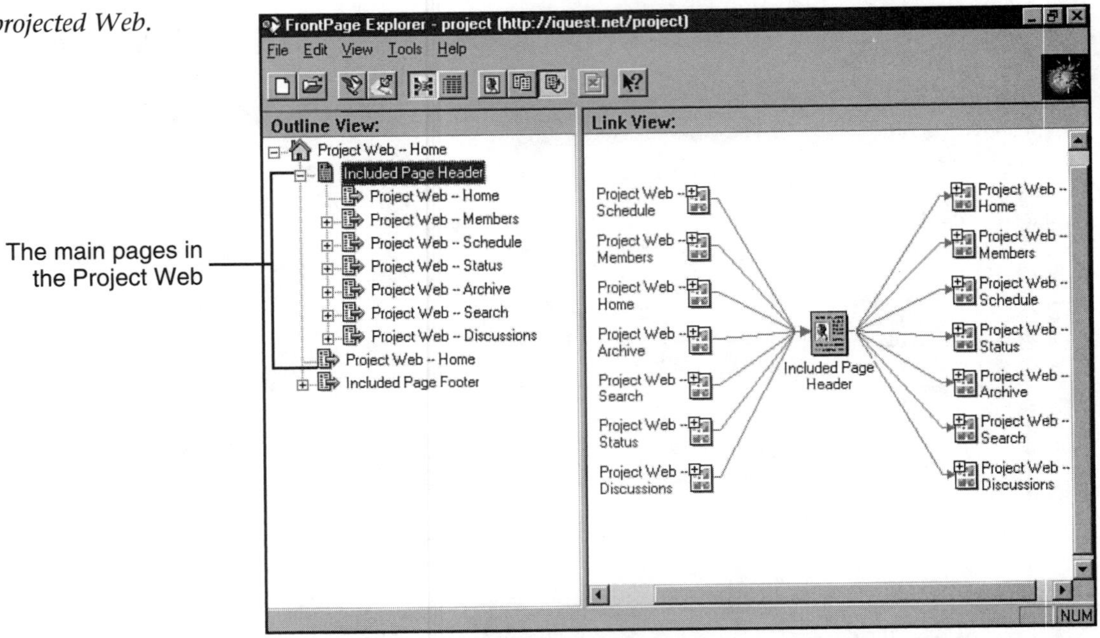

For managing a project, this web is basically complete. Notice that it includes a Member list (with links to their home pages), a Schedule of Events, a Status page, an Archive (with links to files and papers created during the project), a Search page, and a Discussion page with links to two different discussion groups.

This web is only suitable for managing one project, however. But that shouldn't stop you from creating several such webs, if you need to.

Adjust the FrontPage Webs for a Better Fit

Sometimes, one of the FrontPage Webs will come close to how you'd like to organize your web, but not quite close enough. No problem; it's not that difficult to make changes to your web.

First, go ahead and create the web you like. Then copy your home page over the one that's created by following these steps:

1. Open the current home page for your new web.
2. In FrontPage Editor, open the **File** menu and select **Open File**.
3. Change to the directory in which the home page you've been working on is stored. You'll find it in a directory similar to /FrontPage_Webs/Content/Normal/.
4. Select your old home page and click **Open**.
5. Now that you have both pages open in the editor, you can copy your text and graphics from your old home page into the new one. You might want to arrange both windows so you can see them by choosing **Tile** or **Cascade** from the **Window** menu.
6. When you finish transferring your information, be sure to save your new home page.

Why Can't I Simply Replace the New Home Page With My Old One?

If you attempt to copy your old home page over the top of the one created for the web, you'll mess up all the links in your new web that lead from the home page. (In other words, you'd end up with a bunch of junk.) So although it takes longer, copy your stuff from your old home page to your new home page manually, because, well, it works.

The Included Pages Thing

One thing FrontPage does that is kind of nice is that when it creates a web, it provides a header (stuff that appears at the top of each page in the web) and a footer (stuff that appears at the bottom) for you. To add more character to your web site (such as adding a logo to the header or a pet phrase to the footer), simply change either the Included Page Header or the Included Page Footer page.

If you create your web using one of the wizards, then you have one other web page you can change, called Web Colors. Stored in this page are all the background color, background graphic, text color, and link color choices for your web. To change any one of these items throughout your entire web, simply change them *once*, in the Web Colors page. When you save your changes to this special page, those changes are automatically copied out to all the pages in your web.

Where Using a FrontPage Web Falls Short of Expectations

If you need to add a new page to your FrontPage Web, and you want it to look like the other pages in your web (with the same colors, header, footer, and such), you'll need to make sure that you use the Include bot to insert the proper header and footer into the new page. See Chapter 17 for help with bots.

In addition, if your web uses the Web Colors page, you'll have to link it to your new page so your new page will use the same colors as all the others in your web. See Chapter 9 for help with this.

Both of these items may seem like a pain, especially if you plan on adding several pages to your new web. There's no reason that you should do all that work manually, especially when there are templates around. Interested? See Chapter 18 for help in creating one.

Basing Your Web on a Web You've Visited

One feature in FrontPage that is nice is its capability to snarf (uh, copy) a web site from the World Wide Web. Don't jump for joy; the process is a bit convoluted, as you'll see in a moment. In any case, once it's copied to your hard disk, you can use its basic structure as a basis for your own dream web.

Copyrights, 101

Keep in mind that just about anything can be copyrighted, including pages on the web. Just because you can copy a web to your hard disk doesn't mean you can use it any old way you please. That is, not unless you'd like to be sued.

As a result, you should consider the contents of a public web to be copyrighted, unless you can prove that something is specifically in the public domain. This means you can examine the structure of the web you copied, and even use it as a basis for your own web, but you should not, *under any circumstances*, attempt to use any of the web's contents, including all text, graphics, sounds, and so on, without permission.

Anything you want, you have to work for, so be warned: the process involved in copying a web is not exactly "snatch and grab."

A Saner Alternative?

If you don't feel up to copying an entire web site to your hard disk, you can copy only a page or two—a process that you'll find much easier. See Chapter 3, "Opening Your Page Later On," for help.

Ready to copy a web? Then follow these steps:

1. Open Windows Explorer and create a directory for the new web under the /FrontPage Webs/Content/ directory. For example, create a directory called /FrontPage Webs/Content/CopyofaWeb.
2. Start up your Web browser and connect to the web site you want to copy.
3. Visit each page and copy them, one at a time, into the directory you just created. For example, in Netscape, connect to a page, open the **File** menu, and use the **Save As** command to save it to your hard disk.

Not a Complete Copy

Keep in mind that using the Save As command does not save embedded graphics to your hard disk. You need to copy those separately. For example, in Netscape, simply right-click a graphic you want to copy, and select **Save Image As** to copy it to your hard disk.

4. When you've copied all the pages you want (that is, if you haven't already stopped because you've decided that this is *way* too much work), start up FrontPage Explorer. Open the **File** menu and select **New Web**.
5. Select **Empty Web**, and click **OK.**

   When you're asked to type the *name of the Web*, type the name of the directory you've been using and click **OK**—in this case, type **CopyofaWeb**. FrontPage, being smart, will notice that the directory isn't really empty, and it'll create a web called **CopyofaWeb** that contains the pages you copied to your hard disk.

Now that you have your copied web, you can study its structure. Have fun—you've earned it.

How do you go from this copied web to your own (legal) web? Well, using the copied web as an inspiration, make a duplicate of its directory structure using Windows Explorer. Then you can "create" your web in FrontPage Explorer using the Empty Web trick.

Fill this new web with your own *original* stuff, such as your home page, by simply importing the page into the web:

1. In FrontPage Explorer, open the **File** menu and select **Import**.
2. Click **Add File**, locate your home page, and click **OK**.
3. Click **Import Now** to bring it into your new web.

There, now! That wasn't so difficult, was it?

Local Copy

If you're trying to import a local web, such as one on your company's network, this whole process is a lot simpler.You can simply copy the files directly to your hard disk over your network (that is, if you have security access to the files), and then "create" the web using the Empty Web trick in FrontPage Explorer.

But I Only Want to Copy One WWW Page to My Web

As mentioned in Chapter 3, you can copy a page from the Internet into your web, but the process is a bit tricky. First, open the page in the FrontPage Editor using the **File, Open Location** command. Connect to the Internet; then type the URL of the page you want to snatch and click **OK**. The page appears in the editor, however, it's not really copied to your hard disk, because FrontPage is now acting like a Web browser. Pages you view with a Web browser are not copied to your hard disk, so that's why this page isn't copied to your PC.

So how to save the page to your web?

Don't bother to use the **File, Save** command, since all it does is copy the *location* of the page into your web (as a link). To view a page saved in this manner, you have to be connected to the Internet.

To really save your page, use the **File, Save** command, *but with a twist:* when the dialog box comes up, click **As File**. Click **OK** to save the page to your hard disk in HTML format. You'll be asked if you want to save graphics too, which of course you do, so click **Yes to All**.

Now the page is on your hard disk, but not in your web. To bring it into your web, import it. Switch over to FrontPage Explorer, and then open the **File** menu and select **Import**. Click **Add File**, and locate your page. Click **OK**, and you're returned to the Import File to Web dialog box. Click **Import Now** to import the page into your web. It is now the same as any other page in your web; you can edit it as you want.

Starting from Scratch: Some Tips

Creating your web from scratch will take a lot more work, but you guarantee that the result will be exactly what you want. You already started your web, although it's not terribly big at this point, since it consists of only a home page.

To create a web that looks like your plan, you need to add pages and create links from them to the home page, and other pages (per your plan). You'll learn how to add pages and links as needed in the next chapter; but here are a few tips for constructing your web quickly and easily:

- Start by concentrating on the look of your home page. Spend some time getting the background and text colors just right. Why? Because once you get your home page exactly the way you want it, you can use your color choices to make your new pages match the home page. (More on that in a moment.)
- Next, add a header or a footer to your home page. A *header* is information that repeats at the top of each page in your web. You might use a header to repeat your logo and to show your name at the top of every page. You can also add a footer (which repeats at the bottom of each page in your web). In your footer, you might add a copyright notice.
- To make it easy to insert the same header and footer information on each of your new pages, create separate header and footer pages; then fill them with the text, graphics, and other items you want to repeat. Once you create and save these separate header and footer pages, open your home page and use the Include WebBot (and the instructions in Chapter 17) to insert their contents into your home page at the appropriate spots.
- Use a linkbar (toolbar) to link all your main pages to the home page. A *linkbar* is basically a graphic with hotspots that, when clicked, act as links. You'll learn more about linkbars in Chapters 13 and 18. Incorporate your linkbar into your header or footer page; this will make it easy to include the linkbar in each of your web pages.
- Add whole *sections* to your web quickly by using one of the FrontPage Webs, if one of them suits your purpose.

As you add more pages to your web, you can make them look like your home page, by following these steps:

1. Create a new page following the steps in the next chapter.
2. Open the **File** menu and select **Page Properties**.
3. Under **Get Background and Colors from Page**, click **Browse**.
4. Select your home page and click **OK** (it's probably called index.htm, and it's hiding in the \FrontPage_Webs\Content*webname* directory, where *webname* is the actual name of your web). You're returned to the Page Properties dialog box.
5. Click **OK**. Your new page will take on the colors and background of your home page.
6. If you created separate header and or footer pages as described earlier, then insert them into your new page with the Include bot, following the steps you'll learn in Chapter 17.
7. Repeat this process for any other pages you add to your web.

Another trick you might want to use to save time in creating your web site is to make a *template* from your home page. Simply open your home page, and then use the **File, Save As** command to save a copy of it as a template (see Chapter 18 for help). Open the copy and delete the text that pertains to the home page itself, and you'll be left with a "shell" that you can use to create new pages that are twins to your home page. (Be sure to save your changes, of course.) To create a new page using your homemade template, open the **File** menu and select **New**. You'll see your template listed; select it and click OK. A blank page appears, looking like your home page, minus the text and graphics.

The Least You Need to Know

You have a good idea of how to organize your web. What do you do now?

- You can base your web on one of the FrontPage webs and then change it to suit your needs.
- You can copy a web from the WWW to your hard disk, although the steps are rather involved.
- You can create a web from scratch, using separate header and footer pages to save time.
- You can create a template to make the process of adding new pages to your web much easier.

Chapter 12

Adding Pages and Creating Links

By the End of This Chapter, You'll Be Able to...

- Construct links between web pages
- Create a link to another point on the same web page
- Pull the various pages of your web together
- Create a link to a downloadable file

I waited until Chapter 12 to talk about links, while everyone knows that the real reason there's a World Wide Web in the first place is because clicking links is a great way to find information. A link, as if you didn't know, is a bit of text or a special graphic that, when clicked, sends the user to some other spot on the Web. Before links were invented, the Internet was a difficult place: you practically had to have a programming degree to query information out of some remote database. And half the time, the information you received in response would have only 0.015% to do with anything you really wanted to know at the time.

However, things are different now. With a link, you can say, "Aha! That's what I want!," click it, and go directly to the information you are seeking. And how do you find the link that takes you there? I'll just let some Yahoo tell you the answer to that one.

When creating the links in your web pages, you'll run into a few characters: the link itself, the anchor, and the bookmark. In this chapter, you learn the magic behind these link mechanisms and how to add links to your web pages.

Starting a New Web Page

In Chapter 10, you considered your web's design. You planned and plotted, and now you know exactly where you want to add pages to your web.

In Chapter 11, you learned that you can, even at this late date, start over with a new web based on the template or a wizard that most closely matches your overall plan. Even so, you'll probably need to add pages to your web to make it fit your plan exactly.

In any case, you're here because you've decided to add some new pages to your web site and to add links from those pages to the others on your web.

To add a new page, open your web in FrontPage Explorer; then start FrontPage Editor. Once you start the editor, you're ready to add a new page to the web. Open the **File** menu and select **New** (*don't* click the **New** button). You'll see the New Page dialog box, listing a whole bunch of templates and wizards from which you can choose.

Why Can't I Use the New Button?

You can, but when you click it, it's like selecting the Normal template, which results in a blank Web page.

A *template* is a fill-in-the blanks web page. Like Hallmark, FrontPage has a template for just about every occasion, from an Employee Directory to a User Registration form. If you want to use a template to create your new page, select one from the list, and click **OK**. You'll be asked to name your new page; do that and click **OK**.

I Don't See a Template I Like

If you want, you can create a template to match the other pages in your web exactly. See Chapter 11 for help.

Mixed in with all the templates, you'll find an occasional wizard or two. A *wizard* is a guide that enables you to create a customized web page through a series of dialog boxes in which you make various selections. If you want to use a wizard, select one from the New Page dialog and click **OK**. Make additional selections from the dialog boxes that appear; click **Next** to move to the next dialog box. When you're on the last dialog box, you'll click the **Finish** button; then, FrontPage will create your web page based on your selections.

What's a Link?

In order to understand how to create a link in FrontPage, you have to first understand a few concepts: the role of a bookmark, the role of an anchor, and finally, the role of the link.

A *link* is a section of specially highlighted text or a specific spot on a graphic, which, when clicked, sends the user to some other place on the Web. Now, the place to which the user is sent can be a lot of things, such as a spot located a little bit further down the same Web page. A link can also jump you to another page in your web site, or some page out on the World Wide Web.

In this chapter, you'll learn how to create text links. In Chapter 13, you'll learn how to create a graphic link—a hotspot on a graphic that, when clicked, acts as a link to some place on the Web.

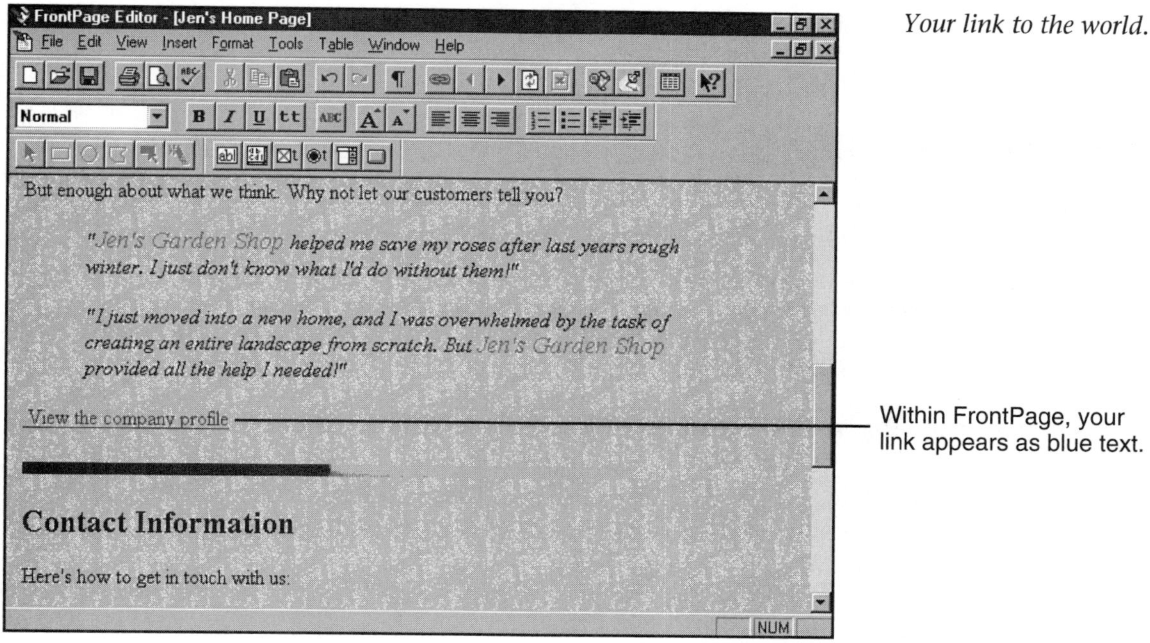
FrontPage Editor - [Jen's Home Page]
File Edit View Insert Format Tools Table Window Help
Normal
But enough about what we think. Why not let our customers tell you?
"Jen's Garden Shop helped me save my roses after last years rough winter. I just don't know what I'd do without them!"
"I just moved into a new home, and I was overwhelmed by the task of creating an entire landscape from scratch. But Jen's Garden Shop provided all the help I needed!"
View the company profile
Contact Information
Here's how to get in touch with us:
NUM
Within FrontPage, your link appears as blue text.

Your link to the world.

What's an Anchor?

An *anchor* is the destination of a link. Typically, when you link to a page, the anchor is assumed to be the top of that page. When the user clicks your link, he's taken to the top of the page you indicated. You can set this anchor somewhere in the middle of a page, as you'll learn in a moment.

The destination or anchor of a link can be other things besides Web pages. For example, you can link to a file so the user can download it. You might link to a sound or video file instead, so that the user can play it on his system.

What's a Bookmark?

A bookmark is optional. Basically, when you create a link to a particular page, the user is linked to the top of that page. To link to a spot somewhere in the middle, you have to set a bookmark. Not only can you set a bookmark on one of your own web pages, but you can also set bookmarks on pages out on the World Wide Web, as you'll see in the next section.

A *bookmark* is a set of characters within a paragraph that you give a name. Instead of connecting your link to just a URL address, you connect it to this named bookmark instead. Whenever the reader of your Web page clicks a bookmarked link, the Web browser transfers him to the specific place *within the web page* where the bookmark was inserted.

Thus, a named bookmark can act as a "landing zone" for one *or more* links, similar to goal posts that mark an end zone.

Setting a Bookmark

Remember that you don't have to use a bookmark *at all* to create a link to a web page. If you want your user to always land at the *top* of a page to which he is linked, then you can safely skip this section. If it's a short page, that's probably fine. If it's a long page with a listing for each of your product lines, and you want to lead the reader to a specific product described some place in the middle or toward the end of the web page, then you should use a bookmark.

Keep in mind that since a bookmark typically marks some piece of important information you want your users to find, you might want to have several links leading to the same bookmark, and that's easy to do with FrontPage. That said, I figure you're still here because you want to learn how to set a bookmark in the middle of a page so you can link to it. Great—keep reading.

1. First, open the web page in which you want to place a bookmark. To open a page on *your* web, open the web in FrontPage Explorer using the **File, Open Web** command. Then, select the page you want to open and use the **Edit, Open** command to open the page in FrontPage Editor.

   If you want to place a bookmark in a page out on the World Wide Web, you have to import (copy) that page into your web first. Fortunately, this is easy. In FrontPage Editor, open the **File** menu and select **Open Location**. Type the URL address for the WWW page you want to use and click **OK**. Eventually, the page will be copied to your system and opened for your use in the Editor.

2. Now that you have your page open, select the text you want to use as your bookmark by dragging over it. You don't need to select a lot of text; one word will do as a mark—typically the first word in a paragraph.
3. Open the **Edit** menu and select **Bookmark**. The Bookmark dialog box appears.
4. Enter a name for your bookmark in the **Bookmark Name** box, or use the name FrontPage came up with. The name can have spaces, but it must be different than other bookmarks listed in the **Other Bookmarks on this Page** text box.
5. Click **OK**. Your selected text appears with a dashed underline beneath it to let you know that it's serving as a bookmark.

A Dash? Is That How Bookmarks Appear to My Users?

No. Although a bookmark appears with a dashed underline within FrontPage, the dashes will disappear when viewed in a Web browser by one of your users.

Now that you have a bookmark pointing to someplace in your text, you can create a link to it. But first, a quick detour into the world of graphic bookmarks and bookmark maintenance.

Making a Graphic Bookmark

You don't have to be stuck using text to create a bookmark if you don't want to. You can create a bookmark to a graphics file (an image). Simply select the graphic first, and then follow the basic steps for making your bookmark: open the **Edit** menu, select **Bookmarks**, enter a name, and click **OK**.

Selecting your graphic in FrontPage can sometimes be a pain. If you click a graphic, it will look selected, but it's not. To select a graphic, you have to highlight it by dragging over it as if it were text. Bizarre, I know, but it works.

Here's how a graphic looks when you select it:

Select your graphic here!

The selected graphic appears in reverse video.

Changing a Bookmark

By the way, to change the name of an existing bookmark, simply highlight it first and select **Edit/Bookmark**. The existing name will pop up automatically under **Bookmark Name**; just type over it with a new name and click **OK**.

Where's My Bookmark?

Changing the name of a bookmark after the fact can be dangerous, since your links point to the name of a bookmark, and not to its location in the text. If you change the name of a bookmark to which some links are pointed, *they won't be pointed there now* because you just changed the name. Just remember to change all your links later to point to the new bookmark name.

To delete a bookmark, select it first; then open the **Edit** menu and select **Bookmark** to display the Bookmark list. Select the bookmark you want to remove, and click **Clear**.

Adding a Link to a Page in Your Web

You can add links to just about anything, as you'll learn in this chapter. For example, you can add a link to a page out on the World Wide Web, to a file, to a graphic, or to a page on your web. Here's how to create a link to a page within your web (if you want to link to a page out on the WWW, see the upcoming section):

1. Open the page in which you want to place the link.
2. Select the text that you want to make into a link. Be sure to select just a few words, not an entire paragraph.

Can I Make a Graphic Link?

Yep, you can make a graphic "hot" so that if somebody clicks it, he links to a particular Web page or whatever. The process is a little bit more involved, so it has its own chapter—Chapter 13.

3. Open the **Edit** menu and select **Link**, or click the **Create or Edit Link** button.
4. If the page to which you want to link is located in your web and is open, click the **Open Pages** tab. If your page is not open *but it is located within the current open web,* click the **Current Web** tab.
5. When you're dealing with an open page, the next step is simple: click it within the Open Pages list.

   If your page is not open, you have to locate it by clicking the **Browse** button and selecting your page from the Current Web list.
6. Once you select the page you want to link to, you can go one step further and select a bookmark. Of course, the bookmark has to already exist; see the "Setting a Bookmark" section for help.

   If you're on the **Open Pages** tab, select your Bookmark from the Bookmark drop-down list. If you're on the **Current Web** tab, you have to type the bookmark name manually into the **Bookmark** text box. Bummer.

7. Click **OK**. Your link text turns blue and takes on a solid underline. You'll also notice that when you move your cursor over the link, the URL (address) that it's linked to appears in the Status bar of the Editor window.

That's it! You'll probably notice right away that you can't test your link simply by clicking it. After all, in the Editor, the link is simply colored text. If you want to test your new link, jump to the "Following Your Links" section for assistance. Also, if you want to change the color of your links, you can. See Chapter 9 for help.

A Fun Way to Link

You can create a link from an open page to any page in your web using FrontPage Explorer, if you want. Just click the page to which you want to link, and drag it into the FrontPage Editor window, where your open page sits waiting. As you drag, your cursor will change to a big **L** that means *link*, I guess.

Anyway, move that big **L** cursor to the point in your open web page where you want to insert the link. The name of the page you select in FrontPage Explorer will appear within your open page—in blue, with a dark underline. The name serves as your text link.

For example, if you drag a Products and Services page into your home page, the words **Products and Services** appear within your home page as your text link.

Adding a Link to a Different Location on the Same Page

If you want to have a link on one page take the user to a location on the *same page,* there's really no difference in the basic procedure: simply open your page as before and select the text for the link. Next, open the **Edit** menu and select **Link.** Finally, open the **Bookmark** list, select the bookmark, and click **OK**.

Now, although it's easy to make, there are some things to take into account when creating a link within the same page, When a web page is small enough to fit inside the entire Web browser window, a link from one spot to another inside the same page is not terribly effective. After your Web browser user clicks your link, its destination bookmark generally shows up at the top of her window, *but only if there's enough material beneath that link to push it up there.*

On a Web page where the text following the link is pretty small, the jump to the link often won't change the user's view enough to make the leap interesting and important. In such a case, you probably shouldn't make the link.

Creating a New Page While Adding a Link

If you want to add a new page to your web and create a link to it, too, why not do both steps in one move? The process is simple:

1. Open the web page in which you want to place the link to the new page.
2. Select the text that you want to make into a link.
3. Click the **Create or Edit Link** button.
4. Click the **New Page** tab.
5. Enter a title for your new page in the **Page Title** field.
6. Type a file name for your new page in the **Page URL** field.
7. If you want to edit the new page as soon as it's created, select the **Edit New Page Immediately** option. If you would rather add a task to complete this page at a later time to your To Do List, then select **Add New Page to To Do List** option instead. Click on **OK**.
8. Select the template or wizard you want to use in creating your new page, and click **OK**.

After FrontPage creates your new page, the link text you select in your existing page will turn bright blue, with a dark underline, indicating that the link is ready to use.

Adding a Link to a Page on the World Wide Web

What makes the World Wide Web *worldwide* is the fact that links transcend individual Web sites. Because the Web is not restricted to the four corners of your PC, you can include links to other people's Web pages within your own web pages.

Before you can attach a link to an outside page, you need to know (or at least have on hand) the precise URL address of the destination page. There won't be a Browse button or a list in this procedure from which you can select the WWW page you want to link to—this is bare-bones-you-have-to-type-it-yourself stuff. So, fire up the ol' Web browser and visit the page to which you want to link. Write down its URL, which will appear in the Location (or some such) box at the top of your browser window.

With your URL handy, here's what ya gotta do:

1. Open your web page and select the text you want to use for your outside link.
2. Click the **Create or Edit Link** button.
3. Click the **World Wide Web** tab.
4. A link to another Web page requires HTTP protocol. So, from the **Protocol** drop-down list, choose **http:** (all other protocols in this list do not transfer the user to a Web page, but to other Internet services such as ftp, explained later in this chapter).
5. Under **URL**, type the exact destination address of the WWW page to which you want to link.
6. Click **OK**.

There's no way for FrontPage to do any error checking here to make certain you've entered a correct URL, so hopefully, you created a link to an outside page. In any case, you'll learn how to test your link later in this chapter.

Making Those Cool Directory Boxes or Toolbars

If you've ever studied Netscape's home page or the Yahoo system, you might have noticed how every page you're on contains a little "toolbar" at the bottom that provides links to any other page in the system. The nice thing about these toolbars is that the same bar appears on every page, in the same spot, so you always know how to get from place to place.

You may be wondering, "If I want to implement such a device on my web, would I have to create all the links *for each page separately*?" Thankfully, no.

FrontPage gives you a way to create one *part* of a page (say, the top or bottom) and have that part *included* on any or all pages in your web. You create one page with the toolbar and *include* that page at the bottom of all your other web pages.

The device that makes this possible is the *Include bot*. You'll learn everything you need to know about this and other bots in Chapter 17.

Oh yeah. In case you're wondering: to create the toolbar, you have to draw one or steal one from somewhere (edit it to suit your web) and save it as a graphic file. You then add *hotspot* links to the graphic toolbar following the steps in Chapter 13. Finally, after saving the toolbar in its own page, you use the Include bot to insert it into each of your web pages.

Adding a Link to a File

You may remember back in Chapter 8, that I introduced you to the concept of importing files into your web. The reason you'd want to do this, I explained, is so you can create links to those files within your web pages. Building a link to a file in a web page is a two-stage process:

Stage I: Import the file into your web, using the steps outlined in Chapter 8. This gives the file a URL.

Stage II: Create the link to the URL of the imported file, as explained next.

A Note of Warning Before You Continue

A link to a file is, by definition, a download process. From the user's end, he clicks your link, and his Web browser begins downloading a file. That seems simple enough, but from your host server's vantage point, things are far from simple. Your server has to locate the file, break it up into bits, and using something called FTP (File Transfer Protocol), it has to flush those bits over the Internet to the user.

Host Server?

The host server is the computer to which you'll eventually publish your web. The computer acts as a "host" to your files, making them available to the Internet. Basically, a host server rents out disk space to you, covering part of the cost of maintaining a full-time connection to the Web.

What does all this mean? Well, in order to link to a file, you have to import that file to your web. And, in order for your host server to figure out what this file is doing in amongst all your web pages, that server has to use the FrontPage Server Extensions.

Now, I didn't mean to hide this from you like the bad news part of a five-year power train warranty. *You can publish your FrontPage web to any server*; but in order to provide a link to a file, the host server you select *must* support the FrontPage Server Extensions. Make sure you ask whether or not your proposed host server plans on supporting FrontPage Server Extensions before you attempt to add links to files.

How To's

Assuming your chosen server *does* support the FrontPage Server Extensions, the first step is to import your file into the web. Even if the file exists on your hard disk, it is not made available to your web site until you *import* it, which you learned how to do in Chapter 8. Now don't jump back there; I'll give you the quickie course on importing (but feel free to return to Chapter 8 if you need more details):

Start up FrontPage Explorer and open your web. Then, open the **File** menu and select **Import**. Click **Add File**. Find your file and click **OK**. Click **Import Now** to import the file into the web. After the file's imported, click **Close**; you'll see the file listed with your web pages in FrontPage Explorer.

Now that your file is part of your big web family, here's how you make the link:

1. Open the web page in which you want to create the link to your file.
2. Select the text you want to use for your link.
3. Click the **Create or Edit Link** button.
4. Click the **Current Web** tab.
5. Click **Browse**. The Editor presents a list of all the URLs belonging to your current web, including those belonging to files you imported.
6. Select your file and click **OK**. You return to the Create Link dialog box.
7. Click **OK**.

Your link to the file is complete. But, what happens when the user clicks the link is anyone's guess. If the user has set up his Web browser to recognize your file's type, then his Web browser will call up the associated program and let it open the file. If no such association exists, then typically the Web browser will ask the user if he wants the file copied to his system, hoping that he can make sense of it at some later date.

Adding a Link to a Sound

A common file type that you might want to include on a web page is a sound file. You don't actually insert a sound file onto a web page like you might a graphic image. Instead, you simply insert a link to the sound file, which is what makes this discussion fit nicely into our chapter on links.

Even though you might include a sound file link on a web page, there's no guarantee that the user's system can play it. However, your chances increase if you use common sound file types, such as .WAV, .MIDI, .AU, and .AIFF.

So What Happens When a User Clicks the Sound Link?

Assuming that his Web browser recognizes the file type, and that he has a program that is capable of playing that type of sound file, when the user clicks the link, he'll wait a bit while his Web browser downloads the file. Depending on his sound player program, the user might hear the beginning of the sound being played while his Web browser continues to download the rest of the file. If not, then the user will have to wait while his browser downloads the file, at which point his sound player will begin to play it.

If the user doesn't have the right sound player, then typically his Web browser will ask him if he wants to download the file anyway, to play later, after he installs the appropriate program.

The process of adding sound to a web page begins with importing the sound file into the web. Again, I'll run through this process quickly, since it's covered in great detail in Chapter 8.

To begin, start in FrontPage Explorer. Open the **File** menu and select **Import**. The **Import File to Web** dialog box rears its head, and here you click **Add File**. Locate your file and click **OK**.

Click **Import File** to start the import process, and then wait awhile for things to happen. Shortly, the file will appear in the Outline View of FrontPage Explorer. You still have to click **Close** to see it, though.

The trick is to build the link to this sound file:

1. Open the page in which you want to include your sound file link.
2. Enter some text, such as, "Click here to hear Jennifer speak." to use as the sound file's link.
3. Select this text; then click the **Create or Edit Link** button.
4. Click the **Current Web** tab, and click **Browse**.
5. Select your imported sound file, and click **OK**. Then click **OK** again.

You now have a link to the sound file. For now, it only works on your computer; but later when you publish the web, your users can play your sound simply by clicking your link.

Following Your Links

Normally, when you click a link in a Web browser, it takes you to your destination. However, in the FrontPage Editor, when you click a link, it simply places the cursor there. That's because, to the Editor, the link is simply colored text.

What if you want to test a link to see if it works? What do you do?

Well, the solution is simple: Just hold down the **Ctrl** key *while* you click the link. You'll notice that your pointer turns from a cursor into a white right-pointing arrow. When you see this funky arrow, you know that you can click this link, and the Editor will behave like a Web browser, taking you to its destination. If it's a remote destination on the Web, and you're linked to the Internet, well, that's where you're going, so you better be connected to the Internet, or you'll get an error.

For example, I wanted to test the sound file link I added. When I pressed **Ctrl** and clicked the link, Windows 95 started the Sound Recorder.

Testing, one, two, three.

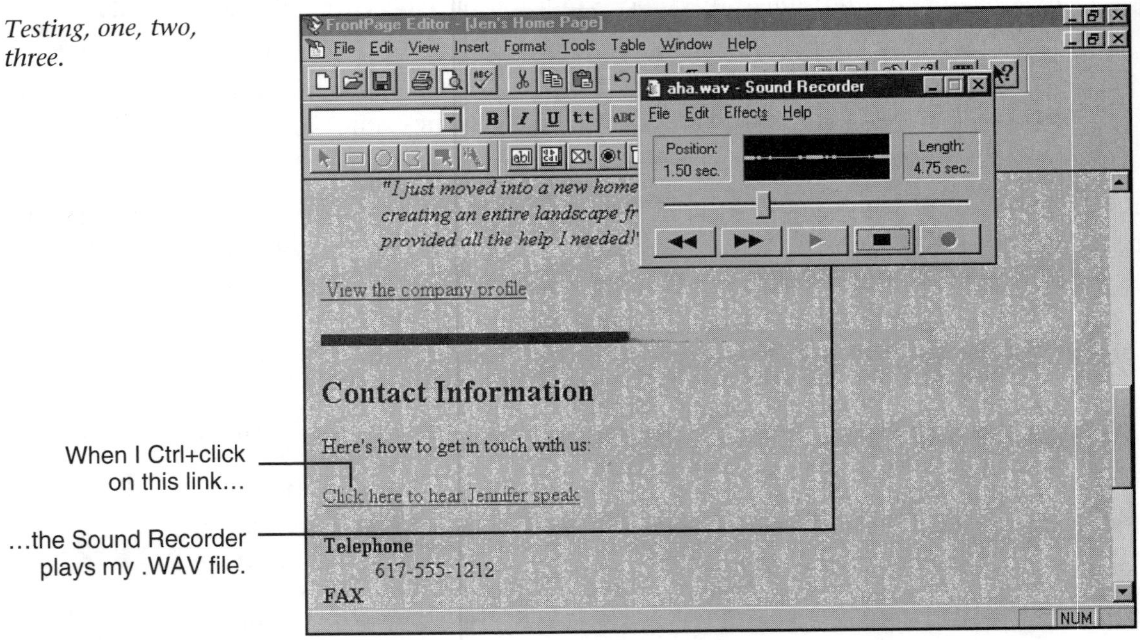

When you test your link, if it takes you to a different page, you can return to your previous page by clicking the **Back** button that you'll find on the Standard Toolbar. You can move forward again (just like you might in a Web browser) by clicking the **Forward** button.

The Least You Need to Know

Here's what you need to know about links, in a nutshell:

- In FrontPage, to make links to a specific spot on one of the pages in your web, you place a bookmark on that page.
- A bookmark is simply some text or a graphic that has been given a name.
- A link is a bit of text or a graphic that when clicked connects the user to the designated page or file.
- You can create links to any other page in your web, or on the World Wide Web. You can also link to a sound file, a graphic, or any other file.
- To create a link to a file for download, you first need to import the file into your web. Once imported, you can easily build links to that file.
- In order to publish a web with links to non-Web-oriented files, such as sound files or program files, your host server needs to support the FrontPage Server Extensions. Otherwise, the only files you can reliably import (and provide links to) are web pages, text files, and GIF or JPEG images.

Part 4
Adding "Wow" to Your Web Pages

In this part, you can make your neighbors jealous by adding lots of awesome things to your web pages, such as graphics links, tables, forms, and frames.

At the end of this part, you may feel that you've fallen head-first into a science-fiction novel, as you learn to use bots (WebBots that is) to do the hard parts of web page creation.

Chapter 13

Giving Your Graphics Hotspots

By the Time You Finish This Chapter, You'll Be Able to...

- Know a hotspot when you see one
- Link parts of a graphic to different pages
- Shape the link areas

So, you have this nice picture of your family on your web page, with Mom, Dad, Fido, and your kid sister Daphne. You want to link this image to information on each of them, but that information is on different pages. You also want the user to click Dad's face to see the page of your web that's all about him, or click Mom to see her company's web site (www.momco.com). You know the user would enjoy clicking Fido to access the web site he created for himself (despite its garish background colors and weak spelling). And finally, the user needs to click Daphne to travel to the form for online reporting of suspected alien invasions.

But, you can't do this just by selecting the graphic and adding a link (as seen in Chapter 12, "Adding Pages and Creating Links"). After all, that creates only one link for the entire picture. Is there some way to link different parts of a graphic to different pages?

I'm not going to answer that question, so you'll have to figure it out for yourself. I can't give you all the answers! At the moment, I'm too busy with this other question that I have to answer.

What Is a Hotspot?

A *hotspot* is an area on a graphic that links to a page. By putting several hotspots on a graphic, you can link different parts of a graphic to different pages. (Oh, I guess I answered your question for you! Okay, for extra credit, what's the capital of Minnesota?)

When you use most Web browsers and come across a graphic that has hotspots on it, your mouse pointer changes as you run it across the graphic. When the pointer is an arrow, clicking doesn't do anything. When the pointer becomes a hand with a pointing finger, however, this means that it's on top of a hotspot, and clicking that hotspot will take you to another page. This just goes to prove that old adage, "the hand is mightier than the arrow."

How Do Hotspots Work?

When you add hotspots to a graphic, FrontPage creates a file called an *image map* that has the information on what parts of the graphic link to each URL. That's why some folks refer to the process of adding hotspots as *image mapping*.

There are two different ways this file can be used. With *server-side image maps*, the Web browser tells the server which part of the graphic was clicked. The server looks this information up in the map and provides the link to the proper site.

With a *client-side image map*, the server sends the whole image map to the Web browser. It's the Web browser that figures out which URL to go to. This is considered a better way to do things, but it doesn't work with many older or less-popular Web browsers.

Creating a Hotspot

In order to create a hotspot, you'll need to have a page in the Editor with a graphic on it. It doesn't matter if it's a JPEG or a GIF graphic. (Just make sure that you don't get them confused and put up a JIF, because that's peanut butter.)

The editor buttons used to create hotspots are part of the Image group of buttons at the end of the first row of Editor buttons. In fact, they're so far at the end that, if you're using Windows in a low resolution mode, some of them will be off the screen. (If this is the case on your system, point to just above one of the visible toolbar buttons, push down the left mouse button, and drag the mouse downward and to the left. A rectangle shape will follow your mouse pointer. Move it so that the whole rectangle is on-screen and overlaps the edge between the bottom of the toolbar and the top of the page being edited. Let go of the mouse button, and a new toolbar row will appear, displaying all the buttons. Check out the figure to see what these tools look like.)

There are three buttons in this group that you can use to define the hotspots. Each button makes a different shape of the hotspot.

- The button with the rectangle on it is called *Rectangle*. Use the Rectangle button to select rectangular hotspots.
- The button with the circle on it is called *Circle* and you use it to select circular hotspots.
- The button with the rough upside-down outline of Senegal on it is called *Polygon*. This button is good for selecting any shape that isn't a rectangle or a circle.

In this picture, the words "who stayed up all night" are selected as a rectangle, the face is selected as a circle, and the ears are selected as a polygon.

Rectangular Hotspots

To select a rectangular hotspot (such as a box of cereal on a picture of a breakfast table), click the **Rectangle** button. The pointer becomes a pencil. Point to the upper left-hand corner of the area you want to select (where the box says "Free Dinosaur inside!"). Hold down the mouse button and drag the mouse to the lower right corner of the area

("Enlarged to make cereal look big"). An outline will appear to show you the area that you are selecting. Release the mouse button when you are completed.

Once you select the rectangle, a Create Link dialog box appears.

Choosing the Link

The Create Link dialog box here is the same one you use when creating text links, which you learned all about in Chapter 12. To summarize, it has four tabs. Use the Open Page tab if you want to create a link to a page currently in the Editor (including a targeted spot on the current page). Use the Current Web tab to choose a page that is already part of the same web as the page you are editing (the Browse button on this one brings up a list of those pages). Use the World Wide Web tab to designate a link to a page not on this web. The New Page tab lets you create a link to a page that is going to be part of this web but hasn't been created yet.

Once you select the appropriate tab and fill in the appropriate information, click the **OK** button. Congratulations! You've created a hotspot! (Before FrontPage, if you wanted to create a hotspot, you either had to start up a popular nightclub, or make your dog radioactive.)

Rectangular Rearrangements

If you didn't position your rectangular selection just right, you can always change it. Click the picture to select it, and the outlines of the hotspots will all appear. Next, click in the rectangular hotspot area. Squares will appear at the corners of the hotspot, as well as at the centers of the edges.

Click the square at the center of the top or bottom edge and drag it up or down to make the rectangle taller or shorter. Click the square on one of the side edges and drag it sideways to make the rectangle wider or narrower. Dragging one of the corner squares lets you adjust both the height and the width at the same time. All this dragging may seem a little awkward at first, but eventually, you'll become so quick at this you'll be a regular drag racer!

Circular Spots

To make a circular hotspot (for example, to create a hotspot for a quarter on a picture of a pile of change, point to the center of circle (George Washington's ear), hold down the mouse button, and drag to the edge of the circle. A thick outline of the circle appears as you drag it.

Once you release the mouse button, the Create Link dialog box appears. Choose your link; then click the **OK** button.

Piling Up Hotspots! By overlapping two hotspots linked to the same URL, you can make the user think they're a single hotspot. For example, you can create a lollipop-shaped hotspot by using a circle hotspot for the candy and a rectangular hotspot for the stick. This is often easier for you, and for the computer, than trying to use a polygon hotspot.

Resizing the Round Spot

To change the size of the circular hotspot at any time, click the graphic, and the outline of the hotspots appear. Click in the circle, and four squares will appear outside the circle, where the corners of the circle would be if a circle had corners (which only the cheap ones do). Drag one of these squares toward or away from the square in the opposite corner, and the circle will change size, growing or shrinking in the direction that you drag.

When you drag a square, remember that the circle will still stay a circle. You can't stretch it into an oval or other more interesting shape (such as a figure eight or Mel Gibson). Also remember that because the opposite corner stays in the same spot, the center of the circle (midway between the corners) will be moving.

Polygonamy

The polygon tool lets you select shapes made of many flat sides. By selecting a number of points, you can select shapes that hold pretty close to a curve. To select such a shape, click the **Polygon** button. The pointer becomes a pencil (or at least that's what Microsoft says it is; I think it looks more like a crayon, but I am not the defacto standard setter for the microcomputing world. You can call it what you want). Click one point of the outline of the shape you want to outline. Point the pencil (crayon!) at the other end of that edge of the outline; then click and a line will appear between the two points.

Continue clicking the points around the edge, building the outline. Work your way all around the outline. Once you create the last point around the edge, click the whatever-writing-implement pointer on the first point again, and the outline will close up.

After you complete the outline, the Create Link dialog box appears. Select the URL for the link; then click the **OK** button. Your roughly edged hotspot is now complete.

Don't Get Crossed Up!

When drawing a polygon, don't draw lines that cross (like in the center of a figure eight). In some cases, this will cause the shape of the hotspot to be confused.

Polymorphing

To change the shape of a polygonal hotspot, select the graphic with the hotspot, and the outlines of the hotspots appear. Click in the polygon, and squares appear at all the points you selected along the edge. You can change the shape by selecting any one point and dragging it to where you want it. All the other points stay where they are; the only thing that changes is the edges between the point you're moving and the points before and after that point.

Finding a New Spot for a Hotspot

You can slide any hotspot around by pointing to the center of the hotspot, holding down the pointer, and then dragging it where you want it on the graphic.

Be careful not to let hotspots linking to different URLs overlap. You can't be sure which of the overlapping links will be followed. There's too much randomness and unpredictability in this world; by contributing to it, you're only adding to entropy and could be given sole blame for the eventual heat-death of the universe. (But probably not.)

Make a Not-So-Hotspot

If you want to get rid of a hotspot that you made, select it and then tap the **Delete** button. The outline and the link it represents disappears, never to be seen again! (And I do mean never; the **Edit, Undo** command won't undo this destruction, so be careful, and look both ways before deleting.)

Can You Rethink Your Link?

If you want to adjust what a hotspot links to, double-click that hotspot. The Create Link dialog box reappears, and you can select where you want the link to go.

Can't See the Spots Before Your Eyes?

The outlines of the hotspots don't show up very well in front of some pictures. The outline appears as a color that contrasts with the color behind it, but if you have a picture with a lot of colors or that is naturally filled with lines, the outlines might be hard to tell from the design. Modern Art and modern web tools were not meant to go together.

However, there is a trick that lets you see the hotspots no matter what the image is. Click the **Highlight Hotspots** button (the one with the arrow pointing to the blue rectangle). The image disappears, leaving just the outline of the hotspots. The outline of the currently selected hotspot will be filled in.

Unfortunately, you cannot resize/reshape or move the hotspots while viewing them this way. You can change which hotspot is selected by clicking the one you want to select. To delete a hotspot, select it and hit the **Delete** key; the hotspot disappears (but the picture appears again). To change a link, double-click the hotspot, just as with the standard display.

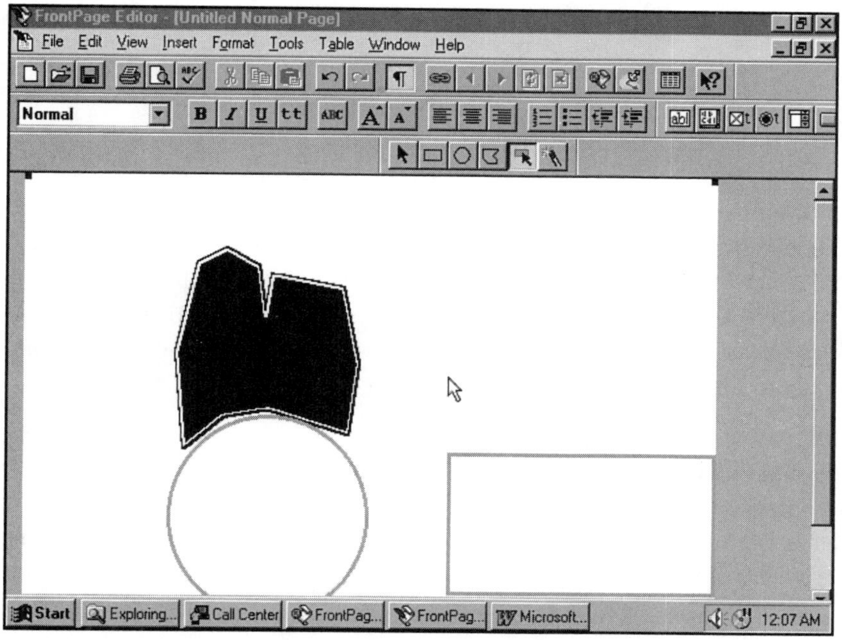

The picture disappears when you click the Highlight Hotspot button, and the currently selected link appears filled in.

Is Your Server Spotty?

The companies that make server software each uses a different format for the image map file that describes the location of the hotspots. Because of this lack of standards (or glut of standards, depending on one's view), FrontPage needs to know what type of server your web will be on.

To set this, bring the web up in the FrontPage Explorer. Pull down the **Tools** menu and select the **Web Settings** command. A dialog box appears with a number of tabs. Select the **Advanced** tab. (*Advanced*, in this case, not meaning "silly detail that you won't need to deal with and is probably too complex to understand anyway" as it usually does. Instead, it means "really basic information hidden away.")

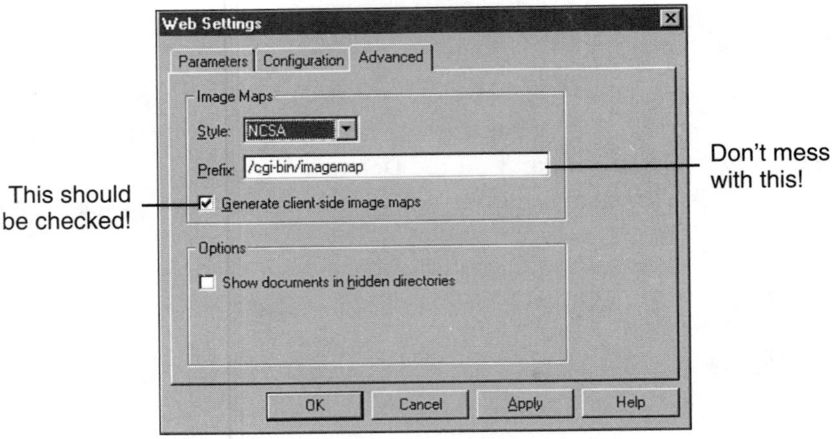

The Image Maps section of this tab has the information you want to deal with. Click the down-arrow button to get a list of possible image map styles. If your server is running the FrontPage extensions, select **FrontPage** from the menu; if your server is running the Netscape extensions, select **Netscape**. (If you don't know if your server has those extensions, call your server guru and ask him. Once he puts the Doom game he was playing on pause, he should be able to quickly answer your question.)

If you don't have either set of extensions, the next step is to check your server's /cgi-bin directory. If you find a file in there called imagemap.exe, then select **NCSA**. If not, but you find a file named htimage.exe, you can select **CERN**. (If you don't know how to check this, call the server guru again. The world needs your web page working more than it needs saving from those evil zombies.)

If you don't have either of the server extensions nor either of the files, you still aren't totally out of luck. Select **<None>** as the style. The hotspots will now only work with browsers that support a feature called *client-size image maps*. But, since the current versions of Netscape and Internet Explorer support this feature, most of the users out there can still use your hotspots.

No matter what your choice, don't mess with the Prefix field, and make sure that there is a check in the **Generate client-side image maps** check box.

Pardon the Pictureless People

Not everyone's browser supports graphics, so even if you have the server software that supports hotlinks, some people won't be able to use them.

On one hand, you can simply choose to ignore these poor wretches of the online kingdom. However, it's really not politically correct to pick on the graphic-impaired, and this is a PC book after all, so we have to recommend that you prepare for this people. The best way to do this is to put text copies of the links somewhere below the picture. Make the text as small as possible. Most of these browsers that don't support graphics show all the text the same size anyway, and this way, it won't be intrusive for the people who do get the picture.

Hotideas

There are many good uses for hotspots. Here are some examples from quality web sites, which might get your own creative juices flowing, or at least clear your sinus passages.

Click the Blue Plate Special

You can create your own on-screen menu of commands with fancy-looking buttons. Use your favorite graphics program to draw a control panel made up of rectangular buttons, place that image on your page, and select each of the buttons as a different rectangular hotspot.

A Real Map for Your Image Map!

Maps that show the dividing lines between towns, states, or countries are ideal for hotspotting. If you make each place its own hotspot, you can link each place to a bunch of information about that location such as "Residents of Riverton, New Jersey, are inexplicably proud that the town was the first American home of the Japanese beetle, which has caused massive destruction of crops."

When making such a map, you have to draw the edges of your polygons very carefully, making sure to follow the borders exactly. You may also run into a problem of some places being too small to click. On a map of Europe, for example, Monaco would be so small that it would be invisible even compared to Liechtenstein, which is 100 times as large. If you had a map of Europe that filled the entire typical user's browser screen, Monaco would be so small that it would take up less than a tenth of a pixel (the little dots that make up the screen image). Monaco is so small that the road sign on its entrance say "Welcome to Monaco, please come back real soon." Monaco is so small that bowlers there have to put a wicked spin on the ball—they had to curve the alleys so that they'd fit in the country! Monaco is so small that at the Customs Office on the way out, they check your suitcase to make sure you're not stealing the country as a souvenir. Monaco is so small that, well, it's hard to fit a polygon around on a map.

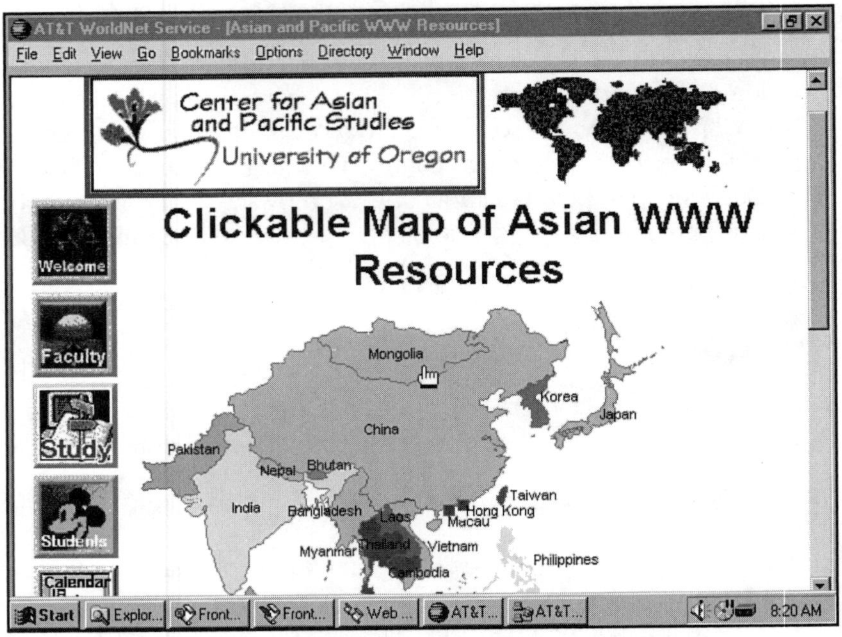

The University of Oregon's Center for Asian and Pacific Studies' site uses hotspots for a command menu and a map where you can click any country and get a list of web sites about that country.

The Least You Need to Know

- A hotspot is a clickable area on a graphic that serves as a link.
- The FrontPage editor has tools to make rectangular, circular, and polygonal hotspots.
- After making a hotspot, you can change its size or shape by selecting the hotspot and moving the squares that appear at its edges.
- You can delete a hotspot by selecting it and hitting the **Delete** key.
- You can change the link of a hotspot by double-clicking it.
- The **Highlight Hotspots** button lets you see the hotspots more clearly by not showing the graphic.
- For hotspots to work properly, you need to configure information about your server, using FrontPage Explorer's **Tools, Web Settings** command.

Chapter 14

Setting Up Tables

By the End of This Chapter, You'll Be Able to...

- Create a table
- Fill in the table
- Make your table look good
- Add and delete rows and columns
- Combine or split cells without blowing up your neighborhood
- Improving the table's appearance

On the World Wide Web, there is information, gobs and gobs of information. If information were physical and edible, no one would ever starve, because we would all be crushed to death first under piles of physical, edible information.

When you're ready to throw your information into the ever-growing pile, it's a good idea to have it understandable and organized, so that it is useful. Tables are good at that.

What Is a Table, Anyway?

A *table* is a grid of information, organized in *rows* (lines across) and *columns* (lines up and down). You may remember your multiplication tables from when you were in school. Each row had a number being multiplied, the column had a number that was multiplied by, and where the column crossed the row was a square (called a *cell*) with the result.

On a web page, tables are good for much more than just mathematical information. Any time you want a grid, or even just to break the page into columns, tables are your tool.

This Table Isn't Big Enough for Everyone

One thing that you must be careful of, however, is that while most people are using browsers that understand tables, they are a relatively recent addition to the web, and there are still many browsers out there that don't understand them. Their numbers are shrinking rapidly, but for a while, there will be some people who can see the information in your table, but it will all run together rather than being broken into understandable chunks. You can show compassion to these people and also make the data available in some other form—or you can laugh cruelly at them.

Creating Your Table

To add a table to a page that you are working on in the editor, click the **Insert Table** button on the toolbar (it looks like a car radiator, and is just to the left of the Help button). An Insert Table dialog box appears. This dialog box has a lot of settings, but don't worry, none of these settings is tough to understand; once you know how to use them, you can make a table fit for a king!

The Insert Table dialog box lets you design the look of your table.

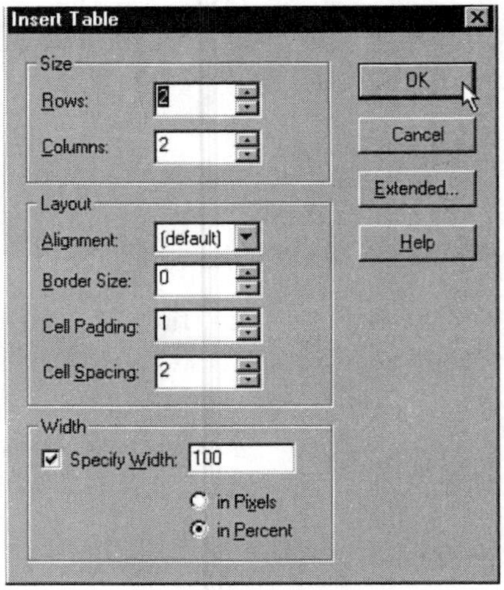

Rows and Columns

In the first two fields, you're going to list how many rows and how many columns this table is going to have. When you're figuring it out, remember to include a column to hold the name of each row and a row to hold the name of each column, like the numbers 1 through 12 across the top and down the edge of the multiplication tables. (You may have gone to a better school where they used 1 through 20; the equipment at my school was so old that they hadn't even invented numbers above 12 when they made up the tables.)

Don't worry if you miscount how many rows or columns you will need. As with everything else, you can change it later.

Align Is Not the Shortest Distance Between Two Points

The next field is **Alignment**. This is where you decide where the table is going to be across the page, which only matters if your table isn't as wide as the browser's display.

Click the down arrow button, and you will find a list of four possible settings. Choose **Left**, and the table will snuggle up with the left edge of the browser window. Choose **Center**, and it will stay in the middle, taking no sides. Choose **Right** and the table will stay on the east coast of the browser window.

The other choice, **(default)**, positions the table the same way that the text before and after it is positioned (for example, if the surrounding text is left-justified, the cell contents will be against the left wall of the cell). Dis way, if de table is not in de right position, it's de fault of whoever set up de text.

Border Patrol

The cells of the table are each surrounded by their own box. The lines on this box are usually shaded, to make it look like the cells are indented. There's another box around the whole table, which is shaded to make it look like the table is raised off the page. The value in the **Border Size** field sets how thick these lines on this outer box are, measured in pixels (the little dots that make up the computer display). The thicker the lines are, the more raised the table looks.

If you set the border to 0, not only does the outside box disappear, but so does the boxes around each cell. Don't worry, this doesn't mean that your data will leak out and run around the place like uncaged tigers, wreaking destruction and leaving cool-looking paw prints. The box is still there, it's just invisible when viewed with a Web browser.

If you have no borders, the Editor will display dotted lines to separate the columns and the rows. These lines won't show up when a browser looks at the final display; they're just there to help you while you're working on the page. (Dotted lines are friendly, helpful, and kind by nature. They should not be confused with dotty lions, however, which are more like uncaged tigers.)

Elevating the Empty Cell

If there is nothing in a cell (no text, no pictures, and so on), the browser will often not draw the box around the cell. This makes it look like the cell is at the same raised level as the table frame. The Editor will sometimes, but not always, show it this way as well.

Are You Ready for a Padded Cell?

The next field is **Cell Padding**. This sets how much space there is between the inside edge of the box around the cell and the text in that cell. If you set this number too low (0 or 1), the text will run into the edge of the cell, which may make it harder to read. If you set it too high, you'll end up with a lot of empty space. The right setting really depends on how much information (and of what type) you are trying to fit in the table. Experiment with this a bit!

Cells in Space!

The **Cell Spacing** field lets you choose how much space is between each cell's box and the boxes next to it, above it, and below it. I find that two is a good number to put in here, although a larger number can give you a keen window-pane effect.

With Width or Without

Width, the last section of the dialog box, deals with how far across the page the table will go. The first field in this section is the **Specify Width** check box. If you don't have a check in this box, the browser will make the table wide enough to fit the text in each column without rearranging it at all. This could mean that you'll have a table that is wider than the browser window, and the visitor will have to scroll around (which may be the most exercise he gets while using the web).

With a check in the box, however, you get to dictate just how wide the table is. You can set this width either as a number of pixels or as a percentage of the available browser window width. Click the radio button for the measurement button you want (in **Pixels** or in **Percent**); then type the number into the **Specify Width** field.

If you set the width, the browser may have to split up the text in some cells across multiple lines, just like the text in this book is broken into lines to fit onto the page. If you end up with a lot of columns with a lot of text in each cell, this could make things very difficult to read, just as if we made this book only two inches wide. (But then, you could carry it in your shirt pocket! Of course, it'd be about five feet tall, making walking through doorways rather difficult.)

Remember, however, that different people are using different-sized browser windows, so that a pixel measurement that fits on one person's screen may not fit on another person's screen. People are also using different size fonts for text, so even cells that don't get broken into multiple lines in a small browser window on your system may be rearranged on theirs.

Set the Table! It's Dinner Time!

Now that you have all of the dimensions of the table ready, just click the **OK** button. The table will appear on the page with all of its glorious gridlines—but with nothing in it!

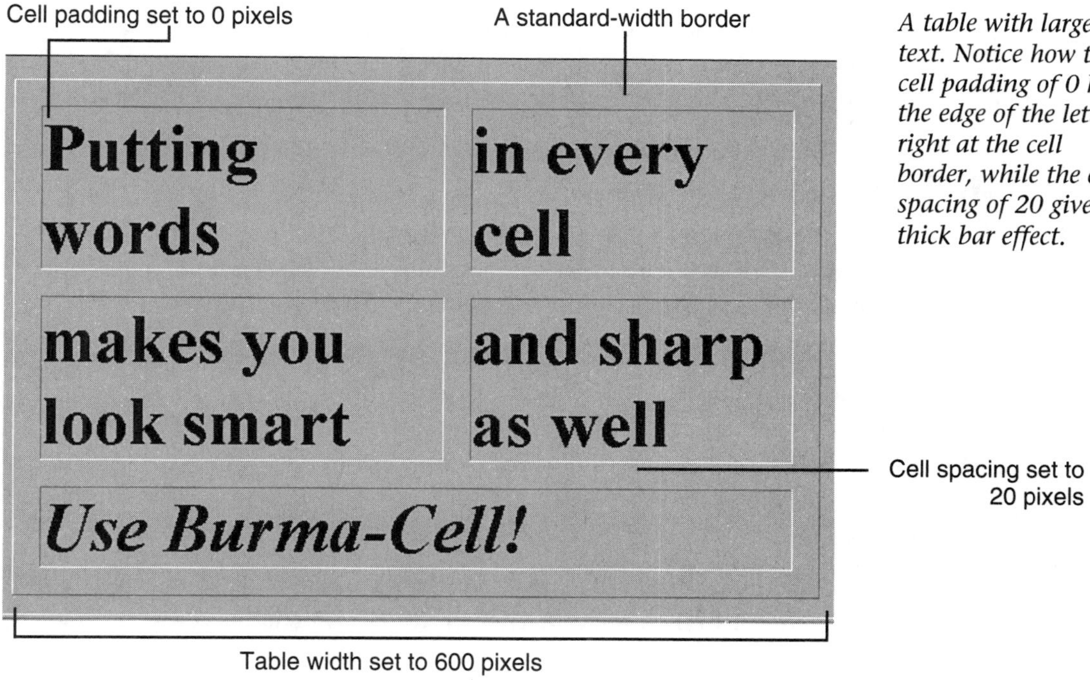

A table with large text. Notice how the cell padding of 0 has the edge of the letters right at the cell border, while the cell spacing of 20 gives a thick bar effect.

> **Techno Talk**
>
> **Tagging the Table**
>
> If you're an HTML guru, you may know of some additional features that tables can have that FrontPage can't put in for you. To add the appropriate attributes (HTML settings) to the table, click the **Extended** button at the side of the dialog box. An Extended Attributes dialog appears, allowing you to build your own additional attributes for the <TABLE> tag.

Stuffing the Cells

A big empty table can be nifty looking, I suppose, but it's not very useful. Imagine the Hollywood Squares without the X's, O's, and current and former TV stars. It just wouldn't be the same! So it's time for you to fill your grid with the online equivalent of Wally Cox and ALF.

What can you put into a table? Well, you can put in anything that you would put anywhere on the page. You can put in text, headlines, graphics, links, Bots, and even other tables!

Choosing the Cell

To start typing into a cell, simply click that cell. Then, you can type into it, or use any of the usual inserting or editing functions to edit it.

To move onto the next cell, hold down the **Ctrl** key and press the cursor down-arrow key. Even though you hit down, this will take you to the next cell across. Once you hit the end of a row, hitting this combination will take you to the first cell on the next row.

Cell-ecting

If you just want to edit the text in a cell, you can use the plain old-fashioned method of selecting (putting the cursor before the first character you're selecting and dragging the mouse to after the last letter you're selecting). This works just fine within a cell.

However, there are times that you want to mess with a whole cell, or even a group of cells or a whole row or several columns. You're far too busy to make changes one cell at a time! If you ever want to truly change the world, you'll have to work at least a whole table at a time.

Selecting One Cell

To select a cell, click within that cell. The cursor will appear there. Pull down the **Table** menu and choose the **Select Cell** command. The whole cell will change color to show that the cell is selected.

Selecting Rows of Cells

Last time you pulled down the **Table** menu, you probably noticed the **Select Row** command among other commands. Thinking ahead, you probably thought "Aha! *That's* how you select a row!"

Well, you're only partly right (that's what you get for thinking ahead). There's a better way, one that lets you pick one or more than one row.

Roll the pointer to the left edge of the table. As the pointer is over the edge, you'll see it change from the normal left-angled arrow to an arrow pointing to the right. Now, an arrow that changes direction doesn't sound like much of an arrow, but in this case, it's quite useful. Move it to the edge of the first row you want to select. Press down the left mouse button, and that row becomes selected (you can tell because it changes color).

Drag the mouse down until it points to the last row you want to select. As you drag it down, each row you pass changes color. Once you point to the last row, release the button. The rows will stay selected.

Selecting Columns of Cells

Selecting one or more columns of cells is a lot like selecting rows while lying down. (And, what better way to spend a lazy day than selecting columns?)

Push the pointer up to the top edge of the first column you want to select, and it will turn into an arrow pointing down. Holding down the left mouse button, drag it over to the last column you want to select. The columns change color to show that they're selected.

Selecting Any Group of Cells

Point to the first cell in the group; then while holding down the **Alt** key and the left mouse button, drag the pointer over all of the connected cells in the group. As the pointer passes over each one, it will change color, showing that it is selected. If you want to add some cells to this that aren't attached to the selected cells, release the **Alt** key, hold down the **Shift** key and click each of the additional cells.

Selecting the Whole Table

To select the entire table, simply click somewhere in the table, then pull down the **Table** menu and choose the **Select Table** command. The entire table changes color to show that you have selected it.

Changing the Whole Table

You can make changes that effect the original table layout by selecting any part of the table, pulling down the **Table** menu and selecting **Table Properties**.

When the dialog box appears, you'll see it has fewer functions than you originally set up.

Here, you can change the alignment, the border size, the cell padding and spacing, and the width. Notice that the area for changing the width is labeled **Minimum Width**, where previously it was called **Width**. This is because tables, like many of us, tend to put on width as time passes. In the case of the tables, it's because large nonrearrangable items have been added. For example, you may have set the original table width to be 100 pixels. However, if you've put an image into one of the cells and that image is 150 pixels across, there's no way that the table can be smaller than that. The more you stuff in the table, the wider it is likely to get—just like yourself!

Make your changes; then click the **OK** button to have them take effect.

But wait! There's nothing here that lets you change how many columns or rows are in the table. This is something you might need to change! Oh, no! I usually don't suggest panicking, but this seems worth it! You panic, and I'll wait for you.

Okay, okay…wait a minute. My editor says I have to tell you that there's really no need to panic (even though it would have been fun to watch). There are ways to change the number of rows and columns, and I promise to tell you about them in the later section, "Making a Bigger Table." Authors never get to have any fun around here.

Making Ex-Cell-ent Cells

You can change attributes of cells to make them look different. To do this, select the cells that you want to change (whether it's one cell, several rows, or even an entire table). Right-click the selected area, and select **Cell Properties** from the shortcut menu that appears.

A dialog box full of useful little toys appears.

Blank Values

When you bring up the Cell Properties dialog box, the current values of the fields are shown. If some of the fields are blank, it just means that you have more than one cell selected, and the cells don't all have the same value for that field so it doesn't know which one to display.

Tossing the Text Around the Box

The first field in the Cell Properties dialog box is **Horizontal Alignment**. Click the field's drop-down button to display a list of three choices. Selecting **Left** shoves your text (or other cell content) over against the left wall of the cell box. Selecting **Center** moves it to the center of the box. Selecting **Right** moves it in a direction that high-level computer programmers and WebMasters refer to as "right."

The second field is **Vertical Alignment**, which (as you may guess) works much like Horizontal Alignment. Selecting **Top** moves the cell's contents to the top of the cell box.

Bottom shoves it to the bottom of the cell. Select **Center**, and the secret Web browser elves will hold the cell's contents at dead-center. The life of a Web elf isn't easy, and is made enjoyable only by the fact that they get to read all of your e-mail.

Header Setter

Also in that top section of the dialog box is a **Header Cell** check box. If you check this box, the text of the cell will display in bold on most browsers. This makes it useful for marking the column titles in your first row or your row titles in your first column.

Ac-Cell-erated Growth

Minimum Width is the middle section of the Cell Properties dialog box. Now, this can get messy, because every cell in a column has the same width, even though they may have different Minimum Width settings. All of the cells in the column will be *at least* as wide as the biggest Minimum Width setting in the column. Because of this, changing any one cell's Minimum Width setting may not have any effect on the column.

If you don't check this box in this section, the cell only has to be wide enough to hold its contents (and remember that text can be split into multiple rows). If, however, you check this box, you can set a minimum width for this cell, either in **Pixels** or in **Percent** by selecting the appropriate radio button. Percent, in this case, is measured as percent of the entire table width. (Percent is usually the better choice, since you don't know what the resolution of the viewer's screen will be.) After selecting the appropriate measurement, put the value (the number of pixels or the number of percent) in the **Specify Width** field.

Dealing with these column widths drives the Web browser elves nuts. They have to check every cell in the column, to see which one is the widest. The width of some of the cells is dictated by the contents, and in others, it is set by these width settings. One column may have some set in pixels and others set in percents, and trying to compare the two is tricky because the percents are percents of table width, but you don't know how wide the table is until you know all the column widths, and you don't know how wide the columns are until you know the table width and can figure a percentage of it.

Ex-Span-d Your Cells

The bottom section of the Cell Properties dialog box houses some powerful controls that let you make cells that are more than one column across or more than one row deep. Why would you want to do this? Well, say you're going to make a TV time-table you see in the newspaper or weekly TV magazines. (No, you don't have to say it *out loud!*)

In one of those time-tables, each column is a half hour slot. However, some shows run longer than a half hour. So, even though each column is rigidly defined, some items have to span more than one column. And, if you were doing a sideways TV timetable that ran down the page, it would be rows you'd be reusing.

There are two values to set here. The first is the number of rows that the cell spans, and the second is the number of columns it spans. On most standard tables, you will leave both of these set to one.

When you do increase these figures, the elves have to shove some cells around to make room. They don't get rid of any cells, just move them. Where they shove the cells depends upon whether you're increasing the row span or the column span.

For example, consider a basic table where each cell takes up only one column and one row. If you take one cell and make it span three columns, all of the cells to the right of that one get pushed over two columns to make room. The elves have to make new columns to fit the last two, although (being lazy elves) they not only leave the rest of the cells in those columns blank, they don't even give them a box, so you can't put anything in there.

If you took one cell and made it span two rows, however, the elves don't shove everything below it down and make a new row. Instead, they make room by pushing the cell below the expanding one, and every cell to the right of it, over one to the right. This pushes the last cell out past the end of the table, so a new column is built for it.

The moral of this story is that elves are pushovers.

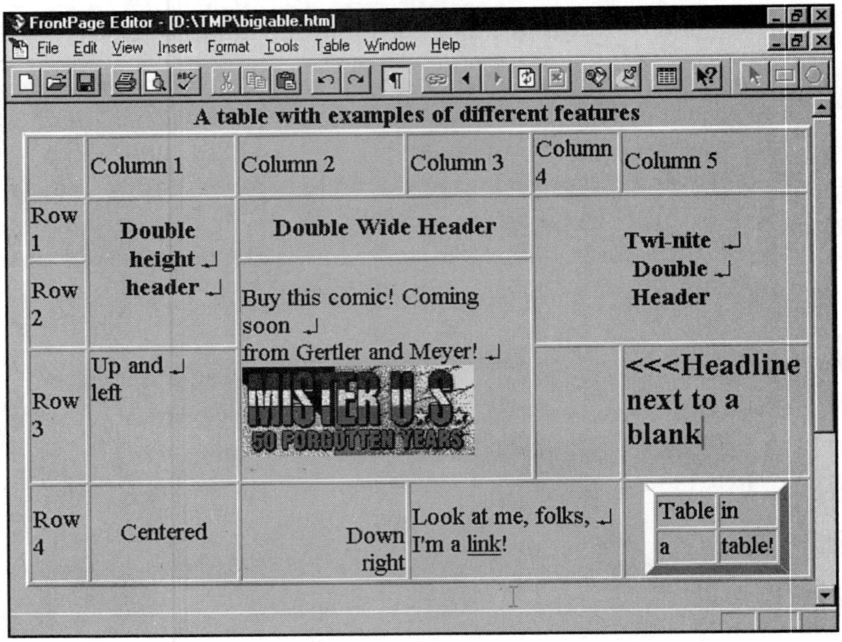

This table shows a variety of cell formats, including spanning multiple rows and columns.

De-Cell-eration

Sometimes, you'll want to get rid of some cells. This is likely to happen if you've been creating cells that span multiple columns or rows, and are left with some spare cells sticking out in new columns. Those cells are pesky things, but you can easily eliminate them. Simply select the cells that you want to delete; then click the **Cut** button. The cells will go away, and if they were the only live cells in the column or row, that column or row will disappear as well.

If there are any cells that aren't being deleted to the right of ones that you are deleting, they will get moved to the left.

Save Some Effort

Wait until you create all of the multirow or multicolumn spanning cells before you start deleting the stray cells that show up at the right.

Making a Bigger Table (Like When the Family Comes for the Holidays)

Information is like potato chips. If you take people who didn't particularly want information and give them just a little bit, they'll soon want more and more, until they're desperately digging at the crumbs of information at the bottom of the bag or trying to fish that broken-off end of information out of the dip.

Because of this need for more and more information, you may need to add more rows or columns, to cover information in more detail.

The Rows Arise

To add more rows, select a cell in the row that you want the new rows to be below. Make sure that it's a cell that only spans one row. Pull down the **Table** menu and select the **Insert Rows or Columns** command. On the dialog box that appears, the **Rows** option should already be selected, as well as the **Below Selection** option. Just enter the number of rows you want to add into the **Number of Rows** field, and click the **OK** button.

If you want to add rows at the very top of the table, select a cell in the first row, select **Table, Insert Rows or Columns**, select the **Above Selection** radio button, and enter the number of rows into the **Number of Rows** field. Click the **OK** button, and the rows will be added.

The Columns Accumulate

Adding columns is a lot like adding rows, only sideways, sort of. Select a single-width cell in the column to the left of where you want the new columns to appear. Pull down the **Table** menu and select the **Insert Rows or Columns** command. When the dialog box appears, select the **Columns** option radio button. The area below that option will change to reflect the Column choice. Type the number of columns you want to add into the **Number of Columns** field; then click the **OK** button. Poof! The new columns appear. (Note: your system probably will not make the sound effect "poof!" but I encourage you to make it yourself to make this whole thing seem appropriate.)

To add new columns at the far left side of the table, select a cell in the first column, and do the same steps just mentioned, except you also have to select the **Left of Selection** option button before hitting **OK**. (In fact, if your system *does* make the "poof!" sound effect, you should check it. It's probably some irritated elves messing with the circuitry.)

The Span Doesn't Stretch

If you insert new rows or columns between two existing ones that a spanning cell stretches across, the span doesn't grow to stretch to where it used to. Instead, the span still covers the same number of rows or columns.

Every Table Needs a Title (Mine Will Be Knighted in the Morning!)

There is a feature designed just for giving a title or other caption to a table. First, select the table. Pull down the **Table** menu and select the **Insert Caption** command. The cursor will appear above your table. Type your title or caption.

You're somewhat limited in what you can do with your caption. You can't include a carriage return; and while you can use text formatting such as bold and italic, you can't use paragraph formatting such as the Heading formats.

Real Captions Go Below

If you want the tables caption to go below the table, you'll first have to select it. To properly select a caption, double-click in the space to the left of the caption. The caption space across the entire width of the panel will change color to show that it is selected.

Pull down the **Edit** toolbar and select the **Properties** command. The seldom-seen Caption Properties dialog box appears. Captions, you will quickly discover, have very few properties (which is, I suppose, why they aren't called "titles." Titles such as "Duke" or "Baron" usually have a lot of property associated with them). In fact, captions have exactly one property, and that's whether you want them placed above the table or below it. Click the **Bottom of the Table** option radio button, and the caption will move to the bottom side of the table.

Tables Are the Key Furniture for Fancy Page Designs

Tables break space down into rows and columns, but there's nothing that says that it has to be a chart. For example, say you wanted a web page with a long story laid out in three even columns, like a newspaper. Build a simple table with zero border width (so you don't see the border lines), enough cell spacing that the columns won't run together, three columns, and one row. Make it 100% of the page width. Put the text for the first column in the first cell, text for the second column in the second cell, and the rest of the text in the third. Make sure that the Vertical Alignment on all three cells is set to **Top**, so that the columns are even across the top (they may be a little raggedy at the bottom). Voilà! You've just taken cutting-edge technology and used it to emulate a low-tech, centuries-old layout!

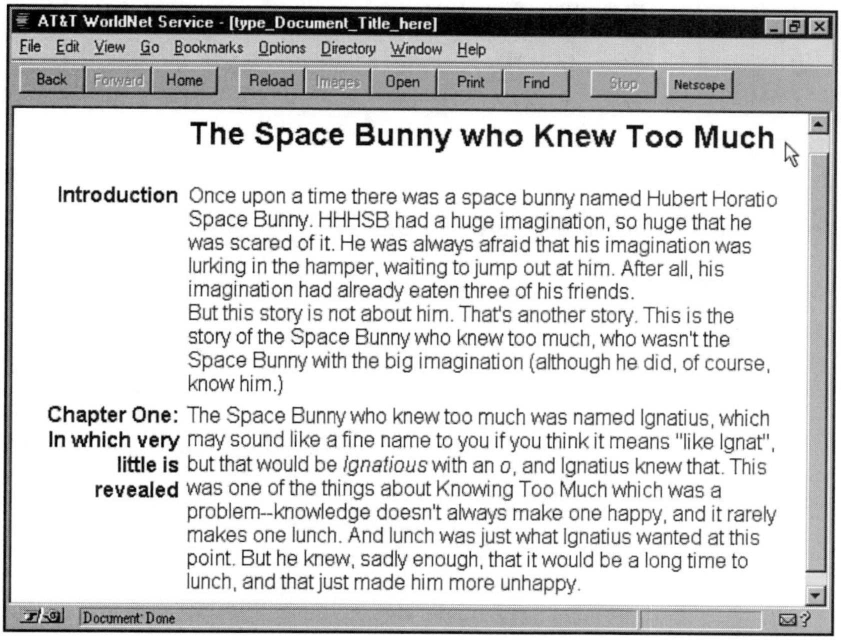

This page is laid out using tables. The headings and the text are separate columns. Each time a new section starts, there's a new row.

An Important Caution

FrontPage can, sometimes, create tables that will be misinterpreted by Web browsers, even by Microsoft's own Internet Explorer (which just goes to prove that no one is fully compatible with anyone). This seems most likely to happen when you start by importing a page with a complex table that was designed outside of FrontPage. Be sure to check all pages with tables by looking at them with various browsers before you publish them.

The Least You Need to Know

- A table is a grid used to hold information.
- Tables are made up of horizontal rows and vertical columns. Individual cells are formed by the intersection of rows and columns.
- Cells of tables can hold text, graphics, bots, or just about anything else you can put on a web page.
- To put a table into a page you're editing, use the Editor's **Insert Table** button.
- You can select any group of contiguous cells by holding down the **Alt** key and the mouse button and dragging the mouse over the cells you want to select.
- Using the **Cell Properties** command on the shortcut menu, you can change the alignment of text within cells, or you can stretch cells over multiple rows or columns.
- You can use tables to create fancy text layouts.
- FrontPage will sometimes output tables that are not properly readable by many browsers.

Chapter 15

Getting Interactive with Forms

By the End of This Chapter, You'll Be Able to...

- Set up a form
- Reform and deform a form
- Process the filled-in form

All of our lives, you've filled out forms. From the moment you put your little footprint on the form at the hospital, you've been filling forms with, well, in-form-ation. You fill out library requests, contest entries, magazine subscriptions, credit-card slips, job applications, hotel registrations, insurance claims, standardized tests, marriage certificates, school enrollments, and order forms for those little china figurines that you can only order from the back of crossword puzzle magazines.

But now, the shoe is on the other foot! (Now there's a stupid saying! We don't know if it was on the wrong foot before or if it's on the wrong foot now! Forget that I said that. Pretend I said "Now the tides have turned" or "What comes around goes around" or some other appropriate direction-switch phrase.) You're the one creating the forms, for others to fill out. Of course, since the forms you're making are going to be on computer, the people filling them out will have the ease of point-and-click use—they won't even need a number two pencil.

However, the forms that you make can be much more exciting than paper forms, because you can design a web form to not only *collect* information, but also to give a *response*. It's really the most interactive part of the web. No waiting six to eight weeks for delivery! No standing in long lines at the DMV! A properly set-up web site can respond in a couple of seconds. (What's more amazing is that folks quickly learn to become impatient with those seconds! Just goes to show that humans are crazy people.)

Forms? What For?

There are many different reasons to have a form as part of your web. The sheer joy of form creation is only one of them.

Probably, the most frequently used sort of form is a *search form*. This is the one that you fill out when you're trying to locate information about a given topic. The search form is the heart of popular Internet search engines like Alta Vista and indices like Yahoo. Many sites also have search engines for their site, which seems really useful until you try to search for the term "comic strip" and find out that the authors of the site always use the term "sequential art" instead.

Forms are also used for ordering things over the Web. Gone are the days when you had to walk down the street, go into the store, buy a thing, and come back from the store. Now, all you need to do is fill in your name, address, credit-card number, expiration date, billing address, home phone, business phone, order password, item catalog number, quantity desired, color desired, the name of who recommended you, choice of delivery options, and e-mail address where future junk e-mail ads can be sent, and like lightning, you will get that thing you want, a mere three to five weeks later!

Another popular use is registering for a site, so that the people running the site can now keep track of who's using the site and how to direct junk e-mail to them.

Then there's the comment form, which lets people tell you what they like and dislike about your site, while you gather their e-mail address for nefarious junk e-mail purposes.

Forms are even used to run discussions over the Web, so that you can send junk ads in real-time!

No matter what your purpose for building a junk e-mail address list (or even if you are using forms for some more legitimate purpose, thank goodness!), FrontPage's form capabilities will let you set up a form that is as easy or as hard to fill out as you want, and can help you make a form that makes your web page truly interactive.

Form Function

Having a base of understanding about the way that forms work on the Web is important so you can build a good one. Otherwise, it's like trying to build a building from the top down.

The web page that the form is on contains all of the information needed to build the form: the names of the various fields of the form, the type of fields (whether it's a text field, a pull-down menu, and so on), possible values for the field, things like that. As with most things on the web, however, it's up to the Web browser to interpret this structure and actually present the form to the user.

The browser takes care of gathering the information as the user fills out the form. When the form is complete, the user presses an on-screen button. At that time, the browser sends the value of all the fields that have been filled out to the server. There are several methods of sending this information, and you have to choose one of these methods when you design the form. The most common is to send a request for a page with a long URL. If you look closely at these URLs, you'll see that they contain the name of a program on the server that will process the form, as well as all of the information that you filled into the form itself. The program processes the form and creates a response page based on the information contained within the fields.

Other forms use other methods of passing information to the host over the Internet. Some even create an e-mail message with all of the form's information in it and e-mail it to a set address.

In order to create a form, you have to specify not only what all the fields are, what type of fields they are, and their possible values, but also how this information will be sent to the server, and what the server is supposed to do with it. (You could, if you're of a sadistic bent, just have the host ignore the information altogether, so that all the time spent filling out the form was wasted! Believe it or not, it's been done before!) Sounds complicated? Don't worry! FrontPage makes it all pretty easy, and if you read through this chapter, I'll make it even easier still!

Form Formation

Before you start your form, you should figure out what's going to be on it. After all, even though FrontPage will let you rearrange the items until the cows come home* after you

*(Note to people who don't have cows: strike out the cow phrase above and copy the phrase "to your heart's content" out of one of the earlier chapters. Or mix them, and leave it as "until the contented cows come home, which is where the heart is.")

put them into the form, it's a lot easier if you arrange them fairly well in the first place. I suggest sitting down with a pencil and paper (or, for you people who hate to sound low-tech, a honed graphite containment rod and a fiber-based transportable markup medium) and make a list of the information that you need. For example, if your form was asking for someone's address, the list would include her:

- Name
- Street address
- City
- State
- ZIP code
- Perhaps even the country (remember, the World Wide Web *is* worldwide!)

Each field you create needs a name. This name isn't for the user to see (you'll pick what he sees as the field name separately), but for use by the computer and by the people who have to work with the filled-out forms. It's a good idea to keep these names short (say, 20 characters) but clear. The name can't have any spaces (so you couldn't name a field **business phone**), but you can use periods, dashes, and underlines in addition to letters and numbers, so it could be **business.phone**, **business-phone**, or **business_phone**.) Be careful that you don't accidentally give two fields the same name!

Next, you have to figure out where this form is going to be. Forms cannot just float around formlessly in space. They need to be on a web page. You can put the form on an already-existing page, or you can start a new page and build links to it. You can build more than one form on a page, although you must group all of the fields of a form together.

Open up that web page with the FrontPage Editor. When you put your first field on the page, the Editor knows that you are working on a form and puts a black dotted box around the form area. (You can expand that area by putting the cursor inside it and hitting **Enter**.) So long as you work within that area, the editor assumes you're working on the same form. If you put a field outside that area, however, it assumes that you're starting another form on the same page. If you want to make just one form, make sure you always hit **Return** to start a new line of the form, rather than cursoring down or clicking where you want the next field to be.

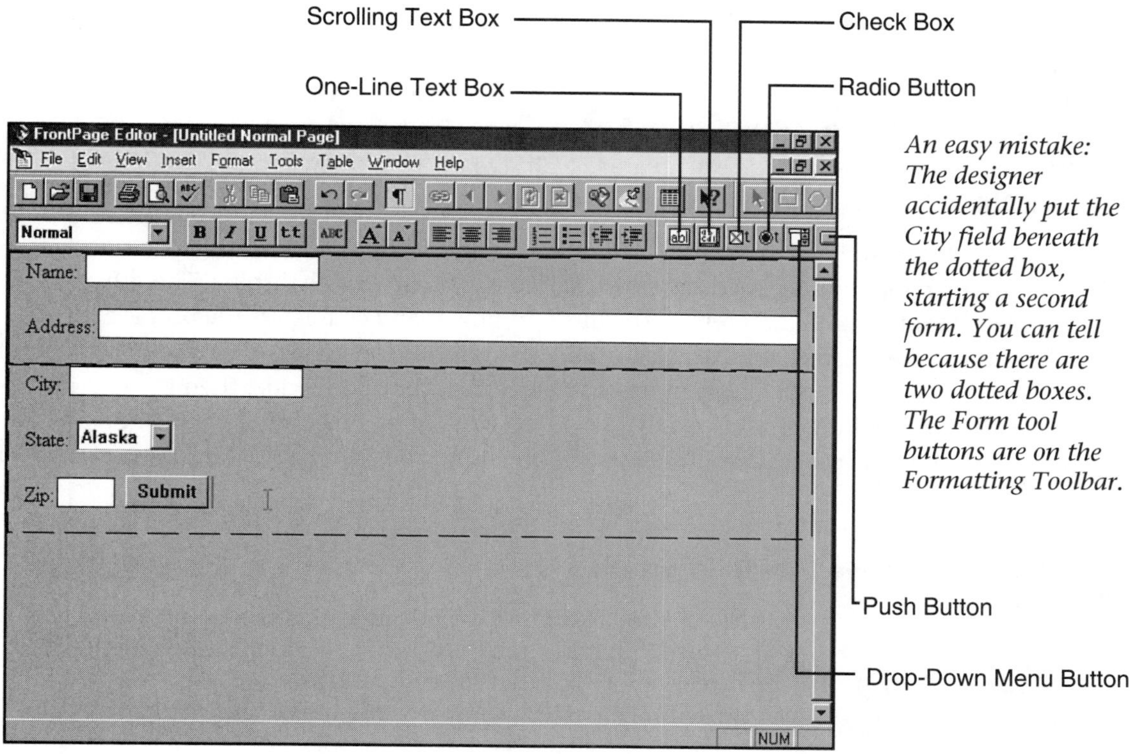

An easy mistake: The designer accidentally put the City field beneath the dotted box, starting a second form. You can tell because there are two dotted boxes. The Form tool buttons are on the Formatting Toolbar.

You can do most of the form work using the six form buttons on the end of the second toolbar. For those of you who are menu fans, you can find basically the same functions on the **Insert** menu, under the **Form Fields** submenu.

The Ever-So-Handy One-Line Text Box

Most forms have one-line text boxes in them. They are good for storing information that is of a limited length, such as name, or e-mail address, or number of times that you've seen Elvis. It's a very simple field to fill out; it's just a box that the user clicks (to put the cursor there) and then types into.

Putting a one-line text box on your form is just about as easy. In the editor, place the cursor where you want the box to appear. Click the **One-Line Text Box** button; it's the one with a white box with the letters **abl** in it (presumably short for **a box likethis**). When you do this, a Text Box Properties dialog box appears.

The first line of this dialog box asks for a name for this field. Fill it in, remembering that it has to be clear, unique, and can't have spaces in it.

The second line asks for an initial value. If you enter something in here, it will already be entered into the field when the user sees it. The user then only has to type in the field if he wants something different. For example, if you had a form that was asking for **Favorite member of the Brady Bunch**, you can have the field come up already saying Cindy. That way, only those weirdoes who are *not* Cindy-fans would have to work to enter something.

There are two number fields to be filled in. One asks for the field's **width in characters**. The number you set here sets how wide the box shows up on the display. The other number, **Maximum Characters**, is the limit on how many characters the user is actually allowed to enter. You can make this number the same as the previous one, or you can make it larger. If the user enters more characters than the box is wide, then the text in the box will start scrolling. The user may not see all of what he typed in at once, but it will all be sent with the finished form.

Keep the Field Small!

You can set the one-line text box's maximum character setting to less than the field width, but you shouldn't. When the user sees a wide field, he thinks he can enter at least that much text. If you have a small number of maximum characters, set the width to the same number.

The final question that the dialog box poses is whether this is to be a password field. When a user fills in a password field, he doesn't see what he types. Instead, with each letter he types, a little asterisk appears in the field. This way, someone looking over his shoulder can't see what he enters into the field (unless, of course, the fiendish perpetrator is smart enough to watch his fingers as he types, rather than the screen). The browser still stores exactly what the user types and sends it on to the computer.

Once you finish, click the **OK** button, and the field will appear on the page!

The Scrumptious, Scrappy, Scrolling Text Box!

If you want to let the user enter several lines (or even several paragraphs!) of text at once, the scrolling text box is the way to go. This is good for creating a space on the form for additional comments, general descriptions, or essays on **Why Cindy is the most psychically powerful of the Bradys**.

To create this field, place the cursor where you want the bottom of the box to appear, then click the **Scrolling Text Box** button (it's the one with the white square with **abcdl** in it, presumably standing for **a box containing data likethis**). A Scrolling Text Box Properties dialog box appears.

The first field of the text box is where you enter the field's name (for example, **Why-Cindy-powerful**). In the second box, you can type an initial value that will appear in the field on-screen, and which the user can choose to change, add to, or leave alone (example: **Just because she is, that's why!**)

The third box asks for the field's width in characters. This limits how big the box is on-screen but doesn't limit how many characters the user can actually type on each line. Finally, the field's number of lines is requested; again, this applies just to the box's appearance; entering the number **5** here will not prevent someone from giving a 73-line explanation behind Cindy's ability to bend spoons with the power of her mind.

A Big Enough Box

A good size for your text box is 60 characters wide and 8 lines long. This lets the user have a lot of space to work in without having any problems fitting it on the screen.

Click the **OK** button, and the field appears with scroll bars across the bottom and up the right side. This will let the user scroll through and look at his entry, if it's bigger than the box can display.

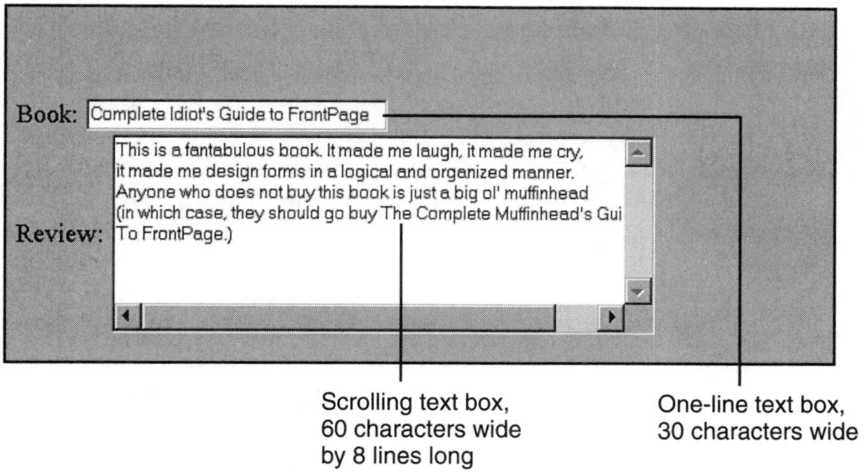

A simple form, seen through a browser. Notice that one of the lines of text in the scrolling text box is longer than can appear in the box, so the sideways scroll bar is active.

Check Box: The Choice of Champions!

The check box is a small box field handy for yes-or-no type situations. The user clicks the check box to take it from being empty (meaning no, I don't choose this thing) to having a check in it (meaning yes, I choose it!), or vice versa. It's most often used in instances where there's a list of items and the user can check off as many or as few as he wants. For example, if you are asking the user **Which of the following TV groups could beat the Brady Bunch in a fair fight?**, you might have **The Golden Girls**, **The Partridge Family**, and **The A-Team** listed, with a check box next to each.

To create a check box, position the cursor where you want the box to appear, and then click the **Check Box** button on the toolbar (it's the one with a picture of a check box with a **t** next to it, presumably standing for **thecheckbox**). A Check Box Properties dialog box appears.

The first thing the dialog box asks for is a name for the check box. Enter a name, remembering that you can use underlines, periods, and dashes, but no spaces (example: **Golden.Girls**).

The second field in the dialog box is asking for a value. Here, you see a way that the check box is different from the text boxes. When the Web browser sends the server information about the filled-in form, for each text box it sends the name of the field, followed by an equal sign, followed by the contents of the field (example: **Favorite.Brady=Cindy**). Even if the user leaves the text field blank, a record of the blank text field is sent (**Why.Cindy.Powerful=**).

However, information about a check box is sent only if the check box is checked. For example, if a user doesn't think the Golden Girls can take the Bradys and leaves the check box blank, the Web browser won't send any information about that field. If he *does* check the box, however, the Web browser will tell the computer that this field is equal to the value you entered in the dialog box. By default, this value is **ON** (which means that the browser would send **Golden.Girls=ON**), but you can set it to anything you want, and this can include spaces (if you enter **Can beat Bradys** in the value field, then the Web browser would send the computer the message **Golden.Girls=Can beat Bradys** if the box is checked).

The last thing the dialog box asks you to decide is whether the box is going to first show up checked or not checked. Usually, forms start without check marks, but if it's something that you'd like to encourage people to check (such as a check box next to **Check here to get on our junk e-mail list!**), choose **checked**. You can count on some people being too lazy to remove the check mark.

Click **OK**, and the check box appears in place.

Rah! Rah! Radio Buttons!

Radio buttons is kind of a stupid name for anything. After all, when you think of radios, you probably think more about knobs than about buttons, so it isn't clear right off what these do.

Radio buttons are named after the preprogrammed channel buttons on the car radio. On low-tech car radios, you push one of them, and it sticks in, and you hear the station it's programmed with. Press another button, and the first one pops out, and now you're listening to a different station. Only one of these buttons can be stuck in at a time. (The buttons on higher-tech car radios have much the same channel-changing effect, but because they're electronic, they don't actually stay stuck in, so you can't tell which stations you're listening to just by looking at the buttons. Ah, the price we pay for high-tech!)

The radio buttons on the form are like that. Out of a group of radio buttons, a user can select one and only one at a given time. The "buttons" are actually circles, and you can tell which one is selected because it has a black dot in it.

Radio buttons are good anywhere you have to select one item from a list, such as title (**Mr.**, **Mrs.**, **Ms.**, or **Your Holiness**) or choosing your favorite type of cookie for a list of three.

To create a radio button, put the cursor where you want the button; then click the **Radio Button** button on the toolbar (it has a circled black dot with a **t** next to it, which presumably stands for **theradiobutton**). A Radio Button Properties dialog box appears.

The first thing the dialog box asks for is the group name. Every button in the group has to have the same name here, and it has the same limits as the other field names.

The next thing required is the value that will be returned if the user selects this button out of the group. This should identify the choice that has been made, such as **Mrs.** or **Your Holiness**. (If you want the user to be able to select no items from the list, just include a button with the value **none**.)

The last decision to make is whether this button should be initially selected. One and only one button should be initially selected. Make it the button that the user is most likely to pick, or the one that you want him to pick (if the question is **How much junk e-mail would you like to get?**, and the three radio buttons are **Lots**, **Some**, and **None**, you should have the first one checked, so that lazy people who don't bother changing the selection will have actually asked you for the e-mail).

Click the **OK** button, and your radio button appears. Keep repeating this for all the buttons in your group!

Keep a Small, Friendly Group!

Radio buttons are best if you have only a few possible choices. If you have a lot of choices (like, say, picking the state from a list of fifty states), using a drop-down menu will be easier to set up, take up less screen space, and will be easier for the user to use.

Dynamic, Delicious Drop-Down Menus

You want to know what a drop-down menu is? You know that **Change Style** box on the left end of the bottom row of the toolbar? That's a drop-down menu. Usually, you can only see the current selection, but if you click the down-pointing arrow button next to it, the whole list of choices appears, and you can choose whichever one you want.

Drop-down menus are good for letting you pick one item from a list, such as picking what state you are in from a list of fifty. Because they only show your choices when you click the button, they take up very little screen space. If you have a lot of items on the list, a scroll bar appears next to the list, which means the user can choose from more options than would fit on the screen at once. These are very handy.

To make one of these menus, put the cursor where you want the menu to appear; then click the **Drop-Down Menu** button (it's the button that looks like, well, a drop-down menu. It's to the right of the Radio Button button). The Drop-Down Menu Properties dialog box opens up.

The first thing it wants is a name for this field. Enter it.

Next is a big block of space listing the items you have on the menu—which is none, so far. Click the **Add** button to put the first thing on the menu. Another dialog box appears. Into the first line of this dialog box, put what you want listed on the menu.

Below this is a check box marked **Specify Value**. Without this check box checked, the web browser will tell the server that the value for this field was whatever item the user selected off of the menu (for example, if this is a state field, and the user selected **New York**, the browser would tell the server **State=New York**). If you check this box, you can then enter some other string for the browser to send the server. This way, you can set up your list so that if the user selects **New York**, the Web browser will send out the phrase **State=NY**.

Finally, there's a pair of radio buttons marked **Selected** and **Not selected**. If you want this menu choice to be the default, click the **Selected** button. Remember, you can only have one default per menu.

Click the **OK** button, and you're back to the Drop-Down Properties dialog box, and there is now a listing for the menu entry you just created. Repeat the process of clicking **Add** and entering the information until you've entered all the items.

If you make a mistake entering a menu item, select it from the list and click the **Modify** button. You can then make changes to the settings for that entry. If you want to rearrange the entries, select an entry that you want to move; then click the **Move Up** button to move it higher on the menu, or the **Move Down** button to move it lower.

ABC for You and Me!

If you have a long menu, it's usually best to keep it in alphabetical order. After all, most of the computer users out there have major parts of the alphabet memorized.

There are two more options at the bottom of the list that can very much change the way your menu works. The first is a field marked **Height**. This is how many lines the menu takes up. If you change this number to something besides **1**, *it won't be a drop-down menu any more!* Instead, most browsers will display it as an always-open scrollable menu that many lines long.

The other option, **Allow multiple selections**, you shouldn't touch. You should just leave it set to **No**, its default. Using a menu like this to select multiple selections is not easy or intuitive for most users; you will just end up confusing them. If you want them to choose more than one item from a list of items, use a series of check boxes instead!

The Positively Purposeful Push Button!

The user needs a way to tell the system that a form is done, and that way is the push button! Each form should have at least one of these push buttons; when the user clicks it, the web browser knows that it's time to submit the form to the server. Additionally, there is a second type of push button, which resets all of the form's fields to their default values when pressed. This latter button is handy, I suppose, if you have users who like to waste their time filling out forms and then removing their selections.

To place a push button, put the cursor where you want the button to appear. Push the **Push Button** button on the toolbar (it's the one with a picture of a push button). A Push Button Properties dialog box appears.

The first field is the place for the field name. You can leave this blank (a victory for the lazy…er, *efficient* people of this world!). The only time that a push button needs a name is when you are going to have more than one submission push button on a form, and you want the server to know which one was pushed. If you're doing that, put the name here. Otherwise, leave it alone!

Below that is a field marked **Value/Label**. Here, put the words that you want to appear on the button. It defaults to the word **Submit**, but **Send the form!** would probably be clearer.

Finally, there are a pair of clearly marked radio buttons that let you choose whether this is a submit push button or a reset push button. Once you've made that selection, click the **OK** button, and your push button will be in place, ready to go!

Prettier, Plusher Push Buttons

If you want to, you can use a graphic of your choice as the submit button! To do this, place the cursor where you want the button, pull down the **Insert** menu, and select **Form Field**. On the submenu that appears to the right, select **Image**. The dialog box that appears whenever you insert a graphic on the page appears; use this to select the graphic that you want to use, and then click the **OK** button.

Next, a dialog box marked **Image Form Field Properties** appears. All you have to do here is to give this graphic a valid field name. Name it **pretty.push.button**, if you want. Click the **OK** button, and viola! Your graphic push button is in place. Do a little dance! Sing a little song! Send off some junk e-mail in celebration!

Where Did They Click?

If you're using an image as a push button, the browser will not only tell the server that this button was used, but also exactly where on the graphic the users click. If you're programming your own handlers on the server, you may be able to use this information to your advantage!

Titanic Text!

Text is probably the most important part of a form. You can have all these blank fields to fill out, and all these check boxes and radio buttons to check, but if you don't tell people what the fields are for and what the check boxes mean, they aren't going to know what to do.

Text on the form is like text anywhere else. You can use the full range of attributes and paragraph formats. The most important thing here is to be clear. The user needs to know exactly what you want filled into the various fields. For example, if you have two fields next to the word **Name**, is it the first name in the first field and last name in the second, or the other way 'round? Maybe there are fields here for two different people. Maybe the second field is for the nickname you were called in school? ("Squidgy")

Don't be afraid to put paragraphs of explanation, if that's what's needed to be clear. Being clear is very important in this world; that's why they've started making clear cola, clear dish soap, and clear gasoline. (Now if I only had a way to tell them apart!)

It's important to make sure its clear which label goes with which field. If you have a row of check boxes with labels, make sure the label is close to its check box and farther away from the next one on the row.

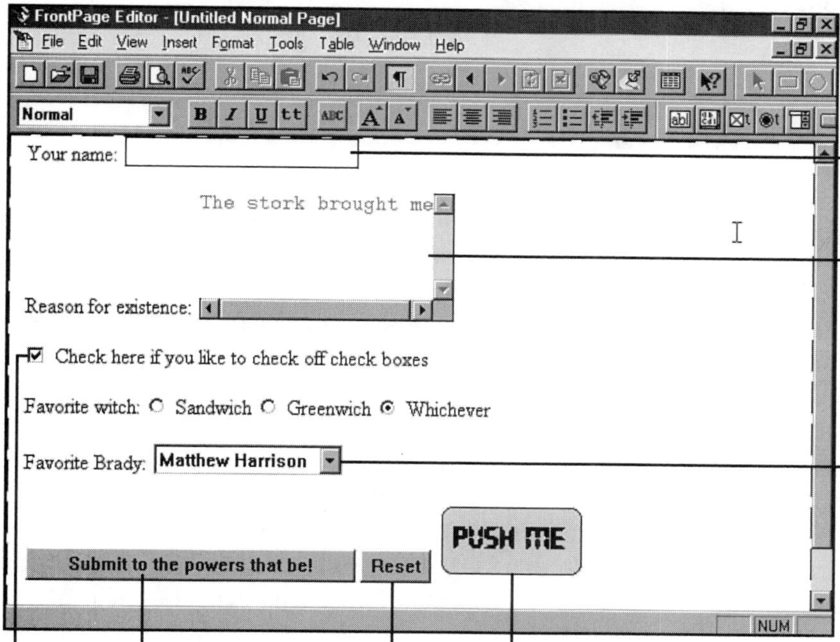

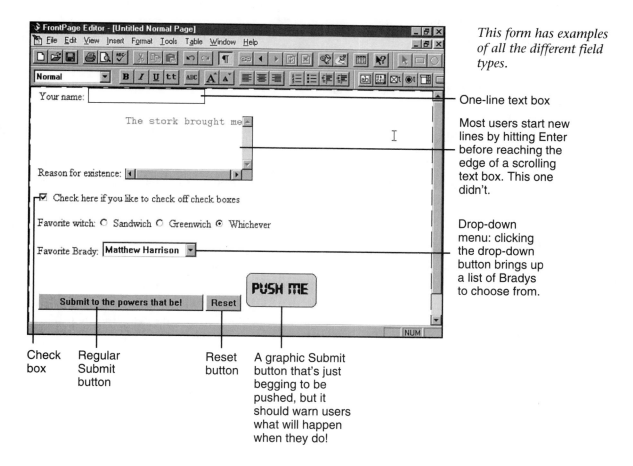

This form has examples of all the different field types.

Crop Rotations: Changing Your Fields

Once you add everything you want, you'll still want to mess and fiddle with it, either because you're a perfectionist or because you've nothing more interesting to do.

To change the setup of any one of the fields, just double-click the fields. The same dialog box you used to set up that field will reappear, and you can make all the changes that you want (and even some that you don't want, if you want).

To get rid of an unneeded field, click it once to select it. Click the **Cut** button, and that field will be out of your life!

More Formal Forms

To make your form look organized, with things lined up in columns and organized in sections, try using a table in the form, putting your fields into the table's cells. This will let you make nice straight columns of radio buttons and the like.

Handling Form Handlers

So far, you've learned to set up the form, which sets how the Web browser gets the information from the user. Now, you have to worry about how the server gets the information from the Web browser. There are a number of different possible ways for this to happen; these methods are called *form handlers*. As the creator of the form, you have to pick the handler for it. Some handlers require certain programs to be on your server; you have to pick a handlers that your server can, well, handle.

To choose a Form Handler, right-click the form in the editor. From the short-cut menu that appears, select the **Form Properties** command. A dialog box appears.

The first field on this dialog box is a drop-down menu that lets you select the Form Handler. The default value for this is **Custom CGI Script**. You select this option if you want to send this form to a server program that you or someone else has written, so that the server can store the information, or compose a response, or whatever else the program does.

Unfortunately, the details on how to create such a program (or even use one that is already on your server) are really far beyond the scope of this book.

Also unfortunately, if your server *doesn't* use the FrontPage extensions, the **Custom CGI Script** option is the only form handling option that FrontPage offers that will work. If your server does have these extensions, you can use custom CGI scripts, or you can use one of the other options listed here.

A Discussion About a Discussion Bot

The next option offered on the pull-down menu is the **Discussion Bot**, designed to involve users in interactive discussions over the Web. When you are using this Form Handler, you need to design the form to allow people to compose their messages for the discussion. For more on how to properly set this up, see Chapter 17, "Working with WebBots" and Chapter 20, "Creating a Discussion Group."

Register This Information About Registration Bots

Another option on this list is the **Registration Bot**. This is a special handler designed specifically to deal with people who are applying for access to the system. The form you set up to use has to have fields for all of the information needed to request access. For more on this bot, see Chapter 17.

I was Saving the Saving Results Bot for Last!

The last option on the list, **Saving Results Bot**, is a very basic one, and in some ways, the most useful. This takes the information the user has filled in on the form and stores it in a file on the server. Once you have that file, what you do to it is up to you!

To set up the **Saving Results Bot**, first select it from the **Form Handler** menu. Next, click the **Settings** button, and a dialog box appears, open to a tab marked **Results**.

The first piece of information this dialog box wants is the name of the file to store the results of the form in. Be sure to include the full file path. If you type in the name of a file that doesn't exist yet, don't worry—the helpful bot will create it for you!

Next, you have to select how the data from the forms is arranged in the file. There are eight different choices, and which one is best depends on what you're going to do with the information. If you're going to look at it through a Web browser, choose one of the three **HTML** formats. If you're going to look at it with a standard editor, choose one of the two **Formatted text** options. If you want to take the file and run it through a database program or something similar, choose one of the three text database options. If your goal was to waste people's time, and you don't care what they filled in to the forms, then it doesn't matter which you choose—just remember to delete the file every once in a while, so it doesn't eat up space on your server!

The next area in the dialog box has a bunch of check boxes listing other possible information you might want to keep with the filled in form, such as the time it was filled in or the type of browser that the person used to fill in the form. Click whichever ones you want to keep track of. When in doubt, click it all; it's always easier to ignore information you have later then it is to use information you don't have!

Finally, there's a spot for a URL for a confirmation page. If you want to let the user know that his form has been accepted, create a page that says just that, and put its URL here!

Once you have all this filled out, click the **OK** button, and you're ready to use your Save Results Bot! Your Form Handler is ready to handle forms!

Revealing Hidden Fields

You can use the lower half of the Form Properties dialog box to set up hidden fields. A *hidden* field is one that is automatically set for the form, that the user does not get to see or change. Some uses of this would be giving the form a name or a revision number that is stored with the results, or inserting an insult into the form that the user cannot see!

To create a hidden field, click the **Add** button. A dialog box pops up, asking for a field name and a value. For example, if you put **Form-name** as the field name and **Stupid pointless form I made up** as the value, every time this form is sent to the server, it will include the line **Form-name=Stupid pointless form I made up**. It's as easy as that!

When you've added all the hidden fields you want to add, click the **OK** button. Your form is now complete—and what a fine form it is!

The Least You Need to Know

- Forms allow the user to enter information, which is sent to the server.
- There are a number of different Form Handlers, which control how the information from the form gets to the server, and what the server does with the information once it gets it.
- There are five different field types used in the design of a form: one-line text boxes, scrolling text boxes, check boxes, radio buttons, and drop-down menus.
- A form must include a submit push button that the user clicks to indicate that he's done filling in the form. This button can be a graphic.
- Once you design your form, you have to use the **Form Properties** command to set up your Form Handler.
- If your server does not support the FrontPage extensions, you have to find or create a program on your server to handle the information from the form.
- If your server does use the FrontPage extensions, you can use a custom program, or you can use the Discussion Bot, the Registration Bot, or the Save Results Bot to process the form.

Chapter 16

Framing Your Web Page

By the End of This Chapter, You'll Be Able to...

- Divide a web page with frames
- Create a frame set and edit it
- Use a template to create your framed page
- Create a framed page from scratch
- Add links to frames

You can use frames to divide a web page into sections. Just as panes divide a glass window into smaller sections, frames divide a single web page "window" into smaller sections of information. You typically use framed web pages to organize a lot of material in a small space so the user can jump directly to whatever he's looking for.

Frames can divide a web page.

Once you divide a web page with frames, you tell FrontPage what you want placed within each frame when the framed web page is first viewed by the user. You typically place a web page into each frame. This allows your user to view several of your web pages at one time and quickly switch between them. However, you can place other things into a frame, including forms (which you learned about in Chapter 15), and clickable images (like the ones you learned about in Chapter 13). You can even place frames into a frame, to create a super-divided look.

Everything's New Again

To create a framed page, you must start anew. You cannot frame an existing page.

How This Frame Stuff Works

As you create your framed web page, FrontPage saves your selections as a *frame set*. The frame set contains information about the size and location of each frame on the framed web page, along with their initial contents. This frame set (or framed web page, if you prefer) has its own URL address. When the user types in this address, he doesn't connect to a single web page but to the framed web page. If you save this frame set (framed web page) with the name index.htm, then it will act as your web's home page. When the user visits your web site, he will be greeted with a framed web page with which to browse your web.

The initial content displayed in each frame also has its own URL. The user's Web browser, in turn, uses this URL to figure out what to display within each frame. You see, when the user types in a URL that links him to a frame set, the user's Web browser will first load the frame set, which in turn divides the window into frames of a specified size and location. Following the instructions the browser finds in the frame set, the user's Web browser will then load the specified items into the appropriate frames.

To create a framed web page, use the Frames Wizard. With this wizard's help, you select the number and size of the frames you want, and you assign a *target* or initial content for each frame. The target is the web page (or form, or graphic, and so on) that loads into the frame initially. As the user clicks your various links, the content of each frame changes (or doesn't change) according to how you created the framed set.

What Can I Do with Frames?

Typically, you use a framed web page to allow a particular page of information to remain on-screen, while the user browses through other pages. For example, you can design your web page so that when a user clicks a link within one frame, the web page to which it links appears in a corresponding frame. With both pages still visible, the user can easily review new information while referring to the information contained on a previous page.

One common use for a framed web page is to create a table of contents, or index, of your web site. When the user clicks a topic within the index frame, that topic appears in the main frame.

On this framed page, the TOC frame remains fixed and constant.

When a user clicks an item in the TOC…

…the corresponding page appears in the main frame.

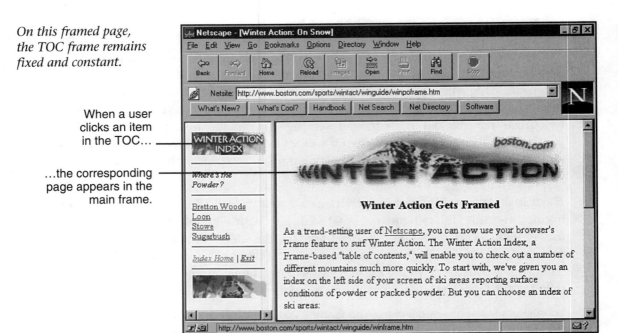

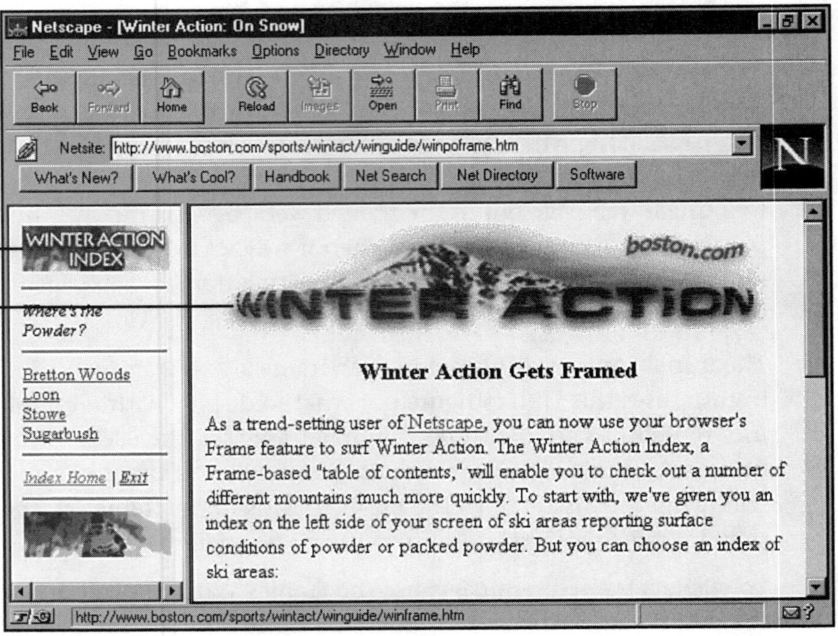

Want to Create a Table of Contents?

A TOC is a special page that requires some specific skills to create correctly. If you're interested, Chapters 17 and 19 explain how to create TOCs.

In this case, the table of contents frame doesn't ever change. This allows your user to switch from topic to topic quickly. But a table of contents is not the only use for this technique. You can place a special message in a *fixed* frame (a frame whose contents do not change) and allow that to remain on-screen at all times. Or instead of an index listing, you can place a graphic map of your web site in the fixed frame, and by creating *hotspot links* on the graphic, allow your user to navigate your web site with ease. (See Chapter 13 for help with graphic links.)

And you don't have to "fix" the contents of any of your frames if you don't want to. For example, you can set it up so that when a user clicks a link within a frame, the contents of *that same frame* changes to that of the link. In other words, the contents of the frame is *replaced* by another web page.

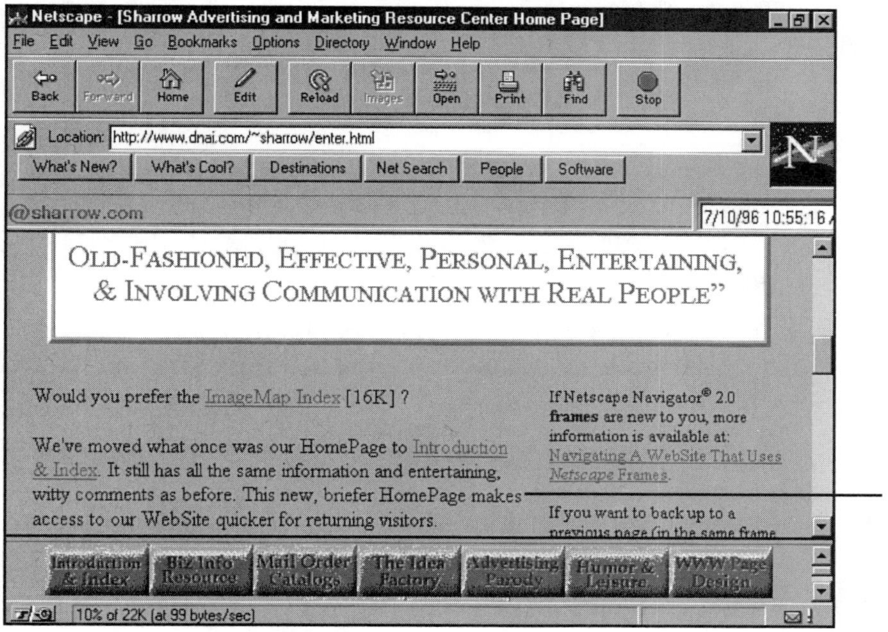

A frame's contents does not have to remain constant.

You can also create a link within a frame that displays the destination page *in a full window*, which removes the frames from the screen. This is an effective technique when presenting important information. You can also use this technique to display the contents of a long document that might appear cramped and difficult to read within a small frame.

You can also display the destination page in a *separate browser window*, meaning that the user would have *two browser windows* open at one time. With this technique, the user can still access the framed web page, and yet, also view the contents of the destination page in a full window.

You can provide a link that opens a second browser window if you want.

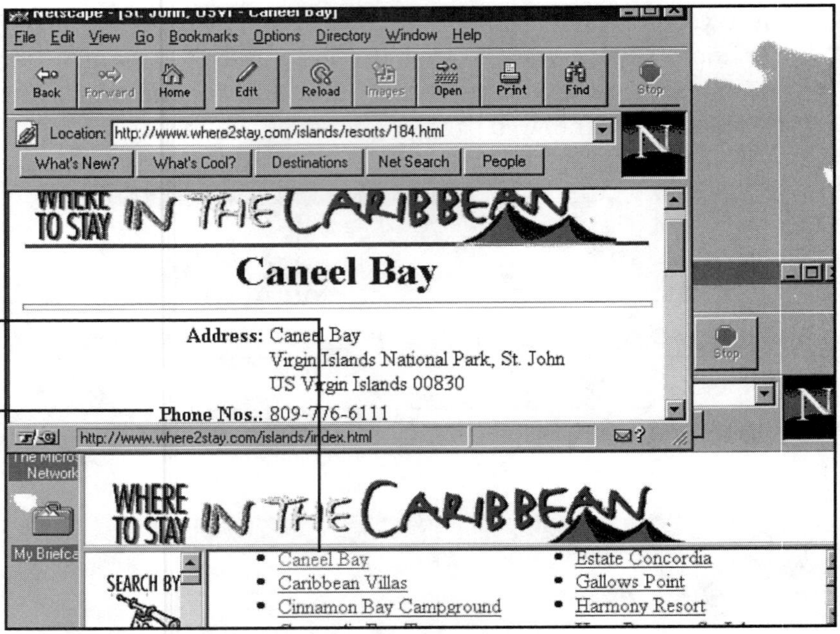

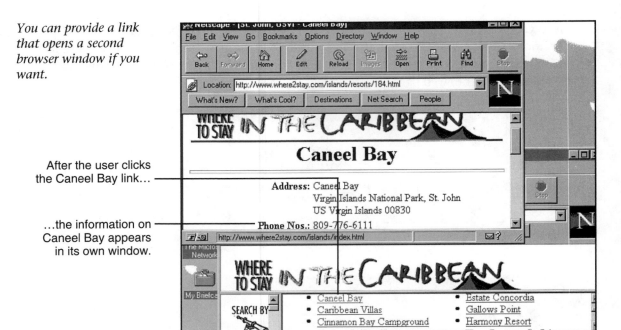

After the user clicks the Caneel Bay link...

...the information on Caneel Bay appears in its own window.

Now that you know what you can do with frames, you're ready to create one.

Creating Frame Sets

A frame set contains information about the size, location, and contents of each of the frames in a framed web page. As stated before, you create a frame set by using the Frames Wizard, which steps you through the process of selecting the number of frames you want and their initial contents.

While using the Frames Wizard, you can start from scratch in designing your framed page, or you can cheat a little and select a *template*. A template, as you've learned by now, provides a rough skeleton that you can change to fit your exact specifications.

Can't Do That

Remember that you can't frame an existing page. You can only create new pages with the Frames Wizard.

Using a Template to Create Your Frame Set

To create your framed web page, start with a completely new page. Now, when creating your framed web page, you can use a template (which provides a predesigned frame structure for you) or you can create the frame structure from scratch.

The upside of using a template to create your frame set is that, well, it's easy—most of the work of selecting the number of frames, their sizes, and their locations has been done for you. The downside is that the result may not be exactly what you want. Also, during the creation process, FrontPage assigns a newly created blank page as a target for each frame. A target, if you recall, is a URL that points to the item (the web page, a graphic, a form, and so on) you want displayed in a particular frame. If you already have certain web pages that you want to use to fill each frame initially, then this is a big fat nuisance. It means that right after your create your frame set, you have to edit the thing so you can assign the right web pages (or forms, or graphics) to each frame.

However, if you haven't yet created the web pages that you want to initially appear in each frame, then using a template gives you a head start. Not only will the template create your framed web page, but it will create a blank page target for each frame, and connect them with the proper links.

Read This if You Plan to Replace Your Home Page with the New Framed Page

You can easily (well, almost easily) replace your existing home page with a new framed version if you want. But the process will take a bit of up-front work on your part. Here's what ya do:

1. First, open your home page and use the **File, Save As** command to save it under a new URL (file name), such as oldhome.htm. While you're at it, give the page a new title, such as Jen's Unframed Home Page.
2. Next, create your framed web page, following the instructions given here.
3. When asked for a file name for your new framed page, give it the name index.htm. Index.htm is the page that appears by default whenever a user types in a URL for a location but does not specify a particular page, as in http://hostserver.com/jennifer/. By making your framed page the default, you'll ensure that most people, when entering your web site, will see it *first*.

Your old home page, by the way, can still be used. You see, there are many people out there who navigate the Web using older Web browsers (gasp!) that don't support the use of frames. For these users, you can specify that FrontPage uses your old home page as an alternate home page.

Back to Our Regularly Scheduled Program

After that small sidebar, here you are, back at the show. If you want to use a template to create your framed web page, follow these steps (if you want to create the frame structure on your own, see the next section):

1. Open the **File** menu and select **New**. *Don't click the New button, since that'll produce a new page using the Normal template, which you don't want.*
2. Select **Frames Wizard** from the **Template or Wizard** list box, and click **OK**.
3. Click **Pick a template**.
4. Click **Next>**.
5. Simply select a template from the **Layout** list, and it will appear in the box to the left. When you find one you like, click **Next>.**
6. Select the URL address of an alternate page that you want to display if the user's Web browser is so old that it doesn't support frames. See "Selecting an Alternate Page," for details.
7. Click **Next>**.
8. Type in a **Title** for your framed page, along with a **URL** (file name). If you want to make this page the default page for your web site (the home page), then you should name it **index.htm**.
9. When you finish, click **Finish**. The framed page appears in the FrontPage Explorer.

Can't wait to view your framed web page in all its glory? Jump over to the "Viewing a Framed Web Page" section for help.

Oh, and by the way, if you want to assign some existing page to one of the frames, you have to edit the frame set, as mentioned earlier. Check out the "Editing Your Frame Set" section for help.

Creating Your Frame Set from Scratch

Rather than using a template, you can create your framed web page from scratch, resulting in a unique framed look. However, let me warn you: this is definitely not for the faint of heart. Although I'll provide plenty of hand holding along the way, you might want to consider using a template to create your first framed page—for the practice, if nothing else.

During the process of creating your frame set, you assign a name for each of your frames, so you can refer to them later. (When you use a template, this naming thing is done for you.) This name is typically descriptive of the frame's location on the page, such as **LOWERRIGHT**. Later, when you want to change the contents of a particular frame whenever the user clicks a particular link, you simply refer to the name of that frame when creating the link. Don't worry; you'll learn about this linking business in complete detail later in this chapter.

Special Names

There are some names that you should not use when naming your frames, because they hold a special meaning for Web browsers. These names all begin with an underline, and they include **_blank**, **_self**, **_parent**, and **_top**. You'll read about the purpose of each of these special names when you learn how to create links to your frames. For now, simply avoid using these names and you'll be okay.

To create a framed web page from scratch, follow these steps:

1. Open the **File** menu and select **New**. *Don't click the New button, since that'll produce a new page using the Normal template, which you don't want.*
2. Select **Frames Wizard** from the **Template or Wizard** list box, and click **OK**.
3. Click **Make a custom grid**.
4. Click **Next>**.
5. An image of your framed web page appears, which you can adjust. To accept the default arrangement, simply click **Next>.** Adjusting the number of frames takes some doing, so you might want to skip this for now and return later to edit your frame set. In any case, see "Adjusting the Size and Number of Frames" section for help. When you finish, click **Next>**. (Remember, you can always return to this screen by clicking **Back>**, or by editing the frame set later on.)
6. Now, click each frame, and change its attributes as needed. Again, check out the "Changing Frame Attributes" section for help. When you finish, click **Next>**.
7. Select the URL address of an alternate page that you want to display when the user's Web browser can't display frames.
8. Type in a **Title** for your framed page, along with a **URL** (file name). If you want to make this page the default page for your web site (the home page), then you should name it **index.htm**, *but only after having saved your original home page with a different file name.*

9. When you finish, click **Finish**. Your new framed page will appear in FrontPage Explorer.

To view your framed web page, you'll need to use your Web browser. Skip over to "Viewing a Framed Web Page" section for the how to's.

Editing Your Frame Set

If you created your frame set using one of the templates, then FrontPage created and assigned a new web page to each frame. For some of your frames, this may be great, because maybe you haven't created all your web pages yet. But for example, if you want to display your home page in one of the frames, you're going to need to edit the frame set.

To edit a frame set, simply open it, a process similar to opening a web page. From within FrontPage Explorer, click the frame set, open the **Edit** menu, and select **Open**. If you'd rather do this from within FrontPage Editor instead, click the **Open** button, select the frame set from the list, and click **OK.**

Adjusting the Size and Number of Frames

When editing your frame set, the first dialog box you'll encounter is quite, well, disconcerting. Check this out.

Now what's this?

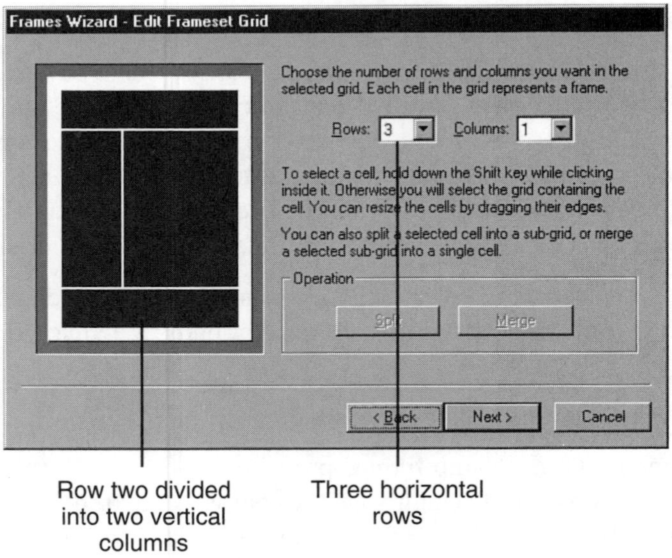

Your framed web page appears on the left, divided into frames. You'll notice in the example that the image shows a page with three horizontal rows. You can divide your page into as many rows (or columns) as needed.

In the example, the top and bottom rows contain only a single column. The second row, on the other hand, contains two columns (vertical segments).

- The sample page consists of two sections. The first section represents the basic structure of the whole page. In the example, that basic structure consists of three rows with one column each. There's a second subsection within the main section (row two) that, unlike the rows in the main section, is divided into two columns.
- When you select a section, the number of rows and columns in that section appear at the top of the dialog box. In the figure, the first section (which contains the structure for the page as a whole) is selected. This section contains three rows with one column each. A second subsection was created within this main section, out of row two. If you were to select this second section, then at the top of the dialog box, you'd see one row and two columns listed.
- You can change the number of rows and columns in any section by clicking that section first to select it. A selected section appears blue.
- To select a section, click it. To select a *cell* within a section, press **Shift** while clicking it. A cell is formed at the intersection of a row and a column. In the example, row two contains two cells, while rows one and three contain only one cell.

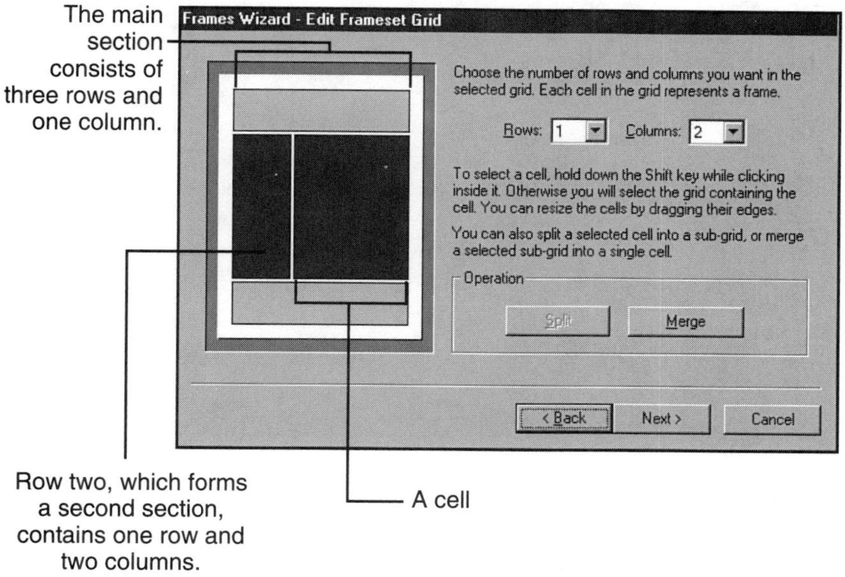

A cell is formed by the intersection of a row and a column.

- After selecting a section, you can change the number of rows or columns it contains. For example, if you select the first section, you can select more columns for the *entire page* by choosing a number from the **Columns** list. To select a different number of rows, choose a number from the **Rows** list.

If you want to change the number of columns in row two, you must select that section. To do that, simply click row two. When you do, you'll notice that only the row two section appears highlighted, and the number of rows is one, and the number of columns is two (see the figure). Once you select a section, you can change its structure by changing the values under **Columns** and **Rows**.

If you want to change row three, and split it into three columns, you have to remember that rows one and three are simply parts of the main section. This main section is divided into three rows and one column, which forms three cells. To select row three, press **Shift** while clicking the row three cell. If you simply click row three without pressing Shift, you'll end up selecting the section it belongs to, which in this case, is the main section.

- You can change the relative size of the cells in a section by simply clicking the line that divides one cell from another, and then dragging the line wherever you want. When you release the mouse button, the two cells resize to fit the boundary you indicated. For example, if you want to change the size of the two cells in row two, click and drag the line that divides the two columns, and drop it wherever you want.

Resize a cell by dragging its boundary line.

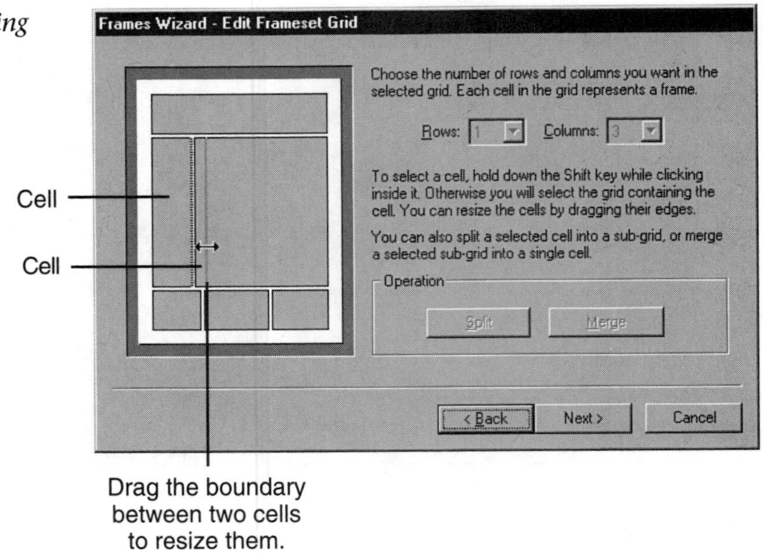

- Say you want to eliminate the individual cells that make up a section? To do that, select the section by clicking it; and then click **Merge** to blend all the cells in that section into a single column. For example, you can select row two by clicking it and then merge it into one cell (one column) by clicking **Merge**.
- You can divide a cell into several cells by *splitting* it. For example, if you want to split the cell that makes up row three into several cells, you have to select the cell first, by pressing **Shift** and clicking it. Then you simply click the **Split** button to split the cell. A cell is always split initially into two rows and two columns, but you can adjust that by selecting other values from the **Columns** and **Rows** lists.

Don't let this dialog box overwhelm you; with a little experimentation on your part, you'll soon get the hang of it. Remember, there's no limit on how much time you can spend getting your frames just right—so feel free to take your time. When you finish, click **Next>** to display the next dialog box.

Changing Frame Attributes

In the Edit Frame Attributes dialog, you can change the attributes for each of the frames. First, select the frame you want to change by clicking on it.

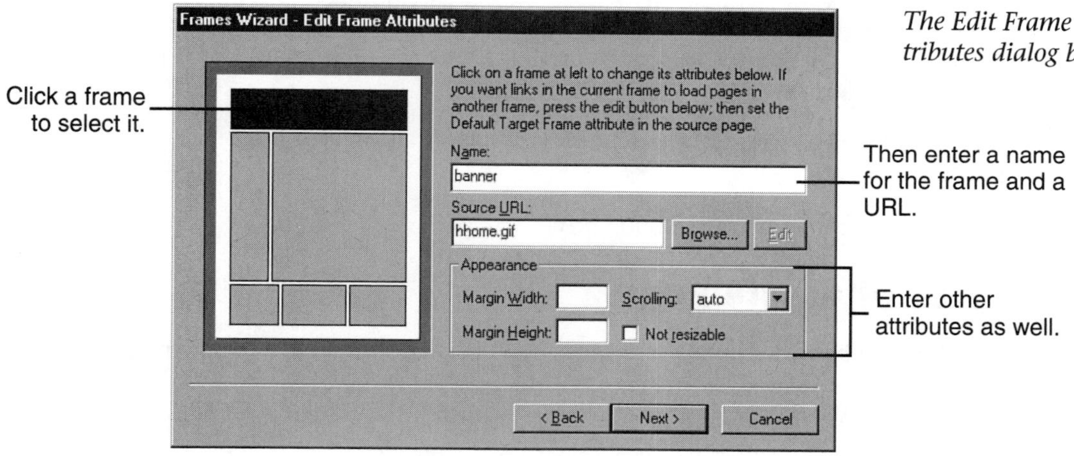

The Edit Frame Attributes dialog box.

Enter a **Name** for the frame, such as **banner**.

If you already created the web page, graphic, or form that you want to appear in this frame when the page is initially displayed, then under **Source URL**, click **Browse** and select it from the list. Click **OK** to return to the Edit Frame Attributes dialog box.

If your Source URL is a web page, and you want the destination of all the links in that page to appear within the *same frame*, click **Edit**, and the source web page opens. Open the **File** menu and select **Page Properties**. Then, under **Default Target Frame**, type the name of the frame in which you want the destination of all the links to appear by default. Click **OK**. You can then close the web page and switch back to the Edit Frame Attributes dialog box.

When It's Not Default

Even though you assign a default target frame in which you want the destination of all the links on that page to appear, you can still override this default for a particular link if you want. See "Creating a Link to a Frame" for help.

Under Appearance, you can change the **Margin Width** and the **Margin Height**. You can adjust the amount of space (the margin) between the text in a frame and the frame itself. The number you enter here is in pixels, those little points of light that make up your screen. Unless you are really feeling picky, just leave these two blank; by doing so, you let the user's Web browser decide on the best margin for its frames.

You can set Scrolling to **auto** (which means that the user can scroll the stuff in the frame when needed) or to **no** (which means that he can't.)

To prevent the user from resizing your perfectly sized frames, you can select the frame and click **Not resizable.**

Click **Next>** to move to the next dialog box.

Selecting an Alternate Page

In the next dialog box that appears, you can select an alternate page for your framed web page. You see, some users have older Web browsers that do not (as yet) support frames. Since you don't want to leave them out of this, assign an alternate page to appear, instead of your framed page. Just click **Browse**, select your alternate page, and then click **OK**. For example, if you saved your old home page under a different name (per the Techno Talk box that appeared earlier), you can use the unframed version of your home page (oldhome.htm in my example) as an alternate. When you finish, click **Finish**.

Changing the Title or URL for Your Framed Page

In the last dialog box, you can enter a **Title** for your framed web page. Under **URL**, you enter the URL address (file name) for the framed page. If you want to make this page the default page for your web, then you have to give it the file name **index.htm**.

Creating a Link to a Frame

Through the process of creating your frame set (your framed web page), you set a default page, graphic, or form to appear within each frame when the page first appears.

If you want the user to be able to change the contents of a frame, you need to create a link to it. You see, when a user clicks an ordinary link, his Web browser responds by displaying the linked web page in a full window. Now that you have a framed web page, you can cause that same web page to display in a *frame* when a user clicks the appropriate link.

You don't have to display a web page in the frame when the user clicks the link. You can also display the results of a form within a frame instead. A form is basically a dialog box pasted on a web page; you use a form to gather information from your user. You can also display the result of the user's choices within your form in a frame.

Your link doesn't have to be text. As you learned in Chapter 13, a graphic can contain hotspots that act as links; when the user clicks a hotspot, a specific web page appears. If you want, you can place a graphic in a frame, and when the user clicks some hotspot on that graphic, you can make particular web pages appear in another frame (or in the same frame).

Special Frame Names

When you create a link to a frame, you have to specify the name of the frame you want to use. There are some special frame names that you can use for certain results. See the "Using the Special Targets" section for more information.

Displaying a Web Page in a Frame

The first part of this business is to create the link. The second part is to tell FrontPage into which frame you want it to place the results of that link.

You learned all about text links in Chapter 12, but here's a quick review: to create a text link, type some text, such as **Great Product Number 1**. Select this text and click the **Create or Edit Link** button. Then click the appropriate tab: **Open Pages**, **Current Web**, **World Wide Web**, or **New Page**. Enter the information required to designate the page you want to display in a frame. For example, to select a page from the current web, click the **Current Web** tab and select a page from the list. (For more help, see Chapter 12.)

Once you designate the page you want to display in the frame, you can select a bookmark on that page if you want. Remember, a bookmark lets you link to a spot part way down a page, rather than just linking to the top of the page.

Remember the Bookmark

If you want to link to some spot in the middle of a page (rather than linking to the top), you have to create a bookmark first. Simply open the page in which you want to place the bookmark and select the **Edit, Bookmark** command. Enter a name for your bookmark and click **OK**. When you create your link, be sure to specify the name of the bookmark you want to link to.

In the **Default Target Frame** box, type in the name of the frame in which you want this page displayed when the user clicks this link. For example, type **lower right**. Click **OK** and you're done! (Remember that there are special frame names you can enter for particular results. See the upcoming section for more information.)

You learned about creating links within a graphic image in Chapter 13, so again, here's a quick review. When you create a hotspot on a graphic, the user can click that spot to jump to the page you designate in the link. You can create several hotspots on one graphic, if you want. To create the hotspot link, make sure that the Image Toolbar is displayed by selecting it, if necessary, from the **View** menu.

Click the graphic to select it. Next, draw the hotspot on the graphic by clicking the **Rectangle**, **Circle**, or **Polygon** tool, which you'll find on the Image Toolbar. Move the tool over the area of the graphic you want to select, and then draw either a rectangle, a circle, or a polygon. (If you need a drawing refresher course, see Chapter 13.) The Create Link dialog box appears.

Click the appropriate tab: **Open Pages**, **Current Web**, **World Wide Web**, or **New Page**. Enter the information required to designate the page you want to display in a frame when the user clicks the graphic link. Once you have your page designated, you simply type in the name of the frame you want to use in the **Default Target Frame** box. For example, type in **mainframe**. Click **OK** and you're through! (Again, you can use any of the special frame names if you want.)

Displaying a Form in a Frame

You can display the results of a form in a frame. First, create the form. (See Chapter 15 because you may need plenty of help with that one.)

Double-click any field within the form to open the Properties dialog box. Click the **Form** button. In the **Target Frame** box, type the name of the frame in which you want the results of your form displayed. Click **OK** two times and you're back at your form.

Creating a Default Target

Just a few moments ago, you learned how to connect a link to a page and to then have that page displayed within a particular frame.

A *default target* is the name of a frame that you want used by default, for any links in which you didn't specify a particular target frame. You can set up one default target for each web page, and for each graphic if you like.

To set up a default target for a web page, first, open that web page. Then open the **File** menu and select **Page Properties.** Under **Default Target Field**, type the name of the frame that you want to use by default. Click **OK**. Now, when a user clicks a link within that page, the result of that link appears either in some designated frame, or if a frame was not specifically designated, in the default frame (default target).

To set up a default target for a graphic, select the graphic by clicking it. Then open the **Edit** menu and select **Properties.** Type the name of the frame you want to use by default in the **Target Frame** box, and click **OK**. When a user clicks a hotspot within the graphic, the result will display in the specified frame. If a frame was not specified in the link, then the result will display in the default frame (target frame).

Using the Special Targets

Earlier, you learned that there are some frame names that mean special things to Web browsers. If you recall, there were four such names:

_blank When you use this frame name as a target in a link, the web page associated with the link appears, not in a frame, but in a new browser window.

_self By using this frame name as a link target, the page associated with the link appears *in the same frame as the link itself.*

_parent When you enter this name as your target frame, the page associated with the link appears in its *parent frame*. A parent frame is a frame that, at some point, was further divided into baby frames. For example, when you create your framed page, you can take a frame and divide it into three columns. When a user clicks a link whose target is this parent frame, then the three small column frames disappear, and the page appears within the larger, parent frame.

_top When you use _top as your target frame, all the frames disappear, and the page associated with the link appears in a full window.

To use one of these special target names, simply type it in the **Default Target Frame** or the **Target Frame** text box when instructed.

Viewing and Testing a Framed Web Page

To view your framed web page and to test its links, you need your Web browser. So fire up your browser—no, you don't need to get on the Internet for this one.

In your browser, enter the URL for your framed web page. For example, you could type **http://*host.net*/*YourWeb*/framepg.htm** (where **host.net** is the name of your host server, or server-to-be, if you haven't actually published your web yet, and ***YourWeb*** is the name of the web that contains your framed web page).

You can look at your framed web page with your Web browser.

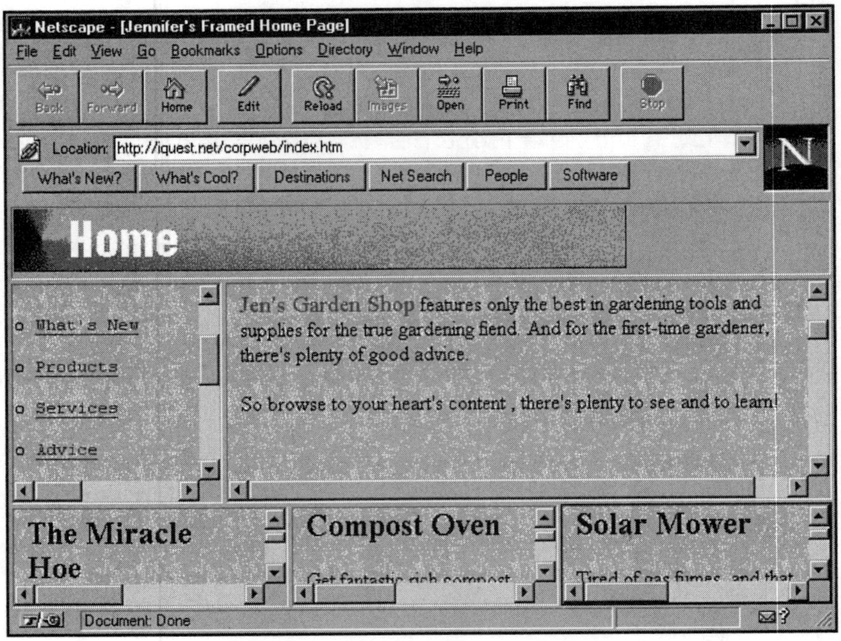

Uh, Houston, We Have a Problem

If you can't get the page to open, it's probably because the Personal Web Server is not running for some reason. No problem; simply click the **Start** button, select **Programs**, select **Microsoft FrontPage**, and then select **Personal Web Server** from the list to start the program. Then try opening your framed page again.

You'll see your page as it appears to your users. (Okay, there'll be some differences depending on the user's Web browser, and so on, but you can't expect perfection here.)

Note the adjustments you might like to make. For example, perhaps a frame is too small, or there are just too many of them. When you return to FrontPage, you can change how your framed page looks by following the steps in the "Editing Your Frame Set" section of this chapter.

To test a link, click it. Does the proper page, graphic, or form display in the correct frame? Again, make a note of any problems.

When you finish congratulating yourself on the terrific job you accomplished, close the Web browser and return to FrontPage.

The Least You Need to Know

Want to start framing? Keep these things in mind:

- ➤ You can't frame an existing page. You must start with a new page.
- ➤ To create a framed page, you create a frame set. The frame set contains the information about the size and location of each frame.
- ➤ You can create a frame set with a template, or you can create one from scratch.
- ➤ After creating your framed page, you can create links to the frames. When the user clicks such a link, the result will appear in the frame you specified.
- ➤ To view your framed page and to test your links, you must use your Web browser.

Chapter 17

Working with WebBots

By the End of This Chapter, You'll Be Able to...

- Use WebBots to insert the date, time, or comments onto a web page
- Manage the data that users enter into your web forms
- Build an automatic registration system for new users of your web
- Create a search mechanism for your web
- Insert a header or a footer on your web

All right, all right. You finally figured out what a template is, and what a wizard is, but what the heck is a WebBot?

A WebBot (short for *Web Robot*; the name's often shortened even more to *bot*) is a program that you can attach to your web pages to automate certain functions, such as gathering data from your user.

In this chapter, you'll take a good look at the many WebBots that come with FrontPage. Some of the bots are so intriguing that they have their own chapters (for example, you can find the Table of Contents WebBot in Chapter 19, while the Discussion and Search WebBots are in Chapter 20). Of course, all the WebBots appear briefly in this chapter, so you can learn what each one does.

No Go

Sorry, but you can't use WebBots in your web if your host server does not support the FrontPage Server Extensions.

The Annotation Bot

If you've ever been asked to look over somebody else's writing (such as an important report, or a résumé perhaps), you may have been tempted to mark it up with lots of comments that (after the person got over his urge to kill you) would eventually make the finished piece more understandable and professional-looking.

You can insert a similar form of comment into the middle of your web page with the *Annotation bot*. For example, you might include a note to yourself about a particular link, or you might leave a note to someone else who shares your Web master duties. An annotation is a section of text that is only visible in the FrontPage Editor window. Because your users will never see it, an annotation can say absolutely anything.

Not So Secret

Okay, since the annotation is part of the final web file, your user *could* see it if she bothers to view the HTML source code for your document—so don't say anything too insulting.

Inserting an annotation is a simple process:

1. Place your cursor where you want your annotation (your personal comment) to appear.
2. Open the **Insert** menu and select **Bot.** When the dialog box appears, select **Annotation Bot** and click **OK**.
3. Type the text of your annotation. Notice that you can't use italics, underlining, or boldface text in your annotation. Also, don't press **Enter**, since that will close the dialog box.
4. Click **OK**. Your annotation appears as purple text in your web.

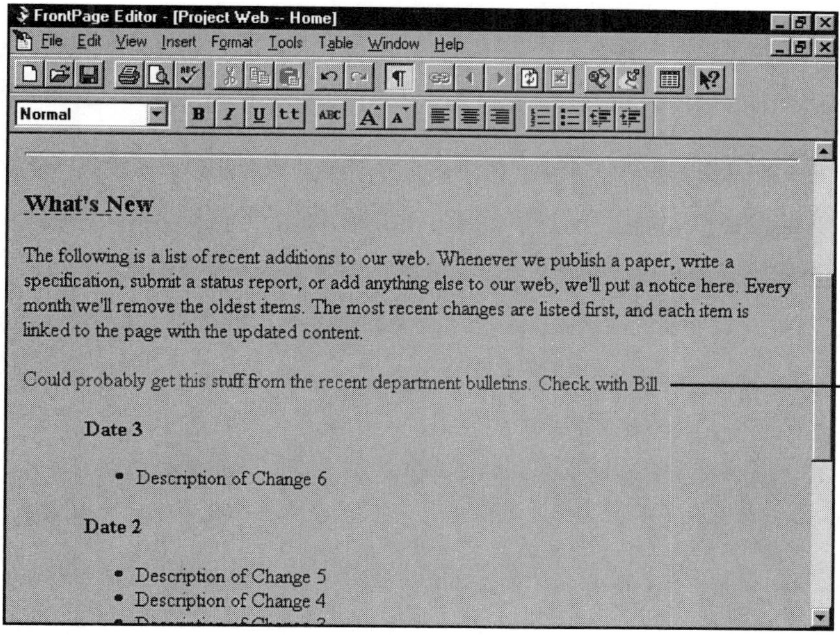

Annotation

Your annotation appears only in the FrontPage Editor.

Better Learn to Like Purple

If you plan to use annotations in your web pages, I strongly recommend that you do NOT use purple body text in those pages, because your purple annotations won't stand out. You can't change the color of annotation text, so go for another body-text color, and save yourself some headaches!

The HTML Markup Bot

If, before discovering the simplicity of creating web pages with FrontPage, you learned a thing or two about HTML, then you may appreciate the opportunity to add an HTML code or two directly into your page without having FrontPage scream and yell about what it might mean. This is the purpose of the *HTML Markup bot*. For example, once HTML version 3.2 is officially released, you can add one of the new codes directly into your web pages, without having to wait for a new version of FrontPage. Or, even though FrontPage doesn't support Java or JavaScript (meaning that it can't check the coding for errors), if you know a small Java program, you can type it directly into the HTML Markup bot. (Sorry, but large programs simply won't fit.)

To Bot or Not to Bot

Sometimes, FrontPage has thought ahead and designed a special place within its dialog boxes for you to enter an HTML code that will then be applied to a particular element. For example, when changing the format of a paragraph (see Chapter 5), you can add HTML codes to that paragraph with the **Extend** button in the Paragraph Format dialog box.

Here's what you do: First, read and reread lots of boring manuals on HTML. Upon discovering some code you want to use, yell "Eureka, Kansas!" and open the **Insert** menu, select **Bot**, choose **HTML Markup Bot**, and click **OK**. In the dialog box that appears, type anything you want (FrontPage does not check it for errors). Then click **OK**.

For example, HTML version 3.2 allows you to set the font for text (of course, if the user's system doesn't have that font, it'll default to the regular text font used now). Although version 3.2 isn't out yet, a lot of Web browsers such as Netscape and Internet Explorer already support these new codes. That means you can use them, too. Suppose you wanted to change the font on a page to Arial (a common Windows font). Open the page and click at the top. Then use the **Insert**, **Bot**, **HTML Markup Bot** command. In the dialog box, type **<font face="Arial">** and click **OK**. You have to insert another code to indicate where you want the use of the Arial font to stop, so jump to the end of the page and click. Open the HTML MarkUp dialog again, and this time, type **</font>**. Click **OK**. You now have two bots in your page, one that tells Web browsers where to begin using the Arial font, and another that tells them where to stop. You must insert both codes for this to work. This font business doesn't work on any system that doesn't have the Arial font. Macintosh systems call their Arial font equivalent Geneva, so to be as universal as possible, you can use this for your first tag: **<font face="Arial","Geneva">** instead.

FrontPage won't show you the text you entered, or try to interpret the HTML codes. Instead, it'll put up a little yellow box with a <?> in it symbolizing the unknown text you manually entered. You'll need a Web browser to test your web page to see whether your experiment is a success or failure. Save your page; then call up your Web browser and have it load up the page for viewing. For example, enter **http://*hostserv.com*/*myweb*/index.htm** to open your home page (replace ***hostserv.com*** with the name of your real host server, and ***myweb*** with the name of your actual web site.

The Substitution Bot

With the *Substitution bot*, you can insert a parameter into your web page and let FrontPage replace (or substitute) the parameter with its current value. That said, let me back up a little and drive over that again. First, FrontPage has several *parameters* available, such as the ModifiedBy parameter. If you insert this parameter into a web page, don't expect to see the words **ModifiedBy**. Instead, you'll see the parameter's current *value* such as Jennifer Fulton. If Betty comes along later and modifies the page, then **Jennifer Fulton** will be replaced by the words **Betty Bigmouth**. When you use a parameter, you can insert important information into a page and know that it will always be kept current.

FrontPage provides many preset *parameters* you can use. These include:

- **Author** When you insert this parameter into a page, it's replaced by the web page's original author (unless you talked some other joker into creating web pages, this is your name).
- **ModifiedBy** This parameter is replaced by the name of the person who last changed this page.
- **Description** When you insert this parameter, it's replaced by your comments about this page (entered when you first saved the page).

But I Want to Comment!

If you didn't enter anything in the description box when you saved your web page for the first time, you can enter (or change) it now. Switch to FrontPage Explorer and right-click your page. Select **Properties**, and click the **Summary** tab. Type in your description in the **Comment** field, and click **OK**.

- **Page-URL** When you insert the Page-URL parameter into a page, it's replaced by the current URL of the page.

In addition to these four parameters, which all apply to a particular page, you can add special parameters of your own that can apply to the entire web. Why bother? By creating a parameter of your own, you make it simple to make a global change throughout your web. For example, suppose you have something you'd like to insert into your web pages, such as the name of your department supervisor, but you know that at some point down the line, it's likely that the name of your supervisor may change. You can create a parameter called "Department Supervisor," enter an initial value, such as Joe Bigguy, and then insert Joe's name into your web pages where needed, using the Substitution bot. If Joe leaves and is replaced by Sue Doesthejob, you can replace Joe's name throughout your web by simply changing the value of the Department Supervisor parameter.

Remember, you can create a parameter for anything whose value might change somewhere down the line, such as the name of your latest and greatest product, the date of your next program release, or the department fax number.

First, you'll learn how to set up your own parameters. Then you'll learn how to use the Substitution bot to insert either a FrontPage parameter or one that you've created into your Web pages.

To create your own parameters, start in FrontPage Explorer:

1. Open the **Tools** menu and select **Web Settings**.
2. On the Parameters tab, click **Add**.
3. In the **Name** field, enter a name for your parameter—something such as "Department Supervisor," "Web master's E-mail Address," or whatever. The name *may* contain spaces, but you can't use any colons (:).
4. In the **Value** field, enter an initial value, such as Joe Bigguy. *You can leave this field blank if you want,* and return here later to fill it in.
5. Click **OK**. That's it!

To change the value of this parameter at some later date, repeat these steps. In the Web Settings dialog box, select the parameter whose value you want to change, and then click **Modify** to change it.

Now, the whole point of doing all that was so you could use the Substitution bot to enter a parameter's value into your web page. This is easy to do:

1. Open your page and place the cursor where you want the...well, the *something,* whatever it is, to appear.
2. Open the **Insert** menu and select **Bot**. When the dialog box appears, select **Substitution Bot** and click **OK**.
3. Select the parameter you want to insert from the **Substitute with** list. You can select one of the FrontPage parameters, or one that you created.
4. Click **OK**. The *current value* of the parameter appears in the web page. As the value of the parameter changes, it will be changed within your page automatically.

The Timestamp Bot

If the purpose of your web is to distribute *current* information, then one question on all of user's minds will be how current that information is. As Martha Stewart might say, it's a *good thing* for web sites to include a little time stamp that shows when information on that page was last updated. Here's how to use the *Timestamp bot* to insert the last modified date:

1. Place the cursor where you want the timestamp to appear.
2. Open the **Insert** menu and select **Bot**. When the dialog box appears, select **Timestamp Bot** and click **OK**.
3. Select either **Date this page was last edited** (if you want the date to change only when a person manually makes changes to the page) or **Date this page was last automatically updated** (if you want the date to also change if it is updated automatically by FrontPage).

Uh, FrontPage Can Change My Page?

Sure, it can. If you use certain bots, such as the Substitution bot or the Include bot, and their value changes, then FrontPage will make a change in your web to reflect that.

4. Under **Date Format** and **Time Format**, you'll see examples of the current date and time displayed in various formats. Choose the ones that look right to you. (In **Time**, by the way, **TZ** means Time Zulu, which the military uses to indicate that something is in military time.) To omit either the date or the time, choose **none**.
5. Click **OK**, and FrontPage inserts your date into the page. As changes are made to the page and saved, the date will change automatically.

The Form Bots

In Chapter 15, you learned how to insert forms onto your page so you can get information from your users. This data is saved in a web page that you can then use in a database of your own. Or, using the WebBots in this section, you can do something *automatic* with the data a user enters, to make your web pages a bit more… what's that word again? Oh yeah: *interactive*.

The Registration Bot

If you want your web to be restricted to certain registered, approved users (and you have the right to do that), then you need to use the *Registration bot*.

This bot creates and maintains the registration database for your users. However, you don't just drop it into your web page and leave it, like you did with the other bots covered thus far. Nope. You have to do a little housekeeping work with your web first. Nothing much; basically, you're turning the option to restrict your web to **ON**.

Suppose you want to add a user registration form to your Web, where new users will enter their full names, the user names (or nicknames) they want to use, and their chosen passwords. To accomplish this task, follow along here.

First, as promised, you need to turn on the "restricted access" option for your web:

1. Make sure you save and close any open pages in FrontPage Editor. Then switch to FrontPage Explorer, open the **Tools** menu and select **Permissions**.
2. On the Settings tab, select **Use unique permissions for this Web**.
3. Click **Apply**, and then click the **End Users** tab.
4. Select **Registered users only**, and click **OK**.

Now that you've told FrontPage that you want to restrict access to your web, you're ready to create your registration database:

1. Open the **File** menu and select **Open Web**.
2. Click **List Webs**. Wait a moment or two (or twelve) for something to show up in the Webs list. Select **<Root Web>** and click **OK**.
3. Now that you have the Root Web open, you'll create your user registration database. Click the **Show FrontPage Editor** button.
4. Open the **File** menu and select **New**. Choose the **User Registration** template and click **OK**. What you'll see next looks something like this.

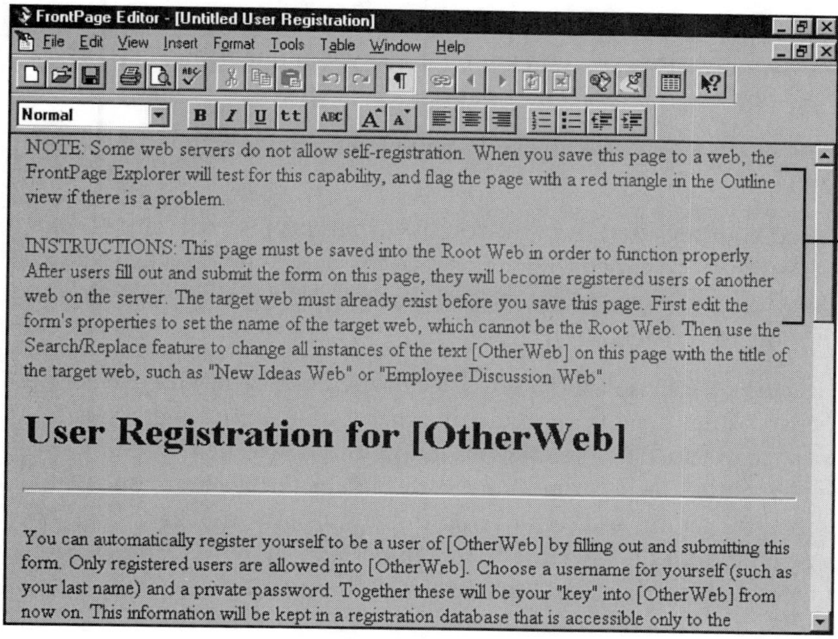

Will our mystery guest please sign in?

Now that you have a registration form in your web, it's time to make it *yours*. Follow these steps:

1. You'll find your form at the bottom of this page. Right-click anywhere inside the form, and select **Form Properties**.
2. Click **Settings**.
3. Under **Web name**, type the name of your web. The *Web name* is the name you gave your web when you first created it.
4. Click **OK**; then click **OK** again. No, you're still not done.
5. Now, click back at the beginning of the text, open the **Edit** menu, and select **Replace**. Under **Find what**, type **[OtherWeb].** Under **Replace with**, type the name of your web as you want it to appear on the registration page, such as Engineering Projects Web. Click **Find Next** to find the first instance of [OtherWeb], and then click **Replace All**. Click **Cancel** to dismiss the Replace box.

At this point, all you *have* to do is to save your page. However, before you do that, you can add more fields to the registration form, such as fields for the user's address or office telephone number. Skip back to Chapter 15 if you run into any trouble.

While you have the page open, you might want to replace the stupid text at the bottom with more official stuff that identifies you and your company. For one thing, take off that silly **©Copyright 1995**—don't they know what year it is?

Once you finish making changes, save your page but don't close it. One final thing, and you're through (I promise).

You need to add a link to your registration page. You see, when people try to access your web, they'll be denied until you've added them to the database, which you'll learn how to do in Chapter 23. Anyway, you need to give them some way to access the registration form, or they won't be able to register!

Return to FrontPage Explorer, and open the home page of the Root Web. You can get rid of the free Microsoft advertising if you want, and any other junk you find there. Once you modify the home page of the Root Web to your liking, then type the text you want to act as a link to the registration page—something such as **Register Here** will do. Highlight your text, open the **Edit** menu, and select **Link**. In the list of open pages, you'll find **User Registration Page** (you didn't really close it, remember?). Choose that and click **OK**. You now, after a bazillion steps, have a working user registration system.

Gee! Could They Have Included More Steps?

Before you go to pieces about how long that procedure was, let me take this opportunity to tell you how *excruciating* the act of creating a user registration system was before the advent of Microsoft FrontPage. Just a year ago, a simple registration database alone could sell for several hundred dollars. And to use it, you needed a Ph.D. So consider yourself lucky.

What happens when the user tries to access your web? Suppose you have a web called **Projects**, which you've restricted access to. When the user types in **http://hostserver.com/JenWeb/Projects/**, he'll be told in no uncertain terms that he's not registered. If he then types in **http://hostserver.com/JenWeb/** in a desperate attempt to get access, he'll see the home page of your Root Web. (Of course, if the user doesn't figure this out, there's little you can do about it, since he won't see the Projects home page if he doesn't have access to that web.)

Because you added a link to the Registration page, he can click it and register like a good boy. Then, when you retrieve your database and get his information (explained in glorious Chapter 23), you can add him to the database. Next time this user tries to enter http://hostserver.com/JenWeb/Projects/, he'll get in. Of course, he'll have to enter a password.

The Confirmation Field Bot

The User Registration page has a nice feature: when the user clicks the **Register Me** button, the information she typed is automatically saved to an HTML page, allowing her to verify that everything's correct before continuing. However, there's a little glitch: the page that FrontPage generates is plain gray, so chances are, it won't match the look of the rest of your web pages. If this bothers you, you can create your own custom confirmation page, using the **Confirmation Field** bot.

There's a two-stage process involved: first, you make the actual Confirmation page. You're not limited as to what you can do here; just make sure you use the **Confirmation Field** bot to create the thing, as explained in a minute. Next, you simply tell FrontPage that you want to use your own customized Confirmation page and not the default version.

To create your Confirmation page, open the **<Root Web>** in FrontPage Explorer: click the **Open** button and click **List Webs**. Select **<Root Web>** from the list and click **OK**. Simply create (then save to the Root Web) your confirmation page exactly the way you want it. You might create something like this.

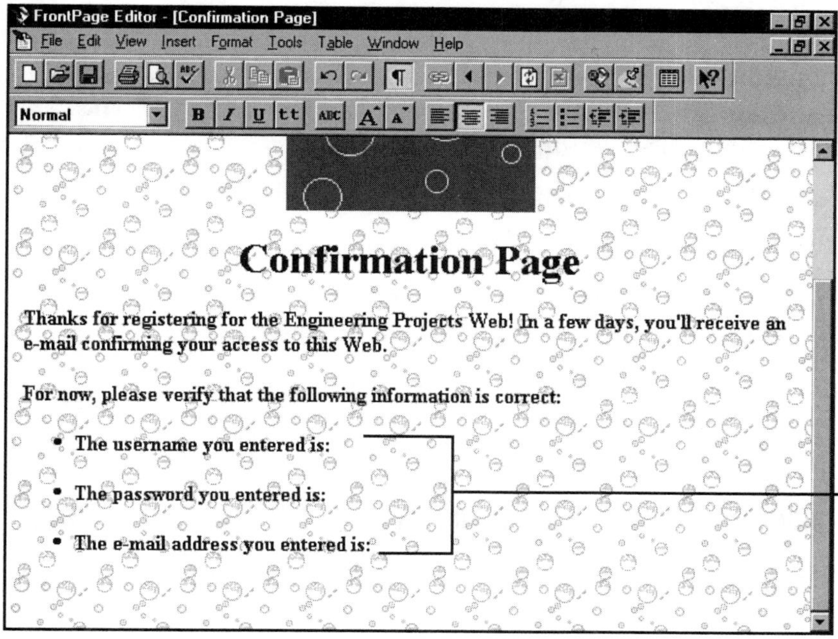

Please confirm.

Notice there are blank spaces where the user's data should show up—as in, **The password you entered is**...Now you're ready to tell FrontPage what needs to go into each of these blank spaces:

1. Click the page where you want an item from the Registration Page to appear. For example, click after the words **The password you entered is...**
2. Open the **Insert** menu and select **Bot.** When the dialog box appears, select **Confirmation Field Bot** and click **OK**.
3. Type the name of the database field whose contents you want to be echoed here. "Wait a minute," you're saying, "how am I supposed to know what *that* is??" If you used the standard registration form inserted at the point where you clicked. For example, type **Password**. Here are the common field names:

Username	The user's chosen password.
EmailAddress	The user's e-mail address, which may be blank.
Error	An automatically contrived error message generated by the FrontPage Server detailing any error that might have occurred.

   If you changed the Registration Form by entering additional fields, then you need to remember what you called them (or go back and open the Registration Form page so you can take a quick peek.)
4. Click **OK**. You'll see the name of your database field entered into your page, surrounded by [square brackets]. For example, you might see something like, **The password you entered is...[Password]**.
5. Repeat steps 1 through 4 for each database field you want displayed on your Confirmation page. When you finish, make sure you save your Confirmation page.

Great. Now all you have to do is to tell FrontPage to use your Confirmation Page, instead of the one it normally generates. Here's what you do:

1. Open the User Registration Page. (You'll find it in the Root Web.)
2. Right-click the form (inside the dashed perimeter line) and select **Form Properties** from the pop-up menu.
3. Under **Form Handler**, make sure that it says **Registration Bot**. Then click **Settings**.
4. Click the **Results** tab. You'll see something like the following figure.

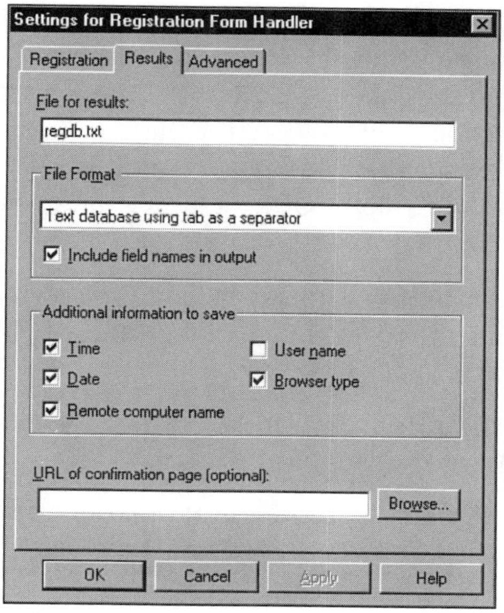

Getting the registration page to recognize your confirmation page.

5. Enter the file name of your Confirmation Form in the **URL of confirmation page** field, or click **Browse** to locate it.
6. Click **OK** and then click **OK** again. Now, FrontPage will recognize your creation as the official confirmation page.

Your Own Non-Confirmation Page

You can create a customized error page that will appear should a problem come up while the user is trying to register. Create your page as before and insert the Error confirmation field using the Confirmation bot. (Be sure to save your error page to the Root Web.) Next, return to the Form Properties dialog of the User Registration Page. You'll find the **URL of failure page** under the **Registration** tab.

The Save Results Bot

You can also use the Save Results bot to save your form data into an HTML document, so that you (and others) can read its contents online.

In Chapter 15, you learned how to build forms. You'll probably remember from that chapter that each gadget you build into a form—such as a text box, check box, or Creating a form is cool, but the data that a user types in is only helpful to you if you can do something with it. If you want, you can use the Save Results bot to tell FrontPage to save the form data in a text file that you can later bring into some kind of database program, such as Access, Paradox, or alphaFOUR, or even a spreadsheet program, such as Excel or 1-2-3.

The Save Results bot can work with any kind of form such as a feedback form, or (even more exciting) an order form for things you're selling. Here's what you do to get the Save Results bot to save the data in a form:

1. Make sure *all* the gadgets and labels you need for your form are already entered. Your form is 100% ready to go.
2. Right-click the form and select **Form Properties** from the pop-up menu.
3. Select **Save Results Bot** from the **Form Handler** drop-down list.
4. Click **Settings**. You'll see the Settings for Saving Results of Form dialog box (what a mouthful!), which looks like this.

Here you build a database for your form.

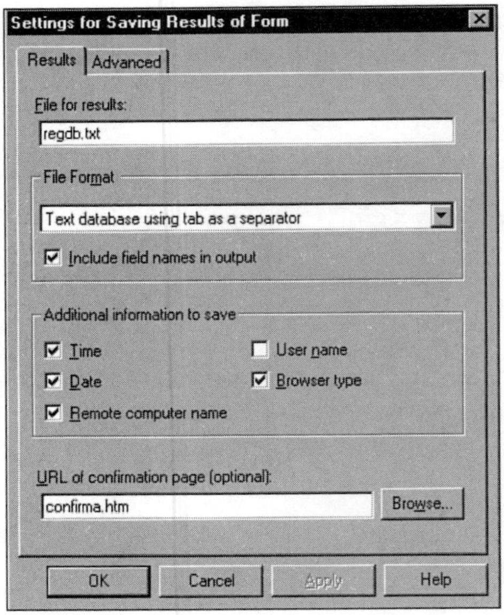

5. In the **File for results** field, type *either* the name of the HTML document you want FrontPage to create OR the name of a text *file* in which you want the form data saved. When entering the name of an HTML document, type the name such as userbase.htm. When entering the name of a text file, type the entire file path, as in C:\FrontPage Webs\Content\userbase.txt.
6. Select the format you want to use in the **File format** drop-down list.
7. If you're saving your data to a text file, then be sure to select the **Include field names in output** option. This causes FrontPage to write the *names* of the data fields (such as "EmailAddress") in the first row of the file. This will make it much simpler to get your data into your database or spreadsheet program correctly. If you're outputting to an HTML document, you don't have to select this option, although you can if you want.
8. Under **Additional information to save**, you can select any of these items about your users that you also would like to know. The user doesn't actually enter this information; your Web server is capable of finding it.
9. Following the steps under the Registration bot section, you create your Confirmation page for your form. If you do that, be sure to enter the name of your Confirmation page in the **URL of confirmation page** text box.
10. On the **Advanced** tab, you can enter the name of a second file in which you want the form data saved. You can also select the format for this file.
11. When you finish making your choices, click **OK**, and you're through.

When a user completes the form, his entries will be saved in the file you indicated. If you selected an HTML file in steps 5 and 6, then your users can view their entries online. If you selected a text file instead, then you can retrieve it from the web using FrontPage Explorer. Simply open the **<Root>** web, select the save results file, and then use the **Edit, Open** command to view its contents and save it to your hard disk.

The Include Bot

If you've ever been to Netscape's web site (and who hasn't?) you no doubt noticed that it's easy to jump to any of Netscape's main pages using a standardized toolbar located at the bottom of each page. Cool, but how can you do something like this in your own web?

You start by creating a link bar (or toolbar). You can create a graphic toolbar, or a simple one using text and | characters as dividers between the "buttons" of the toolbar.

Once you create your toolbar, save it in its own web page. Then use the Include bot (wondering when I was going to get to it, weren't you?) to insert the toolbar into the top or the bottom (or the middle, if you want to be radical) of each page in your web.

Here you'll create a simple toolbar of sorts using very small print text. If you'd rather use a graphic toolbar, then see the "Adding a Link Bar to the Template" section in Chapter 18 for help.

To create your toolbar, open a new page, and type the names of your major pages on one line. Type the character | to separate each item.

You'll probably have to reduce the text a bit to get these names to fit, or press **Ctrl+Enter** to create a line break and add the rest of a name on a second line.

Center the line(s) if you like, and then select each word and create a link from it to the actual page it represents. For example, select **Home**, and create a link to the home page using the **Edit, Link** command. When you're through, save the page with a clever name such as Toolbar Page. I created a simple toolbar for my garden web:

A very simple toolbar.

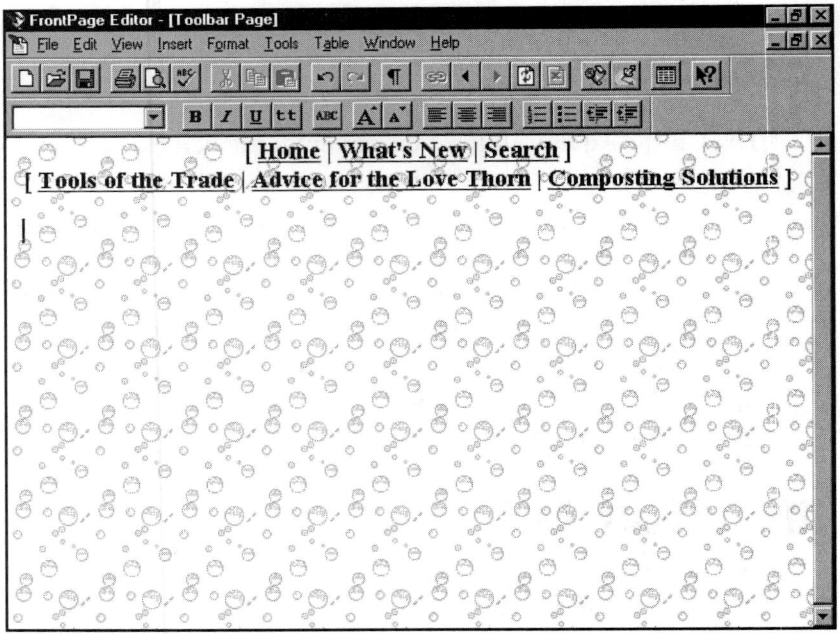

Here's how to insert your Toolbar Page into another web:

1. Open one of your web pages, and click at the point where you want to insert the toolbar.

2. Open the **Insert** menu, select **Bot**, and then when the dialog box appears, select **Include Bot** and click **OK**.
3. Type the URL (file name) of your Toolbar Page, or click **Browse** and choose it from the list.
4. Click **OK**. Your toolbar appears in your web page.

Repeat this process for each of your web pages in turn. You can go back to the Toolbar Page at some point and make changes to it. When you do, those changes will be automatically updated into each of your web pages.

Versatile Fellow

You can use the Include bot to include any information within another page, not just a toolbar. For example, if you want to list the current project participants on several pages in your web, you use the Include bot to insert a page called **Participants** into various pages in your web. As the participants change, you only have to change the one listing in the Participants page and then save it; it'll be updated throughout the web.

The Scheduled Include Bot

Suppose you want to automate your web to work like this: You have a page whose contents you want to insert into your home page, but only during a certain holiday—for instance, a "Happy Arbor Day!" page. It doesn't make any sense to have the message show up when it's *not* Arbor Day, especially since most of the world doesn't really know what day Arbor Day falls on. Instead of confusing the world any further, you can create a special Arbor Day page, and use the *Scheduled Include* Bot to insert it in one or more of your web pages *during a specific interval of time*—say, throughout the entire Arbor Day celebration thing. Before or after that time, your users will *not* see this included page.

The Scheduled Include Bot is one step beyond the regular Include Bot, and so it works a bit differently. Now, suppose you have your special Arbor Day page ready, and that it's saved to your current web. Here's how to have it show up on your web for a specific time:

1. Open the page that you want to include your special information in, and click at the point at which you want it to appear.
2. Open the **Insert** menu, select **Bot**, and then when the dialog box appears, select **Scheduled Bot** and click **OK**.

3. In the **Page URL to Include** text box, enter the URL (file name) of your special page. Again, you can click **Browse** to get help locating it.
4. Under **Starting Date and Time** and **Ending Date and Time**, enter the time when you want the inclusion to begin and when you want it to end, respectively.

Ugh!

You have to type your two dates in *very carefully*, using the arrow key to move from the day part to the month part, and so on. You'll understand once you start fooling around with this mess. Eventually, you'll get some dates entered, and you can relax and spend some time with your family and close friends.

5. If you want another page to appear during those times when your special page is *not* included—for instance, "Happy Non-Arbor Day," then enter its URL (file name) in the field marked **Optional Page URL**. Yes, you can click **Browse** to locate it if you want.
6. Click **OK**. When it's time for the inclusion to appear, it will appear at the cursor.

The Scheduled Image Bot

Suppose the special item you want to include in your web page for a limited time isn't a page but only a graphic image. You can have that image displayed when you want using the *Scheduled Image* Bot.

What's nice about the Scheduled Image Bot is that it works exactly the same way as the Scheduled Include Bot (so I won't bore you by going over all the nasty details again). Place the cursor where you want the image to appear; open the **Insert** menu, select **Bot,** and then select **Scheduled Image** from the dialog box that appears. In the next dialog box, you enter the URL (file name) of the image (either a GIF or a JPEG), try, try, and try again to enter the dates correctly. And if you want, enter the URL of an image to be shown whenever the scheduled image is absent. Click **OK**, and you're under way.

For example, you can use the Scheduled Image bot to include a small "new" graphic next to an item in a list, but only for a short time, since after awhile, the item will no longer be considered "new."

The Search Bot

For webs that contain massive amounts of text, such as long discussion groups and informational services, the *Search* Bot is a blessing. It allows your users to ask your Web server where to find a page that contains some particular phrase of text. Your Web server (provided it supports the FrontPage Server Extensions, that is) will respond with an automatically generated page that contains links to all pages *within your web* that contain the word the user is searching for. (No, you can't use the Search bot to create a search tool to rival Yahoo or Excite!—no matter how hard you try.)

In Chapter 20, you'll see this tool used in the context of a discussion group, where the Search bot is set up to search only within the discussion group directory on the Web. But here's how to have the Search bot search all your pages.

First, create a Search page, and link it to your home page and other pages in your web. One super way to do that is to create a link bar (toolbar) with a link to this Search page. See the section on the Include bot for help creating a toolbar.

Your search page doesn't have to include much, except maybe a title and some instructions. The Search bot takes care of creating the form into which the user will type his query. So, when you're ready to add the form to your search page, position your cursor at the point where you want it to appear. Then open the **Insert** menu, select **Bot**, select **Search Bot**, and click **OK**. You'll see the Search Bot Properties dialog box.

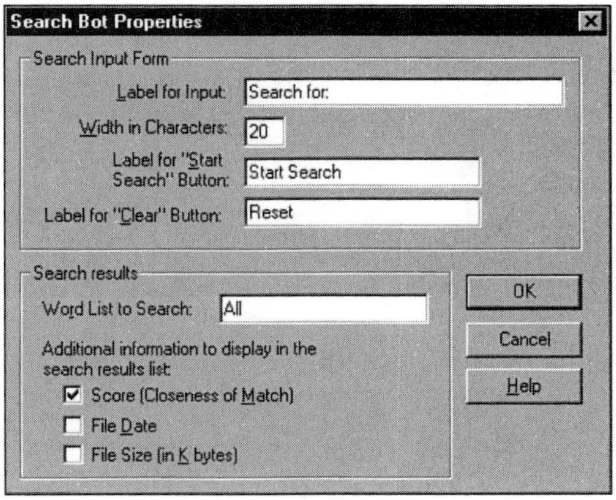

Searching for clues.

There's not a lot to change here:

➤ In front of the text box into which the user types the word (or words) he wants to search for are the words, "Search for:" Change this if you like, in the **Label for Input** box.

➤ Limit the amount of text to search for by changing the number of characters in the **Width in Characters** box.

- To start searching, the user will click a button labeled **Start Search**. If you want it called something else, then change what you find in the **Label for "Start Search" Button** text box.
- Under **Search results**, enter the name of the directory in which you want FrontPage to search. When this is set to **All**, FrontPage searches all your web pages. But if you change this to something such as **Discuss**, then FrontPage will only search your discussion directory (provided it's called **Discuss** of course.)
- Select additional information you want displayed as the result of a search, such as its score (a rating of its closeness to the search query), the file date, and file size (useful if you have a lot of pages on your web site that might match a particular search).

When you finish, click **OK**. The Search form appears in your page, ready to go! Here's what a user might see, if he uses your search form to search the pages of your Web.

The search results.

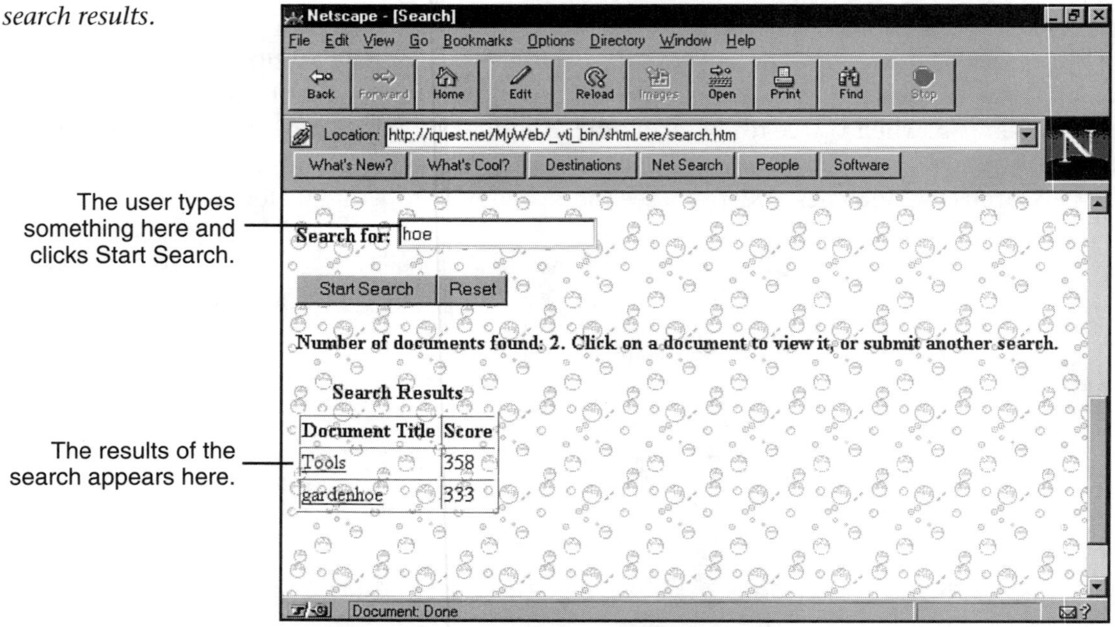

The Table of Contents Bot

The Microsoft FrontPage package contains two other bots, which I'll cover in depth in some of the future chapters. To be complete, however, here's a brief introduction.

The *Table of Contents* Bot is a wonderful little device that automatically builds an outline of the entire contents of your web (like the Outline View of FrontPage Explorer), inserts that outline at whatever point you choose, and keeps that outline up-to-date at all times.

If you (or someone else) generates a new page for the web, it's added automatically to the Table of Contents. See Chapter 19 for help using the Table of Contents bot.

The Discussion Bot

Perhaps one of FrontPage's most fascinating features is its capability to create discussion groups within your web. This is a service for which companies used to pay thousands of dollars; now, it's on your web, for free!

You can start a discussion group about anything you want—perhaps the main topic of your web, perhaps something completely divergent. The way this works is very similar to newsgroups on the web. A user creates a message that contains a comment or question about the main topic. He saves it to the discussion group, and then other users can come along and add their comments to his comment. You'll find Chapter 20 devoted to discussion groups.

The Least You Need to Know

WebBots can perform a fascinating array of functions:

- Use the **Annotation** bot to add hidden comments to a web page.
- Use the **HTML Markup** bot to insert HTML codes into a web.
- Use the **Substitution** bot to insert the value of a parameter (such as the author's name) into a web page.
- Use the **Timestamp** bot to insert the date when the page was last changed.
- Use the **Registration** bot to create a web where only registered users have access.
- Use the **Confirmation Field** bot to create a confirmation page for a form.
- Use the **Save Results** bot to save the data in a form to either a web page or a file that you can use in a database or spreadsheet program.
- Use the **Include** bot to insert the contents of one web page into another.
- Use the **Scheduled Include** bot to do the same thing, except for a specified period of time.
- Use the **Scheduled Image** bot to insert a graphic into a web page for a specified period.
- Use the **Search** bot to create a Search page.
- Use the **Table of Contents** bot to create a TOC.
- Use the **Discussion** bot to create an entire discussion group within your web.

Part 5
Creating Templates and Specialty Pages

In this part, you learn how to put yourself on auto-pilot by creating your own templates, *which are predesigned, fill-in-the-blanks web pages.*

Have you ever noticed people wandering around your web site completely lost? In this part, you learn how to add a table of contents. And, once users find their way out, they may have plenty to tell you, so you might want to consider adding a discussion group as well, which you'll learn how to do.

Chapter 18

Creating Templates

By the End of This Chapter, You'll Be Able to...

- Create a template from scratch
- Create a template from another web page
- Use a template to create web pages that look alike
- Change how an existing web site looks

A *template* is a predesigned web page in which you simply fill in the blanks. The idea behind a template is that it's reusable—in other words, after taking the trouble to create one, you can reuse it to create similar-looking web pages.

A well-designed template contains only the elements you want to reuse each time, without all the nasty particulars, such as the main text for that page. You might design a template with your logo and company name at the top, and a linkbar (a toolbar with links to all your major web pages) at the bottom. By reusing the template every time you create a new page for your web, you can save a lot of time by not duplicating the same tasks over and over.

Not for Web Sites

Even though FrontPage comes with several neat templates to help you in designing web *pages* (which you can reuse to create each of the pages in your web site), you can't create your own web *site* template with FrontPage. (In other words, you can't create some magic template with which you could stamp out multiple copies of the same web site.)

Instead, to get the customized look you want to see throughout your web, you need to create a template for your web *pages*, and then use that template over and over to create your own customized web site.

Why Create Your Own Templates?

When creating a web site, FrontPage lets you select from these options:

- Corporate Presence Wizard
- Customer Support Web
- Discussion Web Wizard
- Personal Web
- Project Web

Suppose that you want to create a web site devoted to fly-tying, which is one of your favorite hobbies. You might choose the Personal Web. But to your horror, you discover a site designed like this.

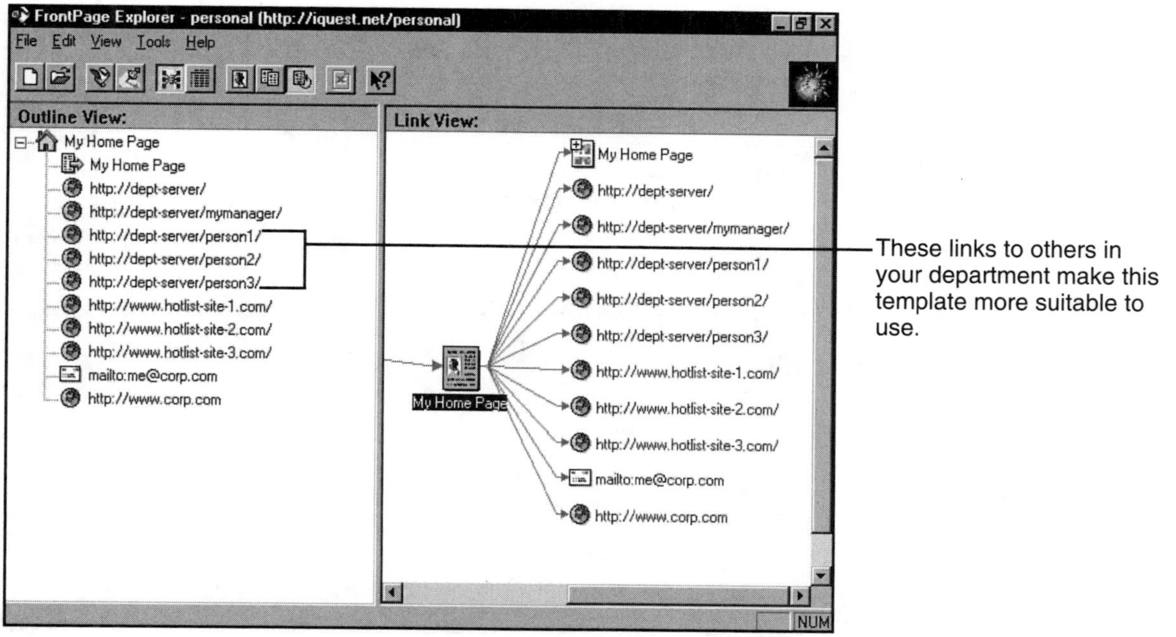

But what if FrontPage includes a web site template that suits your needs, but not your tastes? For example, what if Project Web site is exactly what you're looking for, but the look is nowheresville? What then?

You could create the site and then change each page, which would be a nuisance. Or you can create your web site from scratch, using a template (which has the look you want). Although it's personal, this site is suited only to work-related activities.

The links tell you what you need to know about what FrontPage considers "personal." Although this site would be perfect for use on your company's intranet, or maybe even your home business, it simply isn't suited for personal passions such as fly-tying, golf, gardening, or any of a million different hobbies. And to top it off, the look is *soooo* boring!

These two pages, created with a FrontPage template, look a lot a like.

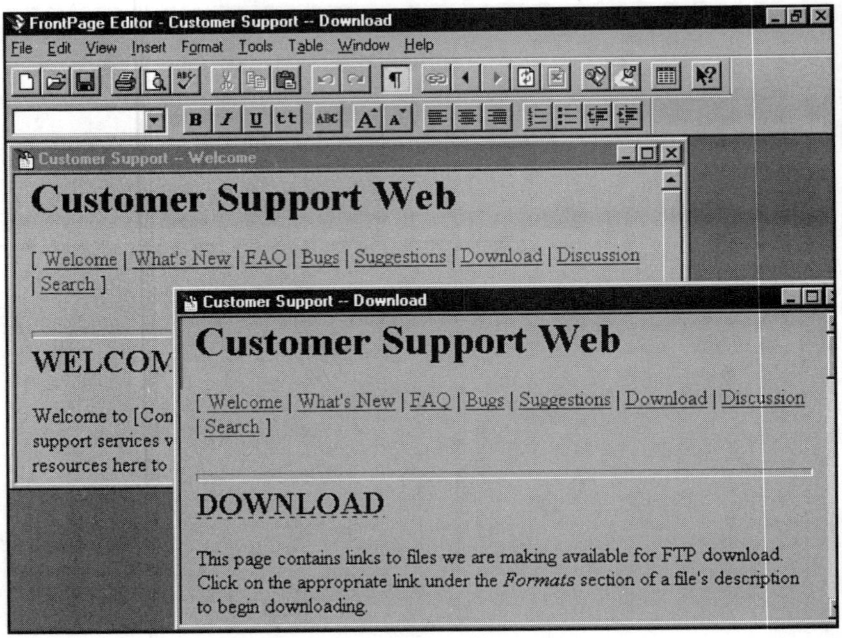

To get your fly-tying web site off the ground, you have to start from scratch. And in that case, you're going to need a lot of help—the kind of help that only a template can provide.

Also, when you use a template or wizard to create your web, FrontPage creates all the pages it thinks you need, and makes them all look alike. That's great.

The only problem comes when you want to add a new page to the web. Your new page will not share the same look as your other pages; it will have a plain grey background instead of the fancy colors, headers, and footers, of your other pages. Even if you find a web site template or wizard you love, to add matching pages to it, you'll need to create a page template.

As stated earlier, the basic reason for creating your own templates is to save time. Sure, creating the template initially will take some effort, but the more pages you create with it, the more time you save.

Check This Out...

Hey, I Kinda Like That Look!

If you created your web site with a wizard (for example, the Corporate Presence Wizard), then the reason all the pages look alike is no accident. Each page in the web gets its background color and link colors from a single page called Web Colors. The common linkbar at the bottom of each page comes from a page called Navigation Links, and the logo at the top of each page comes from the Included Logo page. To change any of these things for your web (such as the background image), you simply change it once, in the appropriate page (in this case the Web Colors page). That changes the background image for the whole web.

If you do want to add pages to such a web, you must add the proper links to the Web Colors, Included Logo, and Navigation Links pages, so that your new pages will look like all the others in the web site. (And later in this chapter, you'll learn how to do exactly that.)

Another way to solve this problem is to create a template with the links to Web Colors, Included Logo, and Navigation Links, and use it to make new pages. I'll show you how to use this method later on too.

Design Considerations

When you use Microsoft's templates and wizards to create custom pages, you don't really have to worry too much about design considerations—the work has been done for you.

However, if you venture out on your own by creating your own templates, there are some elements of web page design that you should know. For example, when designing the perfect page for a template:

- Make sure that your first heading is the largest one, so that it captures your audience's attention.
- Design your other headings with a proportionally smaller text size.
- Consider adding a common link area that provides quick access to the other main pages in your web. You can do this with a graphic downloaded from the WWW or one you created.

Copyrights: 101

Remember, just because you can snatch a graphic or a page from the WWW, that doesn't mean you can use it willy-nilly. If something wasn't created by you, you should treat it as *copyrighted*, which means that you can use it for inspiration, but you can't use it as is without getting permission first.

- Use a background that reflects the mood of the page (from conservative to funky). However, in your zeal to make the Web's most cool lists, don't use a background that's so busy it makes it impossible to read your text. Instead, you might want to choose a solid color background, and add interesting graphics to fill your page. You can also use a solid color, textured graphic to fill the background.

A busy background detracts from what you want to present.

The background fights the graphic for attention.

The regular text, and even the heading, is difficult to read.

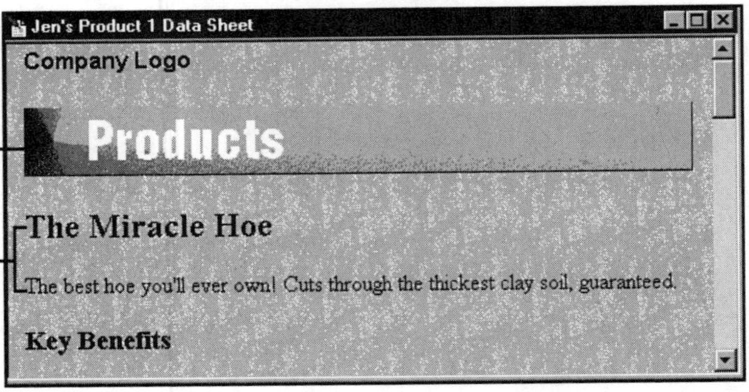

- Choose a text color that is easily read and contrasts well with your background image or color.
- Create an identity for your pages by adding a common logo or banner at the top.

Need Some Inspiration?

Then visit a "cool" Web site, by checking out Netscape's list (**http://home.netscape.com/home/whats-cool.html**), Yahoo's (**http://www.yahoo.com/Entertainment/Cool_Links/**) or Point (**http://point.lycos.com**).

Creating Templates for New Web Pages

Creating your own template is not difficult. You create a web page that you want to use as a template, and then you save the page using the **File, Save As** command.

How do you create a web page to use as a template? Well, you can start from scratch by clicking the **New** button. You'll get a nice, blank web page for your trouble. Then, following the wise wisdom relayed in previous chapters, fill in the elements of your sample page: maybe a header or a footer, and a few graphics here and there. Remember not to add any text or graphics that will change on each page—a template, as you recall, is supposed to be reuseable, so you don't want to fill it up with stuff you don't want to reuse. *However,* it is a good idea to add some fake text or graphics *to hold the place* of real text or graphics you'll add later.

To save some time, you can use one of your existing pages as a template. Simply save the page in template format using the **File**, **Save As** command; then delete the elements that you don't want to reuse.

If you don't relish designing your page from scratch, then import a page you like from the WWW, and modify it to suit your needs. After you do that, save the thing as a template (which you'll learn how to do in a minute).

Changing Templates

If a particular FrontPage template is bothering you, you can replace it with a customized version. Simply create your version of the template, and give it the same name as an old one.

To save your page as a template, follow these steps:

1. Create a web page you want to save as a template. (If you want more help with this creation process, see the next section.)
2. Open the **File** menu and select **Save As**.
3. Click **As Template**.
4. Give your template a nice **Title**—it'll show up later in the New Page dialog box with all the other templates. (The title can have spaces, by the way.)
5. Enter a file name under the **Name** field.
6. Type in a short **Description** (this will show up in the New Page dialog, too), and then click **OK**.

To use your new template, simply open the **File** menu and select **New**. You'll see it listed with the other templates. Select your template and click **OK**. Your new page will look exactly like your template. Add whatever you want to the new page, and save it by clicking the **Save** button. The next time you want to create a new page, simply repeat this process, and it'll look like the template too.

A Practice Session: Creating the Perfect Template

What's it like to create a template? Well, follow along and you'll see how to create a template from scratch:

1. In FrontPage Editor, click the **New** button.
2. Get rid of that boring background by opening the **File** menu and selecting **Page Properties**. You can select a color for your background by clicking **Use Custom Background Color** and then clicking **Choose**. I'd rather use a textured graphic which I created, so I'm going to click **Background Image** and then click **Browse** to select it. If you haven't imported the graphic into your web, as you learned to do in Chapter 8 , then you'll need to click **From File** to locate it. If you're connected to the World Wide Web, you can download a file by clicking **From URL** instead. (Of course, you must know the exact URL for the graphic, not the page it's on).
3. From this same dialog box, you can change your text color if needed, in order to make it contrast with the background color or image you choose.
4. Type in some placeholder text for your page title. I used the Heading 1 style for this one.
5. I wanted to insert a line under the title, so I placed the cursor at the end of my title text, opened the **Insert** menu and selected **Horizontal Line**. I made changes to the line to thicken it, using the Properties dialog box.
6. Enter some placeholder text for the body of your document. I used the Normal style for this text.
7. Press **Enter** a bunch of times, then insert another line at the bottom of the page, similar to the first.

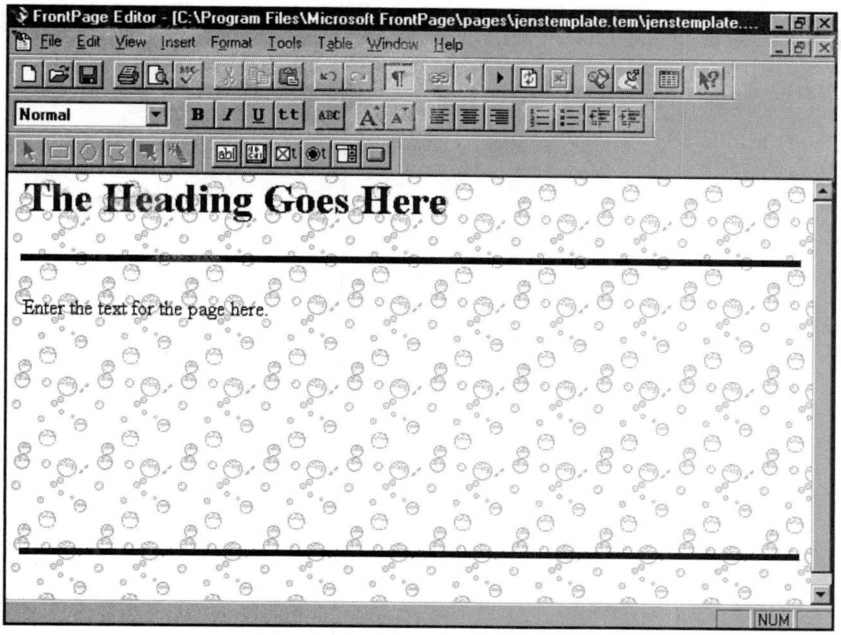

Now it's starting to look like something.

8. I decided at this point to insert my logo at the top of the page. So I clicked to place the cursor in front of my heading; then I opened the **Insert** menu and selected **Image**. Because my graphic logo was not yet part of the Web, I clicked on **From File** to locate it. After selecting the graphic, I clicked **OK** to insert it.

   Once the graphic was inserted, I pressed **Enter** to place the heading on a separate line. Then I centered both the heading and the logo by selecting them and clicking the **Center** button. The following figure shows what the template looks like now.

9. You're not done yet, but go ahead and save your page as a template, so you won't lose what you have. Click the **Save** button. Click **As Template.** Enter a **Title** and a **Name** (file name) for the template. Under **Description**, type something like **Jennifer's Bubbles Template**. Click **OK**. You'll be asked if you want to save any embedded graphics; if so, click **Yes to All**.

Insert a logo at the top of the page.

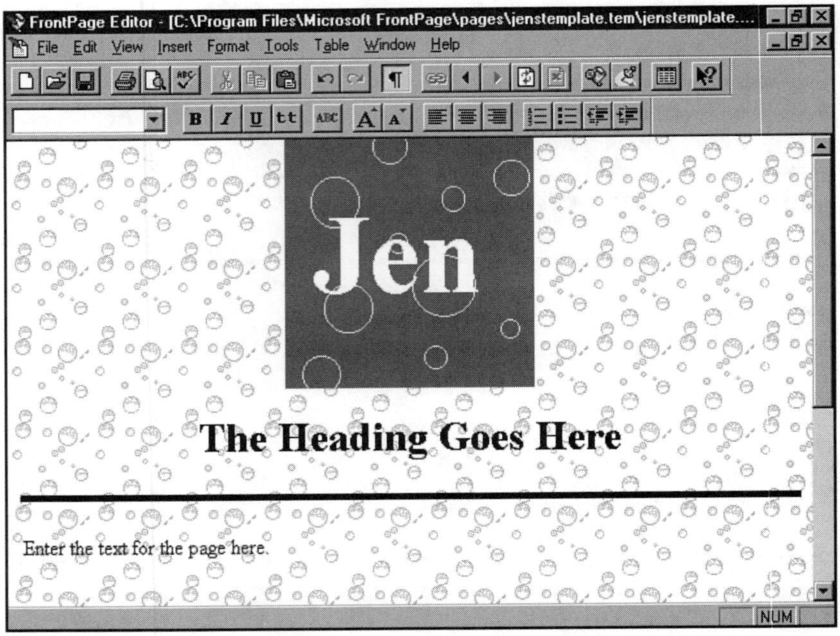

To create a template from one of your existing web pages, follow the steps in this section and the next to add a header and footer, and a linkbar as needed. Then use the **File, Save As** command to save the page in template form. Be sure to give it a new name so it doesn't overwrite the original page.

To use a page from the WWW as a template, connect to the Internet and use your Web browser to save it to your hard disk. In Netscape, use the **File, Save As** command to save the page. Then right-click on each graphic and use the **Save Image As** to save them to your hard disk as well. Once that's done, switch to FrontPage Explorer and use the **File, Import** command to import the page into your web. At this point, open the page with FrontPage Editor, delete unneeded text, and make enough changes so you don't violate any copyright laws. Once done, use the **File, Save As** command to save the page as a template.

Adding a Linkbar to the Template

Using Windows Paint, I created a simple graphic to use as a linkbar for right now. I don't want to insert the graphic into my template now because, for one thing, I want to replace the linkbar with something cooler once I learn how to draw (or I find something better on the Web). If I insert it into my template and then create a bunch of pages with it, I'll have to manually replace the linkbar in each of those pages if I create a newer, nicer-looking one.

But Paint Creates Only Bitmap Images—How Can I Use Them on the Web?

You can't, but when you insert a graphic, FrontPage automatically converts it into JPEG or GIF format for you. Go ahead and use simpler drawing programs such as Windows Paint to create your linkbar if you like.

Also, in order to get the linkbar graphic to work, I'm going to have to create *hotspots*. You'll remember those guys from Chapter 13—a hotspot is a part of a graphic that, when clicked by the user, links him to some specified web page. I can't create the hotspots on the linkbar until I have the pages to link them to—but I don't want to create the pages until I have a template, so what's a mother to do?

The simple solution is the same one FrontPage uses on most of its templates: you *include* the linkbar graphic in the template. That way, you can make changes to the graphic at any point, and any page created with the template will automatically be updated. You remember the Include bot from Chapter 17? Well, you're going to use it here to include your graphic in the template.

First, you create a page in which the graphic can stay:

1. Click the **New** button, and you'll get a nice blank page in which to work.
2. Insert your graphic using the **Insert**, **Image** command. Because the graphic file did not yet exist on my web, I clicked **From File**, located the graphic, and clicked **OK** to insert it. Again, since the graphic I used was in BMP format, FrontPage converted it nicely to GIF.
3. Select the graphic and then click the **Center** alignment button to center it.
4. Click the **Save** button to save your graphic page. I called mine linkbar.htm.

Now that you have a linkbar page, you can include it in your template. Switch back to the template, and click where you want to insert your linkbar. Then:

1. Open the **Insert** menu and select **Bot**.
2. Select the **Include** bot and click **OK**.
3. Enter the name of the page you just created (uh, linkbar.htm) and click **OK**. After a bit, your linkbar will appear.
4. Select the graphic and click the **Center** button to center it.

Your finished template.

You're done, so go ahead and save the template again by clicking the **Save** button. You can use the template now to create your web pages.

After you create and save the main pages for your web, you can go back to the **linkbar.htm** page at any time and create your hotspot links. First, open up the linkbar page. Then, using the tools on the Image Toolbar, create hotspots for each of the pages represented on the graphic linkbar:

1. Click the graphic to select it.
2. Click your tool of choice, such as the Rectangle tool.

3. Draw the first hotspot. (See Chapter 13 for more help.)
4. Type the name of the page to which you want to link the hotspot, and click **OK**.

Once you save the linkbar page and close it, the linkbar will be updated within each of your web pages. From now on, when a user clicks a hotspot within the linkbar graphic, he'll jump to the associated page.

Creating a Template for an Existing Web

The only problem with templates is that they don't help you much when you've already created your Web (along with most of your Web pages!).

If you have a lot of special pages to add to the web, and you want to make sure that they look like the other pages, you can create a template. Open a page in your web, and delete its body text and any other elements specific to that page. You should be left with a basic shell. Save this shell as a template: open the **File** menu and select **Save As**. Click **As Template**; then enter a new **Title** and a new **Name** (file name) for the template. Enter a **Description** if you want, and click **OK**. Create your new web pages using this template, and they'll look like they belong to your little web family.

Changing the Look of an Existing Web

If you create a web using one of the wizards, then the colors for text, links, and background are stored in a page called Web Colors. All the pages in your web get their colors from the selections in this one page. Likewise, the common logo used throughout the web is stored in a page called Included Logo. To change the look of such a web, you simply change the selections in these two pages.

For example, open the **Web Colors** page. Then open the **File** menu and select **Page Properties**. Make your changes to the background, text, or link colors as needed, and click **OK**. You can even substitute a graphic image for the background color if you want.

To change the logo, open the **Included Logo** page, and delete the graphic you find there. Then insert the graphic you want to use. Save the page, and you're through.

You can use this same idea to change a web created with a template even though such a web *will not include* the nice Web Colors and Included Logo pages. For example, if you use the Personal Web template to create your web site, you won't get much, other than a few linked pages. However, there's no reason why you can't create a page called Web Colors yourself, and use the selections in this one page to change the look of your web. Simply create your Web Colors page and use the **File, Page Properties** command to select your color choices as explained earlier. Save the page, and then close it.

The Whole Truth

Okay, some templates do contain pages such as Included Header or Included Footer, although they don't include the other pages such as Web Colors and Included Logo. These pages, by the way, contain the common header or footer that is used within the web. A *header*, by the way, is stuff that appears at the top each page in the web. A *footer* is stuff that appears at the bottom of each page instead.

Now, open each page in your web, one at a time, and do the following: Open the **File** menu and like before, select the **Page Properties** command. Select **Get Background and Colors from Page**. Click **Browse**, and select the Web Colors page you just created. Whammo! The colors and background of the current page change to that of the Web Colors page. Repeat for all your other web pages.

To create a common logo, you can simply insert one into each page. But if you want something more spectacular, such as a complete banner with a logo, your company name, and maybe even a horizontal line underneath, then you need to follow these steps: Start with a new page, and insert the logo you want to use. Add your company name as well, a horizontal line if you want one. When you finish, save the page with a name like *banner.htm*.

Then open each of your web pages in turn, and insert the banner page using the Include bot: open the **Insert** menu and select **Bot**. Select **Include** and click **OK**. Type the name of your banner page and click **OK**. Repeat for each web page.

To create a header and a footer page, follow the basic steps for creating a logo page; then use the Include bot to insert it into each of your web pages.

The Least You Need to Know

By now, you should feel like a template-creator extraordinaire. But in case you're thinking that you might have forgotten something, here's a list of the important points to remember:

➤ A template is a predesigned web page. You can use a template to create web pages that all have a similar look.

➤ If none of FrontPage's templates or wizards give you what you're looking for, then you're stuck creating your web site from scratch—and to do that, you're going to need a template.

- To create a template, create a web page that contains all the common elements you want to save. Open the **File** menu and select **Save As**. Click **As Template**. Enter a **Title**, **Name** (file name), and **Description** for your template, and then click **OK**. You'll be asked to save the graphics within the template. Save them all in one big swoop by clicking **Yes to All**.
- To add a linkbar (navigation bar) at the top or bottom of each page in your web, create a linkbar graphic first. Then insert the graphic into its own web page and save that as linkbar.htm. Finally, use the **Include bot** to insert the linkbar.htm graphic into each web page in turn.
- To add the links to the linkbar, open the linkbar page and create a hotspot on the graphic. When asked for the name of a page to link to, type the appropriate name and click **OK.** Repeat this process to add additional hotspots on the linkbar graphic for each of your main web pages.

Chapter 19

Adding a Table of Contents

By the End of This Chapter, You'll Be Able to...

- Add a table of contents to a new or existing page
- Understand when to create a TOC from scratch
- Invent three-letter acronyms of your own

A table of contents is a listing of the pages in your web. Through the table of contents, a user can easily locate the specific page he's looking for. And because a table of contents provides links to each page in the listing, a user is only one click away from any page on your web.

You May Not Need to Read Further

If you create your web site using a wizard, then a Table of Contents page is automatically created for you. But you can make changes to the TOC if you want—see the "Changing Your Table of Contents" section for more information.

If you created your web site using one of the templates (or you created it from scratch), then you can easily add a Table of Contents page by following the steps in this chapter.

A table of contents provides links to the pages in your web.

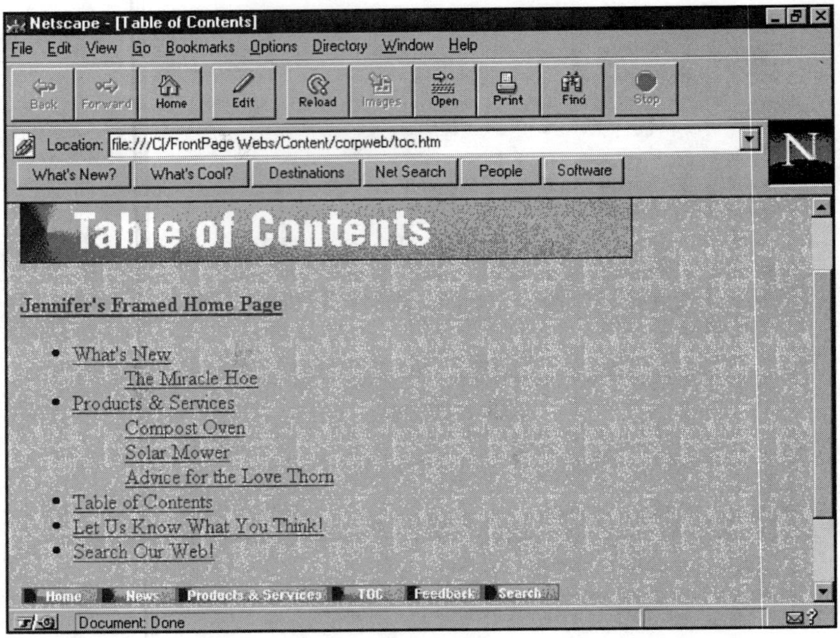

Here Are Your Options

You can create a table of contents for the entire web that lists every page, or you can create a TOC for a single part of the web, such as the section of the web that describes each of your company's main products.

To create the table of contents, use the *Table of Contents* bot. During the creation process, you'll specify the starting page for the TOC outline. The TOC is then created beginning with that page. For example, suppose you had a web site structured like this:

Home Page: Welcome

What's New
Our Products
Adventure Division
The Great Outdoors
Joe's Brand Fishing Equipment

Meet Our Employees
  Sales
  Customer Service
  Management
  Other Personnel
Search

To create a TOC for the Products section, you can specify that the beginning page is **Our Products**. You'll end up with a table of contents that looks like this:

Our Products

- Adventure Division
  - Boogie Boards
  - Surf Riders
  - Ski Equipment
- The Great Outdoors
  - Tents
  - Cooking Equipment
  - Sleeping Bags
  - Campground Equipment
- Joe's Brand Fishing Equipment
  - Fishing Rods
  - Fishing Reels
  - The Best Flies
  - Miscellaneous

Unwanted Duplication

The table of contents is generated by following links. FrontPage starts at the page you indicate and then adds an entry to the outline for every linked page. If a page is linked to from several pages (as the home page often is) then it may appear in the table of contents several times. To avoid this problem, you can opt to display each page only once in the TOC.

Expect Some Visitors

If you've provided links to pages out on the WWW, expect them to show up in your table of contents. Sorry, but there isn't an option to exclude these "visitors" on your TOC.

Haven't I Seen This Somewhere Before?

Here's a downside to letting someone do your work for you: you probably noticed from the earlier figure that the Table of Contents page shows up as an entry within the TOC itself! Pretty silly, but since FrontPage generates its TOC from links beginning with the starting page (which in this case, was the home page), and since the Table of Contents page is linked to the home page, it inevitably shows up in the listing. Kinda stupid, but there you go.

One way to fix this problem is to add the TOC to an existing page instead of creating a separate page for it. For example, add the TOC to the end of the home page; then add a bookmark to mark the table of contents within the page (see Chapter 12 for information on bookmarks). Add links to the TOC bookmark on all your other pages, including one at the top of the home page. Because the table of contents is not a page within your web, it doesn't show up in the TOC.

More Detail Than You Might Want

You might get more detail than you want with the TOC generated by the Table of Contents Bot. For example, consider this one portion of a rather detailed web site:

Jim the Tool Guy Home Page

- Power Tools
  - Drills
    - Standard Drills
    - Craftsman
    - Stanley
  - Cordless Drills
    - Black and Decker
    - Bosch
    - SKIL
  - Professional Drills
    - Dewalt

  - Circular Saws
    - Standard Saws
      - Craftsman
      - SKIL
    - Cordless Models
      - DeWalt
    - Heavy Duty Saws
      - Makita
      - Porter Cable
- Lawn & Garden
- Electrical

Although having all that detail would be great for an ordinary Table of Contents page that you plan on showing full screen, using such a TOC for a framed home page just wouldn't do. Unfortunately, you can't specify the level of detail that you want when creating a table of contents with FrontPage. It lists every page in your web, beginning at the page you specify. So if you specify the home page, expect a very detailed TOC.

> Techno Talk
>
> **What's a Guy to Do?**
>
> If you need a less detailed TOC to use within a frame, create one from scratch. See the "Creating a TOC From Scratch" section for help.

Creating a Table of Contents Using FrontPage

You can insert your table of contents into an existing page, or you can create a new page for it. For example, you can add a Table of Contents section at the bottom of your home page, or you can create an entirely separate page called Table of Contents.

> Techno Talk
>
> **Avoid Duplication**
>
> If you want to avoid the problem discussed earlier, where the Table of Contents page shows up as an item within the TOC listing, here's an easy solution: add the table of contents to the bottom of your home page, rather than creating a new page for the TOC.

Adding a Table of Contents to an Existing Page

To add a TOC to an existing page such as your home page:

1. Open the page in which you want to insert the table of contents.
2. Click in the document where you want the TOC inserted.
3. Open the **Insert** menu and select **Bot**.
4. Select **Table of Contents** and click **OK**.
5. Make whatever changes you need to in the Table of Contents Bot Properties dialog box. If some of these options are confusing, see the "Changing Your Table of Contents" section for information.
6. Click **OK** and your table of contents appears.

Well, not exactly. What appears is a bunch of links, which, when the TOC is generated for the user's Web browser, will show the titles of your actual web pages.

Here's your TOC—uh, well, sort of.

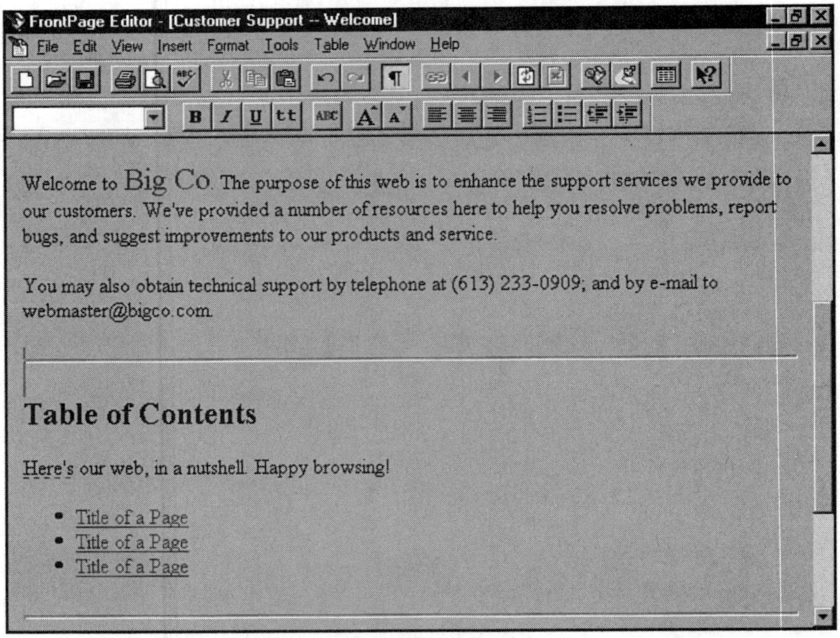

Type some text just above the TOC to explain what it's doing in your home page. You might want to create a bookmark for the TOC and provide a link to that bookmark at the top of the home page. To do that, select some of the text you used as a lead-in to the TOC. Then open the **Edit** menu and select **Bookmark**. Type a name for your bookmark (such as TOC) and click **OK**. Return to the top of your home page, and type some text for the link, such as **Click here to jump to our Table of Contents**. Select this text, open the **Edit** menu, and select **Link**. On the **Open Pages** tab, select your bookmark from the **Bookmark** list and click **OK**. Your link is now active.

To view the table of contents and to test your link, fire up your Web browser, and open the home page, by typing its URL (such as http://hostserv.com/MyWeb/index.htm). You'll notice that the item, Table of Contents, does not appear in the listing. Cool!

Creating a Table of Contents on a New Page

If your table of contents is long, you may want to put it on its own page and provide a link to it from your home page. Keep in mind that by putting the TOC on a separate page, it will appear as an item in the table of contents listing.

Can't say that no one warned you.

To create a TOC on a new page, you basically follow the same steps as before, but with a little twist. To start, open the **File** menu and select **New**. Select the **Table of Contents** template and click **OK**.

You're done—well, kinda. You should delete the instructions at the top of the page and change the lead-in text as you like. Then save the page. Type in a page **Title**, and change the **Page URL** if you want. Click **OK** when you're done.

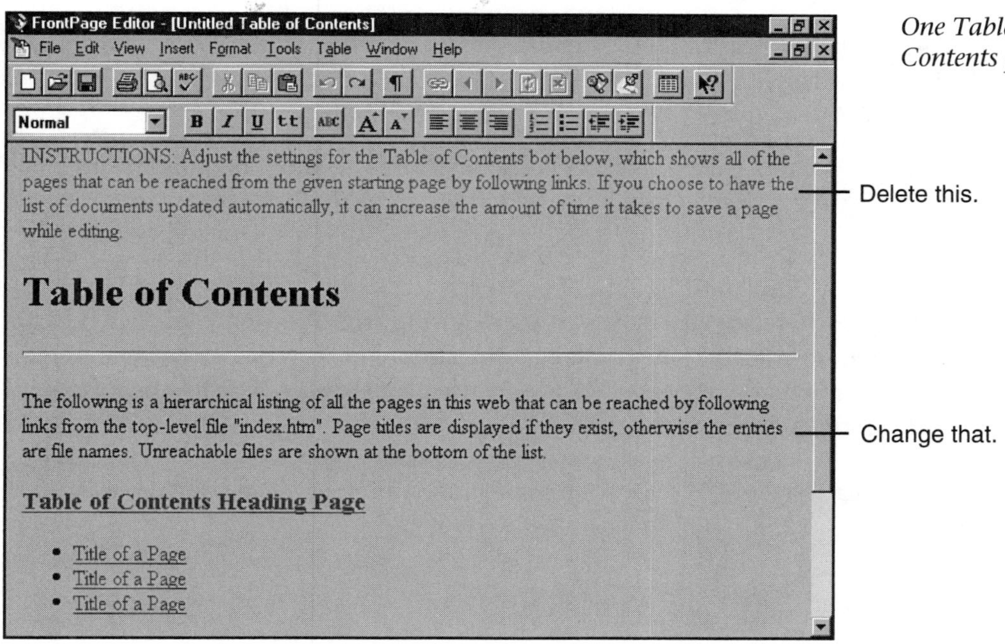

One Table of Contents page to go!

Changing Your Table of Contents

To change the settings used in creating your table of contents, simply open the Table of Contents page. Then double-click the table of contents listing. You'll see this box.

Everything changes.

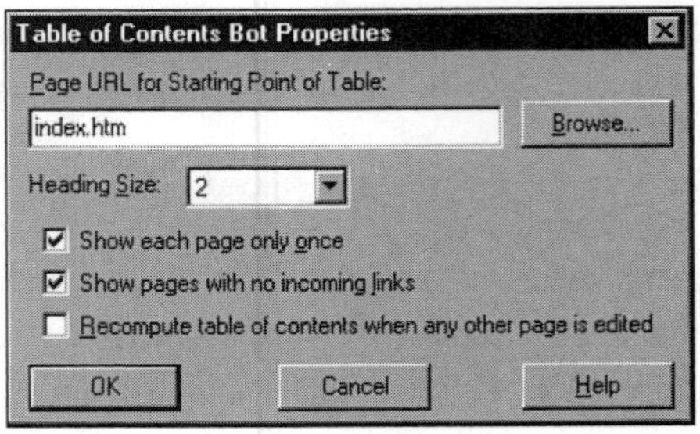

Here's how to make sense of it all:

- ➤ Enter the file name (URL) of the page you want FrontPage to start with in the **Page URL for Starting Point of Table** text box. You can also click **Browse** to select a page from a list if you want.
- ➤ Select the Heading style you want FrontPage to use when listing your start page. Heading 1 is the largest, and Heading 6 is the smallest. If you don't want your start page listed, select **None**.
- ➤ By default, pages appear in the listing only once, even if several pages are linked to the same page. However, you can click the **Show each page only once** option to turn it off if you want.
- ➤ You can list "orphan" pages in the TOC, by selecting the **Show pages with no incoming links** option. An orphan page is one that is not linked to any other page in the web.
- ➤ *Do not* select the **Recompute table of contents whenever a page is edited** option, unless you have a relatively small web, since letting FrontPage do its thing while you're trying to get work done could be quite annoying. You can, however, recalculate the TOC manually whenever you add more pages to your web by opening the Table of Contents page and saving it.

Make your changes and click **OK**. For your changes to take effect, save your Table of Contents page.

Creating a Table of Contents from Scratch

If you want to have power over how your table of contents will look, you'll have to create the thing yourself.

Yech. Why go to all that trouble?

If you want to use your TOC in a skinny frame on one side of your home page, you can't use the Table of Contents created by FrontPage, since even a small web results in a TOC that's too complex to fit there. That's because FrontPage, in its earnestness to do a good job, always creates its TOC with all your pages listed, no matter how minor they may be.

Don't worry that you're stuck creating (and maintaining) your TOC from scratch. There's an easy and quick way to do it.

First, start with a new page. If you want your Table of Contents page to have the same background as your other web pages, you may want to create your new page using a template (see Chapter 18 for help with that one).

Type the **Table of Contents** heading at the top of your page. Press **Enter** a couple times, and click the **Bulleted List** button. You're now ready to add your first entry.

Position the FrontPage Editor window so you can see it and the FrontPage Explorer window. Select a page in the Explorer window that you want to add to your TOC. Drag the page into the Editor window, and drop it on the line with the bullet. A link to the dropped page is created, nice as you please.

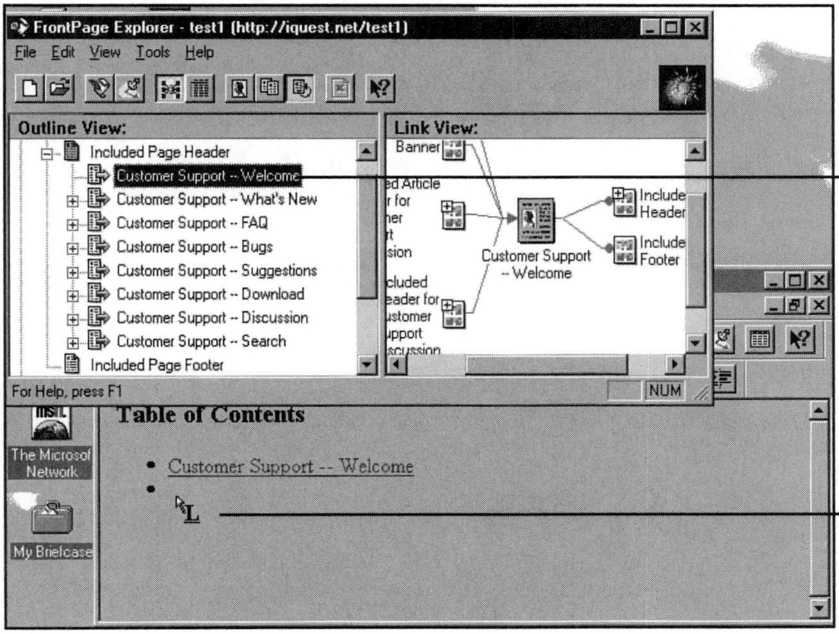

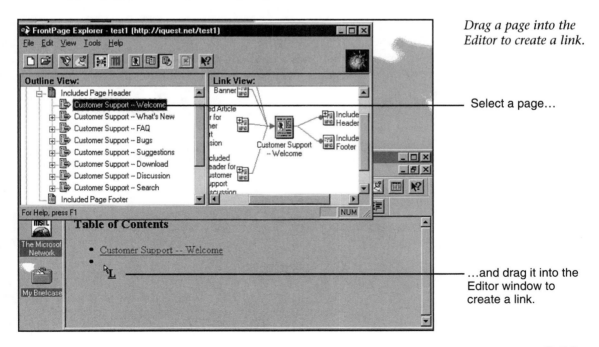

Drag a page into the Editor to create a link.

Select a page...

...and drag it into the Editor window to create a link.

Repeat this dragging thing until you have your complete list. You may have to press **Tab** occasionally, to indent one item under another (that is, if you want to list more than only your main pages in your TOC).

When you finish, save your Table of Contents page. Using the dragging trick, you can add a link to the TOC page within each of your other pages. Simply open each of your web pages in turn, and drag the TOC page from FrontPage Explorer into the FrontPage Editor window.

The Least You Need to Know

To TOC or not to TOC, that is the question. Here are some of the answers:

- A table of contents is a listing of the pages within your web.
- You can let FrontPage create the TOC for you, or you can create one manually.
- When you let FrontPage create your table of contents, you can insert it within an existing page or a new page.
- To create a TOC in an existing page, click where you want the table of contents to appear; then open the **Insert** menu and select **Bot**. Select **Table of Contents** and click **OK**. Choose the options you want and click **OK**.
- To create a TOC in a new page, open the **File** menu and select **New**. Select the **Table of Contents** template and click **OK**. Delete the extra text and type in what you want, and you're done.
- To create a TOC from scratch, start with a new page. Type a heading and begin a bulleted list. Position the Explorer and Editor windows so you can see them both; then drag pages from Explorer onto your page, to create links to each page.

Chapter 20

Creating a Discussion Group

By the End of This Chapter, You'll Be Able to...

- Build and maintain your own newsgroup-like discussion group
- Allow users to post and respond to messages about various topics
- Install a search page that allows users to search for specific information within the discussion area

First, What's a Discussion Group?

At your office, a "discussion group" probably consists of gallons of coffee and fascinating gossip. On an online service such as CompuServe or Microsoft Network, a discussion group is often called a *forum*, in order to give it a more professional-sounding name than "common gossip shared around the coffee machine."

A FrontPage *discussion group* is a close copy of an Internet newsgroup. By including a discussion group in your web, you can gather the opinions of users worldwide, and organize these opinions into a logical, concurrent sequence.

You can set up a discussion group as a way for clients to comment on the products you sell and seek help from other clients. Or you can create a discussion group for other people like yourself, who are starting up a new business, or working at home. You can also create a discussion group where fellow fishermen swap opinions about the one that got away. For any purpose—business or pleasure—discussion groups can be a lot of fun.

A FrontPage discussion group is made up of four parts:

Article The message (comment, or question) that a user creates and then leaves in the discussion group.

- ➤ A **submission form** page with which a user enters a new *article*.
- ➤ A **confirmation page** that allows the user to look over her new article before she officially submits it, giving her one last chance to stop the presses.
- ➤ A **table of contents** page that lists all articles in the discussion web in order.
- ➤ A **search form** that enables users to find individual messages based on their contents.

As an option, you can allow *threaded replies*, which allow users to comment on articles left by other users, forming a thread that can follow later. The *thread* here is the thread of the discussion, or the *logical order* in which the articles were first submitted. For example, one user might leave a question about how to deal with Japanese beetles on her roses. Another user might reply by stating that Japanese beetle traps work well. A third user, after following the thread leading to both of these messages, might add a comment that such traps only attract more beetles. By following a *thread*, a user can re-create the discussion in order and add comments or questions that follow the path of the discussion.

Creating a Discussion Group Web

You can add a discussion group to whatever web you're currently building. It'll form its own *branch* (a group of related web pages) that is separate from the main web.

You can, of course, create a new discussion group web, rather than adding it onto an existing web. For example, you might want to add an employee suggestions/problems web to your company's network. *Also, if you plan on restricting access to the discussion group, you must create it as a separate web.*

Here's what you do:

1. If you want to add this discussion web to an existing web, open the existing web in FrontPage Explorer. Once that's done, click the **New Web** button.

2. From the list that appears, choose **Discussion Web Wizard.** If you want to add this to an existing web, then select that option and click **OK**.
3. Click **Next>** to start the wizard.
4. Select the options you want to use in your discussion web and click **Next>**. The submission form is where users will write new articles, and without it, you can't have a discussion, so it's permanently checked.
5. Here you get a chance to "name" the discussion. Something descriptive such as "Sports Card Trading," "Employee Benefits," or "Indoor Gardening" will help to limit the topics of discussion. Anyway, enter a name and click **Next>**.
6. You have a choice of what data fields you'll be using throughout the discussion web. All articles will have their own *Subject*. If you choose to include a separate *Category*, you can organize all your articles by categories such as "Retirement Plan," "Medical Insurance," and "Hiring Policy." You can choose to have a *Product* field in place of a category if you're running a customer support web. Choose one of these three setups and click **Next>**.
7. You can allow all users to post an article to the discussion group by selecting **No** or only registered users by choosing **Yes**. To continue, click **Next>**. Restricting users only works if this web is a separate web, and not part of some bigger web. However, if this is part of a bigger web, and that web is restricted, then the discussion group part will be restricted too.
8. Choose how you want the Table of Contents (assuming that you added one to your discussion group web back in step 4) to sort articles—newest messages first, or oldest, and then click **Next>**.
9. If you added a TOC to your discussion group in step 4, then you can have it act as your home page. If this is a new web, this might be a great idea. If you added your discussion group to an existing web, this is a probably a *bad* idea. Make your selection and click **Next>**.
10. If you added a Search form to the discussion group, then you can control how much information you want to appear as the result of a search. If you've ever used a Web search engine such as Excite or Lycos, you're familiar with the idea of a *score*—an estimate of how well each article found matches the search criteria. Make your selections and click **Next>**.
11. Select a background pattern, as well as text and link colors for this web. (Your choices will not affect the main web, if there happens to be one.) Make your selections and click **Next>**.

12. You can choose to use frames in the discussion group if you like. Choose a setup and click **Next>**.
13. Whew! Breathe a sigh of relief and click **Finish**. FrontPage creates a discussion group web based on your selections.

Read This if You Created a Restricted Web

If you restricted your discussion group to registered users in step 7, there are a few more things you have to do to get it working correctly. Again, your discussion group must be its own web in order for you to restrict access to it.

When you click **Finish** and FrontPage creates the discussion web, the registration form page appears.

Restricting the use of your discussion web.

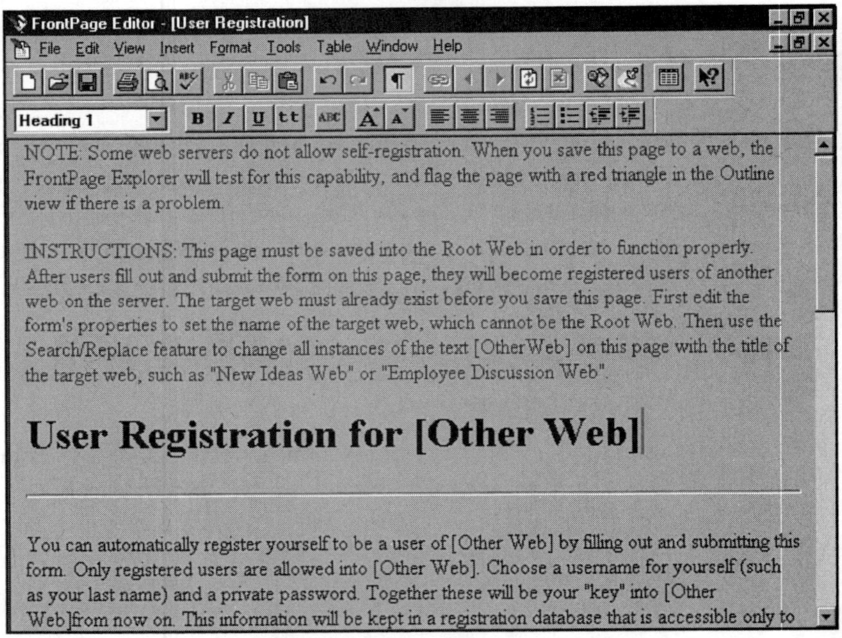

Ignore the form for now, and switch over to FrontPage Explorer. Then follow these steps:

1. Open the **Tools** menu and select **Permissions**.
2. On the Settings tab, select **Use unique permissions for this Web**.
3. Click **Apply** and then click the **End Users** tab.

4. Select **Registered users only** and click **OK**.

Now it's time to deal with the form. Switch back to FrontPage Editor and follow these steps:

1. Right-click anywhere inside the form and select **Form Properties**.
2. Click **Settings**.
3. Under **Web name**, type the name of your web.
4. Click **OK**; then click **OK** again.
5. Click back at the beginning of the text, open the **Edit** menu, and select **Replace**. Under **Find what**, type **[OtherWeb]**. Under **Replace with**, type the name of your web as you want it to appear on the registration page, such as Engineering Projects Web. Click **Find Next** to find the first instance of [OtherWeb], and then click **Replace All**. Click **Cancel** to dismiss the Replace box.

Before you save your page, you might want to customize the registration form using the information in Chapter 15. Make any changes you want, and then save the page to the **<Root Web>**, but don't close it.

You're almost done. You need to change the home page in the <Root Web> so that people can register for your discussion group. Return to FrontPage Explorer, and open the home page of the **<Root Web>**. Type some text for the link, and then use the **Edit**, **Link** command to create the link to the registration form page.

When a user tries to access your discussion group, he won't be able to. But by clicking the link in the home page of your <Root Web>, he can register properly. After a user registers, you need to retrieve his information and add him to the registration database. See Chapter 23 for help.

A Tour of the Discussion Web

Take a close look at the discussion web in FrontPage Explorer to see exactly what it is thou hast wrought. I added a discussion group to my Projects web; if you created a stand-alone discussion group web, then yours may look a bit different than this.

How does this discussion group web appear?

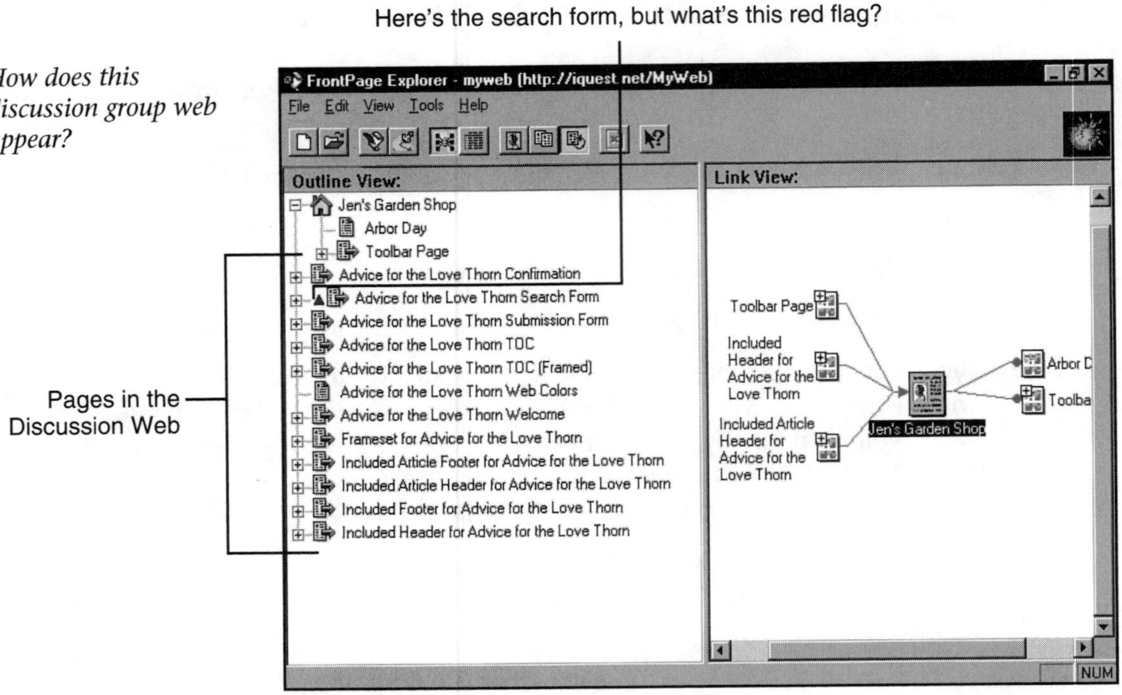

Notice that FrontPage has flagged the Search Form with a red triangle, which usually means that there's some kind of an error. How could there be an error in something that FrontPage created? The answer has to do with the data required for the Search Form to work. Since no one created any messages for this web yet, there are no linked pages for the Search Form to search through. Thus, an "error." Errors like this I could live with everyday.

The Welcome page serves as the "landing zone" through which other webs may link. If your discussion web uses frames, however, you'll want to make the Frameset page the "landing zone" instead.

How a User Sees the Discussion Web

Here's one example of how a user might view your discussion web. Notice that I chose to use frames in my web. In this layout, the top frame contains a table of contents where major topics will be listed (there aren't too many of these at first, but at least you get the idea). At the bottom is the Welcome page with links to the submission form and the Search page.

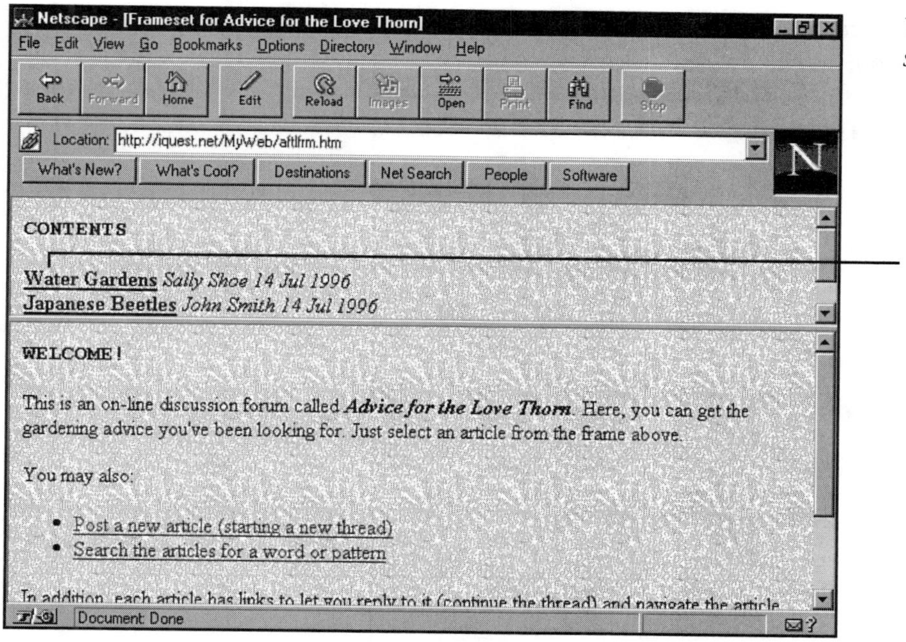

Want to discuss something?

Categorizing Your Categories

If you're using categories in your web, you'll probably notice they are very meaningfully entitled, "Category 0," "Category 1," and so on. Unless you really want your web to be a discussion of whole numbers, you'll want to change the names of these categories. Open the Submission Form, and right-click the Category drop-down list box. From the pop-up menu, select **Properties**. Highlight a category, click **Modify**, type in a new name, and click **OK**. Repeat this process to give the other categories a name. If you need more than five categories, you can add new ones by clicking the **Add** button.

The Discussion Bot

The job of maintaining a discussion web, once it's up and running, is relegated to the *Discussion* Bot. In Chapter 17, you learned how to use the Save Results Bot to save the information users type into your web forms. The Discussion Bot is, for all intents and purposes, the "save results bot" for discussion groups.

To configure the Discussion Bot, open the Submission Form page, and right-click the form. From the pop-up menu, select **Form Properties**. Make sure that **Discussion Bot** has been chosen from the **Form Handler** list. Click **Settings**. This brings up the Settings for Discussion Form Handler dialog box, which looks like this.

The Discussion bot, Part 1.

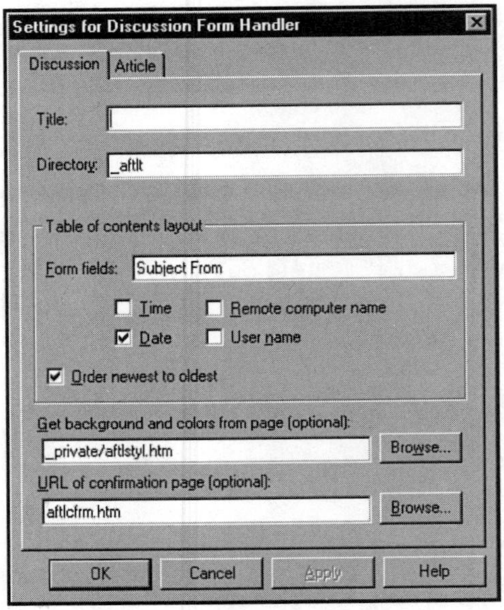

- Enter a **Title** for your discussion web. This title will automatically appear at opportune locations throughout the web, like a logo.
- Under **Directory** is the name of the directory in which the discussion group articles are stored. You can change this, but if you do, make sure you begin the directory name with an underscore (_) character, because that's how your host server will know to hide its contents from your users.
- Under **Form fields**, enter the names of the fields you want to appear in the TOC article listing. You can display the **Subject**, either **Category** or **Product** (depending on your setup), **From** (the originator of the article), and **Comments** (the article).

No Comments, Please

Do not include Comments in your TOC listing, unless you want to have the largest (and most unusable) Table of Contents page in the civilized world.

- You can include other fields in the Table of Contents page, such as: Time, Date, Remote computer name, and User name. *Remote computer name* may be important if your discussion group is operating on a company-wide *intranet* and you want to show the user's computer name on the network for e-mail purposes. *User name* may be important for e-mail purposes too, to distinguish the author's pseudonym ("From") from the name with which he logs on.
- Newsgroups typically list their messages newest first, oldest last. To list your articles the same way, check the box marked **Order newest to oldest**.
- The background, text, and link colors of your discussion web come from one web page, listed here in the **Get background and colors from page** field. If you attached this web to an existing web and you want to make the two the same, select a page from your main web to act as a "sample."
- When a user submits an article, the page listed in the **URL of confirmation page** field shows up, so they can confirm what they entered. You can create your own one instead and list it here.

If you click the **Article** tab in the Settings for Discussion Form Handler dialog box, you'll see this.

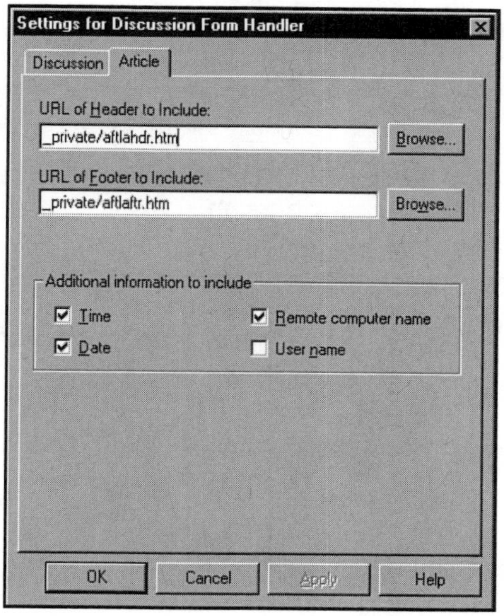

The Discussion Bot, Part 2.

The Discussion tab provides options that allow you to determine how your users will submit articles to your discussion group. It also controls the way your users will *view* those articles. You see, when an article is submitted, it's placed in its own web page. FrontPage makes that web page look like the others in the discussion group, by taking the colors from the page listed in the **Get background and colors from page** field, on the Discussion tab. But there are some other things you may want to change as well to make your article pages look even more like the other pages in your web:

- If you want to make a special header or footer for your article pages, then create either or both, and save them as *separate HTML pages*. You can then enter the URLs for the header and footer web pages in the **URL of Header to Include** and **URL of Footer to Include** fields, respectively.
- Under **Additional information to include**, you can choose extra items that you want the reader of an article to see. For example, the date when the article was created might be a nice thing to include.

The Search Bot

One of the most important pages you can include in a long, long discussion group web is a *Search page*, which allows users to find an article based on its contents. If you were thoughtful to include a Search page in your Discussion group web, then it'll look like this.

Your search is over.

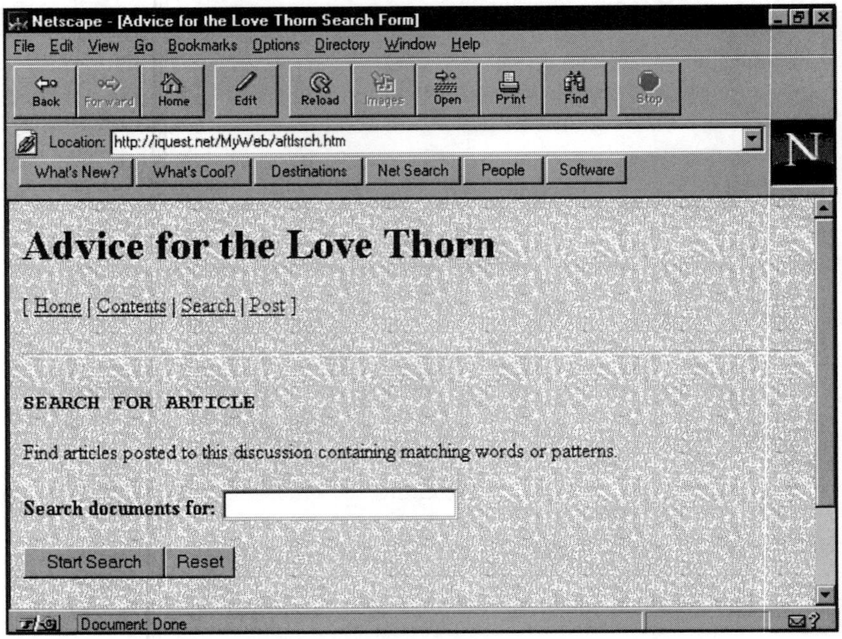

How the User Searches for Information

It's nice to know that FrontPage's search system is endowed with a fair degree of logic. Suppose a user wants to locate all the articles on your web that mention Pete Rose. If he types **Pete Rose** on the search line, then FrontPage will only pull up articles that contain *both* the word **Pete** and the word **Rose**. It won't list articles that contain only the word Pete, or only the word Rose.

However, suppose the user wants to see only articles about Pete Rose while he was playing for the Reds, not the Phillies. The user would enter this instead: **(Pete Rose) and Reds.** Pete Rose is contained within parentheses, so it's treated as a single word, **Pete Rose**. The **and** is a *keyword*, and it tells FrontPage to search for all articles that contain **Pete Rose** and the word **Reds**.

Suppose the reader is interested in two famous Cincinnati Reds, Rose and Johnny Bench. He could enter: **(Pete Rose) or (Johnny Bench)** and get articles relating to *either or both* players. He could make this infinitely complex, by asking for articles on Rose or Bench, which don't mention Marge Schott. He'd enter: **(Pete Rose) or (Johnny Bench) and Reds not (Marge Schott).** FrontPage would pull up only those articles that mentioned either Pete Rose or Johnny Bench (or both) in the context of the Reds and would ignore articles that simply mentioned roses or benches. It would exclude, however, any article where Marge Schott appears. FrontPage recognizes *and*, *or*, and *not* as keywords.

Configuring the Search Bot

You can customize the way your discussion group searches its articles by configuring the *Search* bot. To do that, open the Search page. Then right-click the **Search** form and select **Properties**. I won't bore you with too many details here, since I covered the Search Bot thoroughly in Chapter 17, but you might want to change the fields that appear in the listing of articles that appears after a successful search. Under **Additional information to display in the search results list**, you can select some additional fields to display, such as *File Date* and *File Size*, which tell the reader how long a particular article is. *Score* is a relative number used to rate how closely a particular article fits a user's query. You'll want to include the score only if your discussion group grows so large that a single query is likely to pull a lot of articles from which the reader must choose.

Moderating a Discussion Group

Some Internet aficionados liken the idea of moderating a discussion, chat, or news group to censorship. However, sometimes moderation is needed, in order to ensure that each member has an equal say and an equal hearing—and perhaps, to remove the most offensive discussions from the sight of the general public.

Moderating a discussion often means having to edit its content. FrontPage doesn't give you any special way to accomplish this, and yet, as you'll soon see, it's simple.

First, to view an article (and edit it if needed), open it within the FrontPage Editor. You'll need to use the **File**, **Open File** command, since the articles do not appear in your web. Anyway, you'll find the articles in the **FrontPage Webs/Content/*DiscussionWeb*/_aftlt** directory (where ***DiscussionWeb*** is replaced with the name of your discussion group web). You'll find that each article has been given an eight-digit number for a file name, starting with 00000001.htm. Once you open the article in FrontPage, you can make any changes to it as needed and then save it.

Act Now!

The way the FrontPage discussion group system works with every new article "posted" to the web immediately, the moment someone writes an article and clicks **Post Article**, everyone else on your Web server can see it. If you need to change the contents of an article for any reason, you need to be quick about it. But since it's an HTML file, you can edit it easily enough through FrontPage Editor.

If you're really worried about the comments your users may leave within the discussion group, you can restrict the web. (See the earlier discussion in this chapter for help; and check out Chapter 23.)

If you need to delete an article, you might be thinking that you can simply open the Windows Explorer and send the nasty thing to the Recycle Bin. However simple that sounds, it won't work, because when a user posts an article, it's immediately entered into the TOC list. So even if you delete the file, the reference to it will still be there. However, if some article is truly offensive, (or it reveals some company secret), you can go into the message, delete the offensive text, and replace it with a message like, **Contents deleted on authority of moderator**, or something equally official. (Contact your local intelligence agency for tips on how to delete something and make it sound official.)

The Least You Need to Know

Here's what you should remember about discussion group discussions:

- FrontPage discussion groups are similar to Internet newsgroups.
- A discussion group includes a submission form with which a user enters a new article.

- An article is a message (a comment or a question) that a user can submit to a discussion group.
- Typically, a user can search the discussion group for the article she is looking for.
- Optionally, you can allow your users to reply to articles left on the discussion group.
- When viewed in order, the original article and its replies create a *thread* of the discussion, which a user can follow.
- You can configure the Discussion and Search bots to customize your discussion group web.

Part 6
Publishing and Maintaining Your Web Site

Just like your house, your web site requires constant maintenance. Sure, there's no lawn to mow, but there are other tasks such as verifying your links, adding and deleting files for downloading, and authorizing new users.

Of course, before you can make changes to your masterpiece, you need to publish the thing first, which you learn how to do in this part.

Chapter 21

Publishing Your Creation on the Web

By the End of This Chapter, You'll Be Able to...

- Look at your web site with a Web browser
- Put your site on the Web
- Copy other people's web pages
- Keep other people from copying your web pages

So far, you've been designing your site on your own computer, where only you can see it. Creating a web site that only you can see is just wasting your time. By taking your site and putting it out on the Web where everyone can see it, you won't just be wasting your time, but *other people's* time as well! The World Wide Web is the most efficient waster of time ever developed by mankind, and the addition of your site can only make it better.

Viewing your Masterpiece

Before you unleash your creation on the world, you should try to see it as other people would. Until now, you've been looking at your web pages through the FrontPage Editor. Visitors to your page aren't going to use the Editor to look at your pages unless they plan to steal your page, change it slightly, and put it up as their own work—and if they are, then phooey on them!

Instead, the visitor will look at your site using a *Web browser*, a piece of software such as Netscape Navigator or Internet Explorer designed to display web pages. The designers of HTML have put in careful controls to make sure that your pages will look the same, no matter what brand of Web browser the visitor uses. The designers of the browsers, however, go out of their way to add special features to their products to make sure that their browser can display parts of your page better (or at least differently) from other browsers, making the browser seem more deluxe than the competition.

Some People Are Just Troublemakers!

It may not make much sense that the designers of the HTML standards and the designers of the browsers are working at cross purposes, but it makes even less sense once you realize that often *they are exactly the same people!* There's one for Mr. Ripley, huh?

Anyway, you should check to see what your site looks like using at least one Web browser before you unleash it on the unsuspecting populace. Your page may have things that look fine in the editor but look strange on the Web browser. Ideally, you should look at the site with as many different Web browsers as you can.

The most popular Web browser (and, thus, the one it is most important to test with) is the powerful Netscape Navigator. Navigator is very popular with students because it is free for students—and students are cheap. Gaining quickly in popularity is Microsoft Internet Explorer, which is popular with everyone because it's free for everyone—and everyone is cheap. Following those in popularity is Spry Mosaic and an uncountable number of other graphical browsers (browsers that can display images). Finally, there are nongraphical browsers, ones that cannot display pictures, such as Lynx. Lynx is also used a lot on colleges because it can be used from cheap terminals that do not display graphics—and colleges are cheap.

Once you have one Web browser, getting the others is pretty easy—just download them from the Web! There's a good listing of sites to download browsers from at **http://www.yahoo.com/Computers_and_Internet/Internet/World_Wide_ Web/Browsers/** but you should be aware that this includes browsers for other operating systems besides Windows.

Is Your Page Bug-Bitten?

Some manufacturers will offer two different versions of their browser, a *released* or *current* version (the one people are supposed to use) and a *beta* version. The beta version is the next version of their product that they're still testing. Betas are full of big new features and even bigger new bugs. Testing your site with the beta version (in addition to the released version) lets you see how badly the new bugs mangle your site.

Getting your File Loaded

Start up the browser you want to view your site with, either by pressing the **Start** button and selecting your file from the menu, or by finding it in the File Explorer and double-clicking the file's icon. When the browser appears, pull down the **File** menu. Depending on the browser, the command your looking for may be **Open**, **View File**, or **Open File**. (If you're using an error-filled beta release, it may be **Open Flie**.) A dialog box will appear; either it will be a file navigator, or there will be some button (marked **Open File** or **Browse** or, in the case of a beta, perhaps **Bowser**) that you will click and then a file navigator will appear.

With the file navigator up, navigate over to the directory where you keep your FrontPage Webs (C:/FrontPage Webs, unless you picked another disk or directory when you installed FrontPage, or installed it over a network). Double-click the **Content** folder to open that up, and then click the folder with the name of the web that you want to test. A list of directories and of web page files appear. Double-click the icon for the file that you want to see, and the Web browser will display that page.

Once you have one page displayed in the browser, you can test out the internal links (and, with a connection to the Internet, external links) and go from page to page, seeing how everything looks. Now is a good time to glory in what you have created! Sit back with a bowl full of Jujubees and make satisfied chomping noises as you gaze over your finely honed web site. Be sure to keep an eye out for anything that doesn't look right, and brush your teeth afterward.

Browse the Whole Day Away!

Just leave your browser running all the time when you're using FrontPage. That way, checking your pages while you're working on them is only a couple of mouse maneuvers away!

Shoving It onto the Web

The time has come to share your joy with the world (although you can hog the Jujubees for yourself). Exactly how you do this, however, depends on the server that you will hold your web site. If this server has the software to support the FrontPage server extensions, then you can use FrontPage's **Copy Web** command to copy the pages from your hard disk (or local network server) to the server people will access it from.

Unfortunately (for both you and for Microsoft), most servers do not have the FrontPage extensions, although it seems likely that more and more will in the future. Then again, the makers of other web site authoring programs want the servers to support their extensions as well. Eventually, there may be so many different software extensions on the server's hard disk that there won't be any room left for web pages!

If your server doesn't support them, the people who run the server can you what you need to do to publish pages on the server. Don't worry—you can still use the web pages that you developed! All that time has not been for naught!

If your server *does* support the FrontPage extensions (you lucky devil, you!), then transferring the files is easy. First, connect onto the network (either Internet or your intranet). If your computer is always hooked to the network, then you don't have to do anything (although you may, if you want to, sit around whistling for a few seconds). If you're not sure what to do to connect to the Internet, just start up your Web browser and view a page on the World Wide Web; however you do this, your computer sets up your connection to the Internet.

Once you connect, start up the FrontPage Explorer, and load up (using the **File, Open Web** command) that gorgeous web site that has now become part of your life. Pull down the **File** menu and select the **Copy Web** command.

A dialog box appears, with fields for **Destination Web Server** and **Destination Web Name** (see the next illustration). Type the name of the server into the first field and the name for your site into the second. For example, if your web site address is **http://www.jujubees.com/fan/**, the Web server name is **www.jujubees.com** and the Web name is **fan**. When you enter the Web server name, you may be asked for your user name and password that will let you get onto that server. (After all, if we let just *anybody* place a web site *anywhere*, the Internet would soon be pure chaos—instead of mere intense anarchy!)

Click the **OK** button, and FrontPage will try to work its Web copying magic.

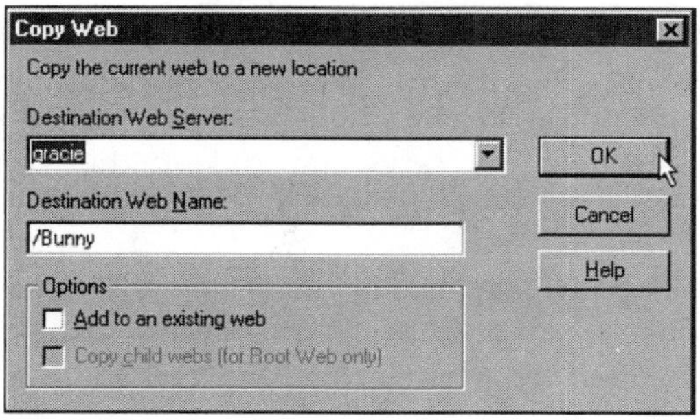

The Copy Web dialog box has separate fields for the Server name you are copying to and the name that the Web will have on that server.

If you're one of those people who is always waiting for something to go wrong, then wait no more! The time has come! If anything is going to go wrong, now is the time. There are a bunch of different possible error messages, many filled with the secret techno-nerd language that mere mortals are not meant to understand. The real problem is probably one of a few simple things:

- You aren't hooked up to the network.
- The server can't be found. (You probably mistyped the server name. Those Jujubees make your fingers sticky.)
- The server can be found, but isn't answering. The server is probably too busy to answer you, or it's disconnected for maintenance. Try again later.
- The server answers, but doesn't have the FrontPage extensions needed. You have to find another way to copy the files onto the server.
- You aren't on the list of people permitted to put files on this server. Either get the server's administrator to put you on the list, or find someone on the list and get him to do the work. (There are advantages to not having permission!)
- There is already a web site with the same name on the server. If you're just trying to update the existing web site, click the **Add to an existing Web** option in the **Copy Web** dialog box and try clicking **OK** again.
- The server doesn't like the Web name. It may be too long or have punctuation in it that the server doesn't like. Computers are a finicky lot—type in a shorter, less complicated name, and cross your fingers that it is accepted. (It's important to cross your fingers *after* you type, not *while!*)

If you stare closely at the geekspeak in the error message, you can probably figure out which of these it is.

If you don't get an error message within about 20 seconds, you can breathe a sigh of relief. It should be easy sailing from here on in. Copying your web pages could take some time, depending on how many files you have, how large they are, how fast your network connection is, how busy the network and server are, and whether you've been making burnt sacrifices to the proper deities of computerdom.

Once the transfer is complete, a dialog box pops up telling you that your web pages has been successfully copied. Click the **OK** button, and this affirmation of your success will go away—but the satisfaction of a job well done will still linger in your heart.

Copyright Means Copying Is Wrong

Once you publish your web site, it's out for everyone to see, which means that if you have something on there that you're not supposed to, now is when someone can find it. You can be careful, or you can surround yourself with a lot of lawyers. I know that I'd rather be careful (10,000 lawyer jokes can't be wrong).

It's easy to accidentally violate someone's copyright. With all of the text and images that go into a big web site, it only takes one wrong piece to get you into trouble.

The surest way to be safe is to create every piece of your web page yourself. Design all your own images, write all the text, and there's no one else who can complain. Unless you're Leonardo da Vinci and Judith Krantz rolled into one, however, this is not the best way to get a great web site.

Failing that, you should make sure you have permission to use everything on your site. Just because you can easily copy a background graphic from someone else's site doesn't mean you're allowed to. If you ask permission (filled with "pleases" and "thank yous" and all those other things your mother taught you about), the person who owns that web site will probably let you use the background. If they don't, it's probably because they invested effort or money into getting a unique background for their page, and it's their right to say no.

Even things that you think your company has the right to may be a problem. There may be a great painting in your lobby, depicting Queen Victoria, Elvis, and John Wayne on the finest black velvet, and you may want to use a picture of that painting as your backdrop. However, just because you bought the right to the masterpiece doesn't mean you bought the rights to reproduce it. You may need to pay the artist a separate fee, as well as possibly a fee to the estates of The King and The Duke. (Queen Victoria is royalty that you can use without royalties!)

What this all boils down to is: Get permission. If you're not sure if you have permission, get a lawyer. If possible, get a cute one!

Snarfing Other People's Pages

Now that you know why you really shouldn't steal stuff from other people's web sites, I'm going to show you how to do it anyway. Maybe, you have permission to use something from someone else's site. Maybe, you're not going to use what you copy on your site, but your just making a copy for your own reference, so you can see how it was made or use it as the basis for a template. Or maybe you are simply nefarious!

The easiest sites to gobble up are ones you have author-level permission for on servers with FrontPage extensions. Use the **File, Open Web** command, selecting their server and Web name to open up their site in FrontPage. Once you have it open, use the **File, Copy Web** command to copy it, selecting your local server as the **Destination Web Server** and some recognizable name as the **Destination Web Name**. Now, the Web is yours, to manage, manipulate, and mangle to your heart's content!

Important Import

Grabbing pages from a server without the FrontPage extensions is a bit trickier. FrontPage doesn't want to deal with those sites, so you might as well close the program and let it rest up while you do your work. It's a hard-working program; it has earned a respite.

Instead, use your Web browser to grab these pages. That's right, a Web browser isn't just a Peeping Tom that peers into other people's web sites—it's also a sneak thief that can steal those sites for you!

Surf the Web to the site you want to snarf (this is called *snarfsurfing*, or at least it should be). Click the browser's **File** menu and select the **Save As** or **Save Page** command. You'll probably want to put it into a new directory. That saves the page's HTML file. To steal picture files, right-click the pictures, and you should see a **Save Picture As** or **Save Image** command. To get the background file, check the **File** menu for a **Save Background** command (some browsers don't have this feature).

Once the files are on your hard disk, you can add the HTML files or graphics to your web, making them look like they're yours. Start FrontPage and open the web you want to add them to. Pull down the **File** menu and select the **Import** command. (Since you've stolen these pages, it's not so much *importing* as *smuggling*, I suppose.) A dialog box pops up. Click the **Add File** button, and a file navigator pops up. Navigate to the files that you stole, select them, and click the **OK** button. These files will now be listed in the dialog box, highlighted.

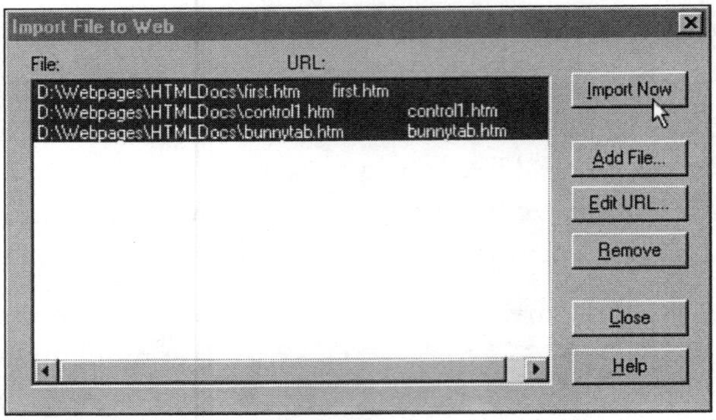

The Import File to Web dialog box has columns (jagged though they may be) for the file name and the URL.

Click the **Import Now** button, and the files will be added to your web. Snicker a sinister little snicker, because you've gotten away with grand theft file! You can now link to these files, add the images to your pages, or just sit around gloating about your evil deed!

Protecting Your Own Pages from People Like You

Now that you know the secrets of being a page and image thief, you may come to a scary realization: these secrets aren't secret at all! Why, they are right here in this book for everyone to read! Now you *could* go around buying up all the copies of this book that you can find, to keep this information from falling into the wrong hands. We here at Que would support this attempt, as we would keep printing more copies until you went broke while we're out cruising the Riviera on the royalty money.

The other course of action is much more sensible, although not nearly so profitable for us. If you take care in several ways, you can reduce the chance that someone will steal your stuff or will see something that you don't want them to see.

They Can't See What Isn't There

If you don't want people to see your file, don't put it on the World Wide Web! The World Wide Web is there in order to give people access to files. If you don't want kids to eat cookies, don't put the cookies on the table with a big sign saying "Don't eat these cookies!" Even putting your files on an intranet is pretty pointless if you don't want people to see them.

Nobody Finds the Missing Link

If you want to have a page (or even a whole web) that only the people that you tell about it can get to, don't have any links to that page (or web). Let the people who need to find it know the URL for it, and they'll be able to find it—but most other people will never even suspect it's there. It won't be *impossible* for people who are looking for it to find it—but people usually don't go looking for things that they don't know exist.

Let 'Em Know the Pages Are Yours

A lot of online theft is innocent; people copy pages and post them elsewhere because they think that no one cares, that the whole reason the page is on the Web is to get distributed. Of course, when they start using a copy of your page, you can't update it with any important new information or corrections. That alcoholic gelatin recipe that you corrected just one day after accidentally using the phrase "quarts of vodka" instead of "shots of vodka" might be reposted elsewhere, causing jiggly drunks for years to come.

The best way of handling this is simply to post your feelings on the page. A little notice at the bottom of the page, "Copyright 1996 Unsolid Inebriants Incorporated. Do not copy without permission." could save you a lot of hassles. (Even if you don't put a copyright notice on the page, you still own the copyright to the page, but putting the notice on serves as notice that You Mean Business.)

You can put a copyright notice on an image itself, but that can be a distraction, reducing the effect of the image (particularly, if it's just a small decoration; you'd quickly end up with a page that is nothing but a bunch of copyright notices!). The page copyright notice should help to warn people that you consider the site yours.

You can also store text messages in GIF files; the text won't be visible to people viewing the pictures on the Web. However, if someone copies it and tries to claim the image was hers, no one will believe her once you show that even her copies of the image have your copyright message built into them. (You'll need a good GIF editor, such as the GIF Construction Set from Alchemy Mindworks Inc., to put that text in the file.)

Even a General Needs a Private Directory

Every web created and published by FrontPage includes a directory named **_private**. This is a handy little hideaway, since people cannot view its contents with Web browsers.

If you want to, you can hide all sorts of wonderful stuff in there, and thrill to the knowledge that your plans for global domination or your Grandma's brownie recipe is right there on a Web server and no one can see it! It also has more practical uses, allowing you to keep files associated with Web on the Web. You might have templates you use for creating pages there, or a file of notes to remind you how the trickier parts of the site work. And there's no law saying that you can't have both relevant stuff *and* brownie recipes there.

To put a file into the private directory, first you have to include it in your web, either by building it there or importing it in. Then, select the file (either in the Outline View or in the Link View). Pull down the **Edit** menu and select the **Properties** command. The Properties dialog box appears.

The URL field (for example, brownies.htm) will appear highlighted. Tap the **Home** key on your keyboard to put the cursor in front of the first letter of the URL. Type **_private/**, so that the field now reads something like **_private/brownies.htm**. Click the **OK** button (*Okay?* It's *great!* Where's the **Great** button?) and that file will now be filed in the private directory.

Be careful that you don't put any files that the web visitor needs (such as pages that other pages link to), because as far as the visitor is concerned, that page isn't there!

The Least You Need to Know

- You should test your web site using a Web browser (or several) before putting it out where everyone can see it.
- Some servers have the FrontPage extensions software running on them. You can install your web on one of those servers using the Explorer's **File, Copy Web** command.
- Most servers don't have the FrontPage extensions on them. You will need to ask the people who run that server how to install your site on their server.
- You have the ability to copy anything you see on someone else's web site, although you may not have the legal right to.
- Everyone else has the ability to copy anything they see on your site.
- FrontPage webs have a directory named **_private** that people can't see into with their Web browsers.

Chapter 22

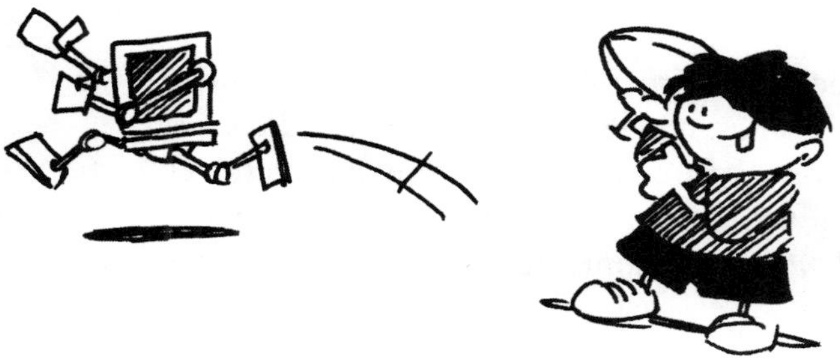

Playing Around with Your Web Site

By the End of This Chapter, You'll Be Able to...

- Check and fix your links
- Move and remove pages
- Change the name of a page or a web

You've built all the pages you planned, linked them together, tested them out, and put them out on the Internet for everyone to see. Does that mean that you are truly done with your project? Of course not! Building a web site is like building a model train layout; even though you might get everything working, you will still want to keep adding new tracks, new buildings, and adding more cars. It soon stops being a project, and starts being a way of life!

And, you can't just let someone else take care of it for you. You know that when you turn your back, he's going to take your two favorite engines and see what happens when he sends them toward each other at full speed down the same track.*

*(Answer: they crash into each other.)

In this chapter, you'll learn about all the tools you need to take that corporate technical support web site you've just developed and slowly but surely turn it into www.model-railroad.com!

Verifying Links

Links make the World Wide Web the special thing that it is. After all, without links, a Web page would just be a document. With links, it gives you the chance to click a selected phrase and find out, in mere seconds, that the web designer misspelled the URL of the link, linked to a valuable resource that has gone away, or linked to a page she intended to build but never got around to! Now that's something that no regular document can give you!

Now you, as a conscientious web developer, would never want to have links that go nowhere, right? (Although, it would be good revenge for all those links that you've followed in the past that never went anywhere...hmmm....) The proper thing to do is to test all your links and make sure they work.

FrontPage makes testing this easy. Load the web you want to test into FrontPage Explorer (using the **File, Open Web** command). Pull down the **Tools** menu and select the **Verify Links** command. FrontPage will find all the links on your site and will start testing all of the *internal* links (the links that go from one part of your web to another part of the same web).

When it's done testing, a display dialog box appears listing all of the bad internal links (links that are supposed to go to a page that isn't there, or go to a target that isn't on the page) and all of the *external* links (links to other web sites). The bad links are marked with a red dot and the word **Broken**, while the external links are marked with a yellow dot and a question mark, to show that they haven't been tested. The URLs being linked to and the name and URL of the page the link is on are listed.

Do the External Links Link?

Now, you know which of the internal links work, but you have to check the external links, which are more likely to be a problem. After all, the computer helped you set up the internal links, but you had to type in the URLs. As a mere human, you are far more likely to make little mistakes such as typos; the efficiency of the computer allows it to make whopping huge mistakes rather than teeny ones.

In order to test the external links, you will need to connect to the network (Internet or intranet) that the linked-to servers are on. If you're in an office situation where you are always linked to the network, then you're fine. If you have to dial in or otherwise connect to the network, do so. (If you aren't sure how to connect, just open up your Web browser and do whatever you do to see any web page that's out on the network. If you can see the page, you're obviously connected to the network, and you can continue.)

Click the **Verify Links** dialog box's **Verify** button. FrontPage will go down the list, trying to link to each of the external sites. (This may take a while, particularly if you have a lot of external links.) If a green dot and the word **OK** appears next to the link on the list, it means that the computer got through fine. If a red dot and the word **Broken** appears, it means that the page couldn't be retrieved. If a blue dot appears, it means you've splashed Kool-Aid onto your monitor.

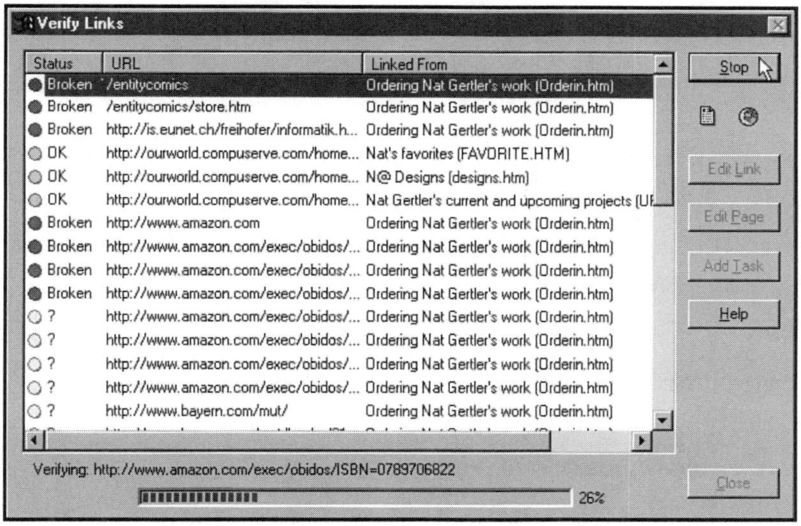

Here, FrontPage is verifying external links. Green dots indicate good links, red are bad links, and yellow are links that haven't been tested yet. The meter at the bottom shows what portion have been tested.

Once the test is complete, you can disconnect from the network. If you have all green dots, it means your links are all properly connected. If you have some red dots, then that just makes it more colorful! Not willing to accept that analysis of the situation? Fine, then; read on.

The Information You Have May Be Wrong

Actually, just because you have a red dot, it doesn't mean that your link is really bad. It might be a bad link, or it might be that the server you're linked to is not running at the moment, or that it is incredibly busy. If you think a link is correct, double-check it later. (If the server is usually busy or usually down, though, your link may be just as useless as if the page you're linking to wasn't there at all.)

However, a green dot just means that you've linked to *something*—it may not be the thing that you wanted to link to! You may have thought that linking to www.peta.org would link you to the People for the Ethical Treatment of Animals home page, when it really links you to something called People Eating Tasty Animals. More likely, you will have linked to where a particular web site used to be, but now all that's there is a page saying **This page has been moved to** and then a link to the new URL.

Because of this, it's a good idea to check external links by actually using your web site and following the links, when you have the chance. It's also a good idea to recheck your external links about once a month, to make sure that your links aren't like what your address book becomes after a few years: a list of places where people you know used to live.

Fixing Links

The right way to fix links is to fry them in a pan with just a little bit of butter. Mmm! Nothing like fresh sausage in the morning!

Oh, wait, you want to fix the broken web links. Well, that's just about as easy and much less fattening.

1. On the **Verify Links** list, select the broken link you want to fix.
2. Click the **Edit Page** button. The FrontPage editor appears, with the page with the link on it.
3. Click the link text (or image hotspot) to select it.
4. Click the **Edit Link** button (the one that looks like a piece of chain).

The Edit Link dialog box appears, just like it did when you first entered the link.

Now, you have a chance to enter your link all over again. It's like being born anew, and you can avoid making the mistakes that you made before! That's right, you can make brand new *different* mistakes! (Or, I suppose, you can get it right.)

Remember that this dialog box has different tabs you can use to make a link to either a bookmark on the current page (the **Open Pages** tab), a different page in the web (the **Current Web** tab), an external link (the **World Wide Web** tab), or to a page that you're going to build into the web but you haven't yet (the **New Page** tab). The **Browse** button on the **Current Web** tab lets you pick easily from the list of all the pages in this web. Using the **New Page** tab lets you link to a page that isn't there yet, which means that the link will still be broken, until you create that page.

Once you enter the corrected link, click the **OK** button to return to the editor. Click the **Save** button to save your changes, then click the **Close** button to leave the editor.

Remember that this method of changing links works no matter how you opened the editor. If you already know that you made a mistake with a link, you don't have to wait until the computer has figured it out as well. Just double-click that page in the Link View, which will bring that page up in the editor. This way, the computer never figures out that you are capable of error!

What's That Edit Links Button?

You may have noticed an **Edit Links** button on the Verify Links dialog box. Clicking this will give you a less friendly link editor, since it doesn't have all the different tabs or the capability to list your existing pages. It does, however, let you fix the same wrong link on a bunch of different pages at once—which is great for people who, while they make mistakes, are at least consistent about it!

Recalculating Links

If you have several people working on the same web at the same time, the changes can become messy. You may have found a broken internal link and fixed it by changing the link. Meanwhile, the second person working on the web may have seen the same problem and fixed it by changing the name of the page that was supposed to be linked to, so that it has the same URL as the link actually pointed to. Meanwhile, the third person working on the web, well, he was asleep. (After all, at any given moment, every third person is asleep. I guess he's just lazy.)

Because of the complications that can occur when several people work on the same thing simultaneously, it's a good idea to have a command that lets you know what the current status is. This command is the **Recalculate Links** command, which you can find on the FrontPage Explorer's **Tools** menu.

When you use this command, the server (not your computer, unless your computer is also the server) handles the job. It regenerates any pages that are based on other pages. For example, if you have one page contained in another page through the use of an Include bot, the server will put the latest version of the included page into the main page.

If you have a text index created by a Search bot, the server will update this index. After all, what could be worse than having an index full of references to pages that aren't there any more?*

The most important thing about the Recalculate Links command is that it updates your FrontPage Explorer displays to reflect all of the changes that everyone else has made to the Web. Because of this, it's a good idea to recalculate your links several times a day.

A large web might take several minutes to fully recalculate, particularly on a busy server. This is a bad thing if you're sitting there waiting for it to be completed, but it's a good thing if you want an excuse to get up and get a cup of hot coffee and a handful of Jujubees. *(Caution: Be careful not to get a cup of Jujubees and a handful of hot coffee!)*

Reorganizing a Web Site

There are many good reasons to reorganize your web site. You may want to add improvements or get rid of old material. You might want to put the files into carefully separated subdirectories where you can find them easily, rather than having them all in one big directory. Or you may simply want to get out of doing less attractive work. ("Fisner, come here, I need someone to help me weigh my ear wax collection!" "Sorry, boss, but it's absolutely imperative that I reorganize the web site! Otherwise, it will merely be... organized!")

FrontPage has tools to let you add pages, delete pages, move files, and other reorganizational procedures.

Adding Pages

Adding pages is something you've already learned how to do. Part 2 of this book showed you how to build a new page using the Editor and include it into your site. Chapter 19 showed you how to add a page that you've created (or stolen from) somewhere else, using the **File, Import** command.

Preparing to Delete Pages

Deleting pages is a messier business, which is as it should be. Remember when you created that page? You were so full of hope for it; it seemed so full of promise. "This is," you thought, "the finest web page that ever there was." You built many links to it, and many links from it. But, that was then; this is now. Now, some other page is exciting your imagination, and the old page is to be cast off like yesterday's news. For shame, for shame!

*(Answer: getting your foot stuck in an elevator door when the elevator is on its way up.)

It must be done. Deleting the web page is easy; it's all those links that are the real problem. If you just delete the pages, all the links that you had to it will be broken. Worse yet, there may be pages that you could only have gotten to from the page you're deleting. If you delete the page, you will be cutting off all connections to those pages, and people can't find them.

To take care of this problem, select the page you want to delete on the Outline View. This will make it the center of the Link View, so you can see all the pages that link to it (on the left) and from it (on the right).

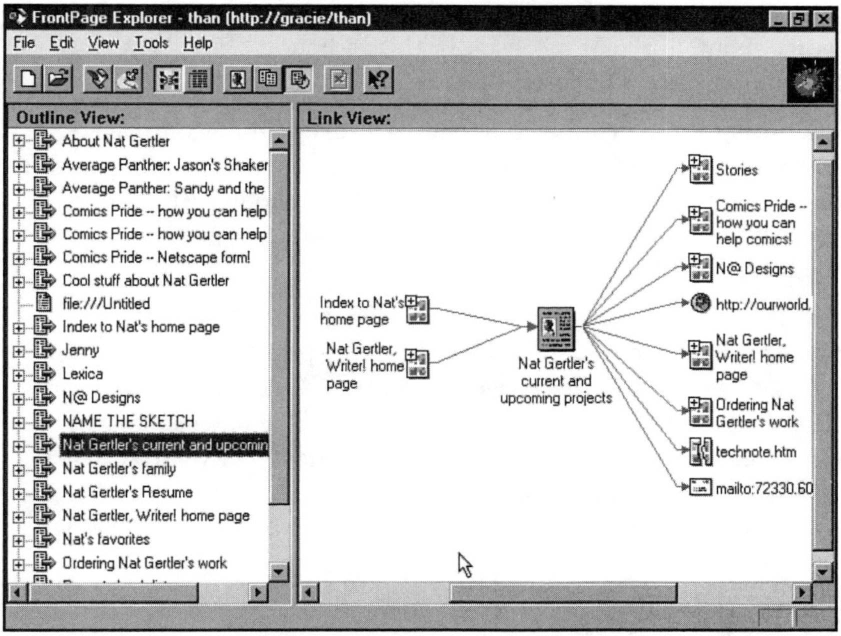

In this link view, you see two pages that have links to the current page, and eight links away from the page. The "broken page" icon next to technote.htm indicates a link to a page that has been deleted.

1. Double-click the icon for the first of the pages linking to the page you want to delete. The page will appear in the FrontPage Editor.
2. Select the link, whether it is in the text or a hotspot on an image.
3. Click the **Edit Link** button. The Edit Link dialog box appears.
4. Click the **Clear** button to remove the link; then click the **OK** button to close the dialog box.
5. Check the text to make sure it makes sense without the link. If the text just says **Click here to go to the most fantabulous page ever!**, then the text is useless without the link. Select the text and click the **Cut** button to get rid of it.

6. Once you edit out the link, click the **Save** button to save the changes; then click the **Close** button to leave the editor.

If you reselect the page you're going to delete in the Outline View, it will be redrawn in the Link View, and you'll now see one less link to it. Repeat this process until you remove all the links (or come to a change of heart and decide that you're going to give your beloved page a reprieve!)

The next step is to check the pages that linked to the deleted page. Expand the to-be-deleted pages entry in the Outline View by clicking the plus sign. If there is no plus sign (and the entry isn't already expanded,) then you have nothing to worry about! (Well, you still have things to worry about, like your mortgage or this addiction to Jujubees you seem to be developing, but they don't have anything to do with this situation.)

Click the Outline View entry for the first linked-to page. The diagram for this page appears in the Link View, and you can see if the page you're deleting is the only page that links to it. If it is, people won't be able to get to this page, so you should either get rid of this page, too (it's a virtual massacre!) or build a link to it from another page. Repeat this for all the pages in the list.

There's one more thing that you have to watch out for, and that's where you have a group of pages that you can reach from each other, or from the page you're about to delete, but in no other way. If page A links to page B and page B links back to page A, both pages are still linked to, but there's no way to get there. It's like having a road between two cities on an island. Even though there are roads into the city and roads out of the city, if you blow up the bridge to the island, no cars can get there! (Unless you have a ferry, but then the whole analogy becomes a mess! That's why you should never bring boats into analogies.)

Dead Pages Don't Need Pictures

If you're getting rid of a page, and there are images that are only on that page, there's no reason to keep them around. Unused images just sit around your web site, taking up space, and making fun of the other, hard-working images. To find out which images aren't used elsewhere, make sure that the **Links to Images** button is pushed in. Entries for all the images on that page will appear attached to that page in the Outline View.

Select the entry for the first image, and that entry shows up in the List View. If there's only one page connected to it, you know that this image isn't used anywhere else. Pull down the **Edit** menu and select the **Delete** command. A Confirm Delete dialog box appears, asking if you're sure you want to delete this image. Click the **Yes** button, and the image will disappear faster than Milli Vanilli.

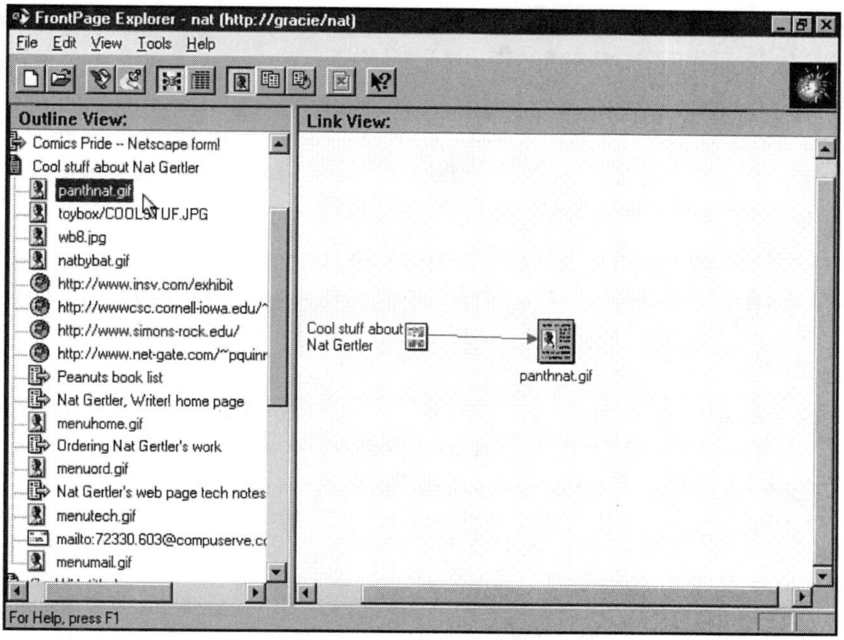

This poor image is only on one page. If you delete that page, then no one will want it around.

The Page Is Always the Last to Go

Now that you have all the links and images worked out, it's time to get rid of the page. Select the page, pull down the **Edit** menu, and choose the **Delete** command. A dialog box appears, asking if you're sure you want to delete the file. It's not too late to click **No** and save the life of a poor, helpless page that never did anyone any harm—but you'll probably click **Yes** and remove the page from existence. Sometimes, it takes a cruel person to build a good web site.

Shoving Files Around

If your web site is made up of only a few pages with a few images, the best thing to do is to keep all the files in one directory, the main directory for your web. That way, you don't have to look very far to find a certain file. On the other hand, if you have a lot of files, then it will make your life easier to put them in *subdirectories*, directories contained in your main web directory. And, if you're like me, making your life easier is one of your major goals.

A logical directory structure is useful. For example, FrontPage's templates encourage putting all the graphics files into a subdirectory called **Images**. If you're setting up a site for your corporation, you may want to put all the pages dealing with your catalog into the **catalog** directory, all the tech support pages into the **techsup** directory, and all of the new product announcements into the **exaggerations** directory.

To move a file into a subdirectory, you don't even have to create the subdirectory first. When you tell FrontPage that you want to move the file, it will automatically create that directory. (Wouldn't it be great if real life were like that? All you'd have to do is say "I'm moving to West Dakota," and kazoom! a new state appears!)

In the Outline View, select the file that you want to move. (If it's an image file, you're going to have to push the **Links to Images** button in, so that it shows up on the list.) Pull down the **Edit** menu and select the **Properties** command. A dialog box appears, with the **Page URL** field highlighted.

Hit the **Home** key, and the cursor will appear at the start of the **Page URL** field. Type the name of the directory that you want to put the file in, followed by a slash (for example, if your old URL was **newtoy.htm** and you're putting it in the **toybox** directory, it should now read **toybox/newtoy.htm**). If there was already a directory name there and you want to move the file from there to another directory, delete the old directory name and type in the new one.

Click the **OK** button. FrontPage checks to see if any pages have links to the file you're moving, or if any pages use it in some other way. If it finds any, a dialog box appears asking you if you want to update the references to this file so that they point to the file's new location. Click the **Yes** button.

FrontPage updates all the references to the file, creates the directory (if it doesn't already exist), and moves the file into it. Remember, however, that it has only updated the references on *your* web site. If there are other web sites out there that link to this file, those links are now broken. If you want to be a nice person, you can warn the administrators of those other sites about the problem. (If, however, you want to be a mean person, you can create a new page in the old location that says **Haha! You fell for the "old dead link" trick!**, but I don't recommend it.)

Shoving the Page Under the Rug

Sometimes, you may want to store a file on your web site that you don't want browsers to be able to see. To do this, use the file moving instructions to move it into a directory named **_private**. Web browsers won't be able to see the files in that directory, which means that you shouldn't do this to files that you have linked to.

URLy Changes

Sometimes, you'll want to change a file's name. Maybe, you want a more descriptive name, or one that is not so easily mistyped, or maybe you are changing it for fun. After all, what could be more fun than changing a URL?*

To do this, select the file in the Outline View. Pull down the **Edit** menu and select the **Properties** command. The Properties dialog box appears, with the file's URL highlighted in the **Page URL** field. Type in the new URL, and remember to keep the same file extension (.htm, .gif, or .jpg) or else the poor Web browsers will become confused and not know what to do with the file. (It's not hard to confuse a Web browser; they're very powerful but ot-nay oo-tay ight-bray.)

If any other pages refer to this file (either are linked to it or include it as an image), FrontPage will ask if you want to change the references to point to the name. Click the **Yes** button, and FrontPage will update all the links and inclusions.

A Web by Any Other Name

Changing the name of your entire web is a very easy thing to do—perhaps, too easy. After all, if you change the web name, you're effectively changing the URL of every file in your site. Every single link from someone else's site to yours will have to be changed. All of your friends will have to spend hours finding their links to your site, changing them, and updating their sites. They will grow irritated with you, and cast you out from their midst. Soon, you will be wandering the streets a lonely and embittered web designer, all because you wanted to change the name of your site. Is all that worth it?**

To set this tragic series of events in motion, pull down Explorer's **Tools** menu and select the **Web Settings** command. When the Web Settings dialog box appears, click the **Configuration** tab. Replace the old name of your web in the Web Name field with the new name; then click the **OK** button.

FrontPage will think for a few seconds, and then pop up a dialog box asking you if you want the web to be refreshed from the server now, so the changes can take place immediately. Click the **Yes** button.

FrontPage exchanges this information with the server. Congratulations!

*(Answer: playing volleyball with a group of vertically challenged lawyers.)

**(Answer: Yes, if you have a really cool new name for your web.)

The Least You Need to Know

- The **Tools, Verifying Links** command checks to make sure all the pages you link to are really there.
- To change a link, bring the file up in the editor, select the link, and click the **Edit Link** button.
- The **Tools, Recalculate Links** command updates the information in the Explorer to reflect the changes made by other people working on the same web at the same time.
- Before you delete a page, you should delete the links to that page.
- Deleting a page may leave you with other pages with no links to them.
- You can change the name of a page or any other file or move it into a subdirectory by selecting the file and then using the **Edit, Properties** command. The internal links to that file will automatically update.
- You can change the name of the web by using the **Tools, Web Settings** command, but you should be very careful about doing this.

Chapter 23

Security Stuff

By the End of This Chapter You'll Be Able to...

- Change your password
- Choose site administrators
- Pick site authors
- Pick *and* choose (and even *select!*) who can visit the site

There are evil people everywhere who want to overthrow the government, crush our civilization, and worst of all, mess up your web site.

Worse than these people are the *really* nice people, who *really* just want to make your web site better—yet don't want to bother you by asking permission.

Permission (If You Choose to Accept It)

Luckily, Microsoft gives you ways to keep these scary people from messing up your web site. Using FrontPage's security features, you can create different categories of people who have permission to do different things. You can even give people access and control over one web but not over another.

Top Bananas: Administrators

The top category is *Administrators*. Someone who is on file as being an administrator for a web has a lot of power. They can create new webs, delete old webs, and control who gets to have permission to do everything else. They are as powerful as the Norse gods, full of compassion and fury.

Second Fiddles: Authors

The second category is the *Authors*. People on the Authors list can create new web pages and change and delete old ones. They're there to do the work. Authors are the salt of the earth.

Everyday People: Users

The next group is the *Users*. Users can use the web site. A good user is humble and appreciates what the administrators and authors have wrought (and continue to wring). While the previous two categories can be applied anywhere that FrontPage is used to *develop* a web site, restricting who can be a user only works on web sites that are published on servers that support the FrontPage extensions.

Untouchables: Nonusers

On a server with FrontPage-compatible extensions, anybody who doesn't have permission can be locked out of your site. This is a fate reserved for lesser beings: criminals, deviants, talk show hosts.

Changing your Password

The thing that keeps just anyone from changing your site without permission is the password system. If someone doesn't know the administrator's password for a given web, she can't sneak on and do administrator things. You have to have an author ID and password to do author things.

Authors and administrators can change their passwords at any time. They *should* change their password whenever they suspect that someone may have found out their password. Even if they don't think anyone's found it out, they should change it every few weeks, just in case someone has found it out without them realizing it.

A site can be set up so that the permissions and passwords for the Root Web apply to all webs, or it can be set up so that the Root Web and the other webs each have separate permissions. Before you can change your password, you have to use Explorer to open up the web you're changing it on. If it's a site where everything has the same permissions, open up the Root Web.

To change your password, pull down the **Tools** menu and select the mysteriously named **Change Password** command. A dialog box appears, with a field marked **Old Password**, one marked **New Password**, and one marked **Confirm Password**.

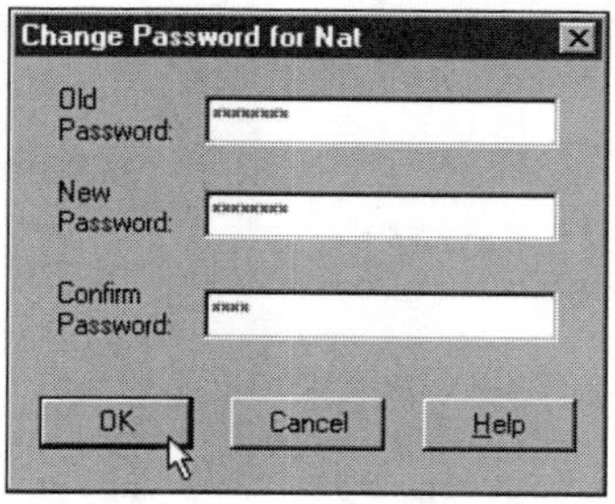

Whenever you enter your password, it does not appear on-screen. Instead, for each letter you type, an asterisk appears in the field.

Type your current password into the **Old Password** field. You must enter your current password so that the system knows that someone else didn't just walk up to your PC and changed your password so that you can't get in and he can. Of course, it also means that if you forget your password, you can't just change it to something else. Obvious tip #37: don't forget your password.

You'll notice that when you type your password, the letters won't show up in the field. Instead, you'll just see asterisks. This way, someone looking over your shoulder doesn't know what your password is.

Next, type your new password into the **New Password** field (again, it will appear as asterisks). Type the same thing a second time in the **Confirm Password** field; since you can't see if you make a typo, the system wants to double-check what you typed. (If you make the same typo both times, you're stuck with it in your password, so I hope you know what that typo is!) Click the **OK** button, and your password will be changed.

Picking the Practicalest Possible Password

A good password is one that you will remember but someone else won't be able to guess. To pick a good password:

- Avoid using just a single word, or even a word spelled backward.
- Use a combination of two unrelated words (such as **catsqueeze** or **throwlemon**) or a combination of words and numbers (**fold317**).
- Avoid anything that has a special meaning to you, like your address or your kids birthday.
- Don't use a variation on your previous password.
- Don't pick anything you have to write down to remember.

Not All Webs Have to Be the Same

By default, the permissions for all the webs on your site are the same as for the Root Web. However, you can give any individual web its own permission list. In order to do this, you have to have administrator permission on the Root Web. Otherwise, all the nefarious villains (not to mention the villainous nefaris) out there would just give themselves authorization to alter your web!

To split one web off for separate permission:

1. Open the web up in the Explorer.
2. Pull down the **Tools** menu and select the **Permissions** command. The Permissions dialog box appears.
3. Select the **Settings** tab, and click the radio button marked **Use unique permissions for this Web**.
4. Click the **OK** button, and your web will now be marked as using a separate permission list.

Adding Administrators

To some, being an administrator is power. To others, being an administrator is a burden. Generous people like to share power, and lazy people like to share burdens. As such, there are many reasons why one might want to enable additional people to be administrators for a web.

To do this, you must already be an administrator for the web. Open up the web in question (either the Root Web, or another web with a separate permission list). Pull down the **Tools** menu, and select the **Permissions** command. The **Web Permissions** dialog box appears. Select the **Administrators** tab, which you'll find is broken into two sections. The top section is to set up administrator accounts individually, and the bottom section is to set up larger filters for administrator accounts, based on *IP addresses*.

Click the **Add** button to add a new administrator. A second dialog box pops up asking for a name for the new administrator, and for the password to be typed in twice. You can type in the name, and feel free to give them the name **goofball** or **catlicker**; after all, you were an administrator first, so you have to keep these newcomers in their place. You should let the person type in their own password. People who make up their own passwords probably have an easier time remembering than people who have them assigned.

Once you finish, click the **OK** button, and goofball's name will now appear on the administrator list. Click the Web Permission dialog box's **OK** button, and the permissions list will be updated on the server.

Defrocking Administrators

To remove someone from the administrators permission list of the current web, you need to be an administrator on that web. Pull down the **Tool** menu and select the **Permissions** command. When the Web Permissions dialog box appears, click the **Administrators** tab and the list of administrators appear.

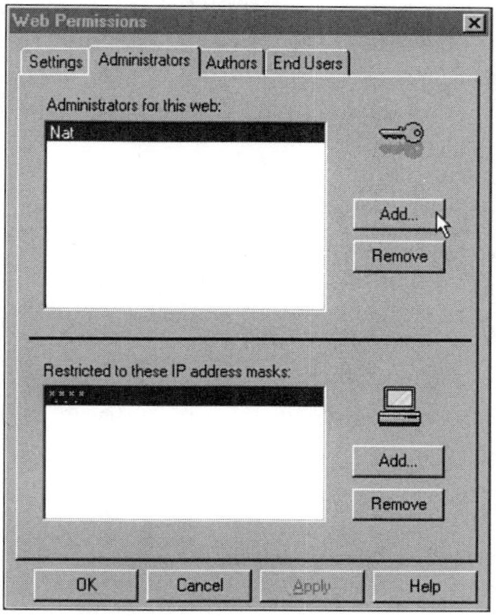

The web permissions dialog gives you control over who controls, creates, and has access to the web. However, you cannot wield that control unless you are an administrator.

Click the name that you want to remove, and it becomes highlighted. Then, click the **Remove** button. As you do so, chuckle sinisterly, and then say "And now you shall be powerless under my maniacal administrative control!"

You're In-Self-Destructible!

There are limits to all powers, even the power of the administrator. The one administrator you cannot delete is yourself.

Configuring Authors

In the world of books, authors aren't very powerful, being constantly under the control and supervision of editors, who are ~~an evil breed that I suspect are serving alien masters~~ very nice people and quite helpful and goodhearted. In the web world, however, authors are quite powerful. They cannot only create new pages, they can also change and even delete existing ones. As such, you should be very careful who you give author permission to.

To give someone author permission, you need to have administrator permission on that permission list. Giving the permission works much the same as giving administrator permission. Open the web you're giving permission for (either the Root Web or another web with a separate permission list), pull down **Tools** menu and select the **Permissions** command. On the Web Permissions dialog box, click the **Authors** tab.

The Authors tab looks just like the Administrators tab, except it has a picture of a hand writing on a piece of paper, instead of a picture of a key. Someone at Microsoft must think that authors hand-write things these days. Don't they realize that during the past ten years, almost all of us have turned to the cutting edge technology known as *typewriters*?

Click the **Add** button, and another dialog box appears. Enter a name for the new author, and let him enter his own password (twice). Click the **OK** button on this dialog box to make it go away, and then click the **OK** button of the Web Permissions dialog box to make that go away as well. FrontPage will then send the updated permissions information to the server, so your new author can get to work immediately.

You cannot give an author account the same name as an administrator account. You really don't need to anyway, since an administrator automatically has the ability to do anything an author can.

Getting Rid of Authors (But We're Such Wonderful People!)

Any administrator can delete anyone from the authors permissions list. That is, assuming they are on the list to begin with. If you're really mad at someone and want to revoke some kind of permission from them, you can always put them *on* the authors list and then immediately yank them *off* of it again, I suppose.

To yank someone off:

1. Pull up the Web Permissions dialog by selecting the **Tools, Permissions** command.
2. Click the **Authors** tab.
3. Select the name of the author you want to eliminate, and then click the **Remove** button. The author's name disappears from the list on your screen.
4. Click the **OK** button at the bottom of the dialog box, and the updated permission list information will be sent to the server.

You, Sir, Can Be a User!

The administrator has the ability to choose if everyone can see the web, or if just select individuals can. The administrator can even choose to let no one see the web, although that may be philosophically problematic. ("If there's a web and no one can see it, is it really there?")

These user permissions controls only work if the web is on a server that has the FrontPage Extensions. If it's on any other server, everyone can see it.

Turning On the User Filter

To turn the current web from an open-to-all above ground site to a secluded secret known only to the privileged few, pull down the **Tools** menu and select the **Permissions** command. Click the **End Users** tab on the Web Permissions dialog box that appears. Click the radio button marked **Registered users only**, and you're ready to run a restricted site!

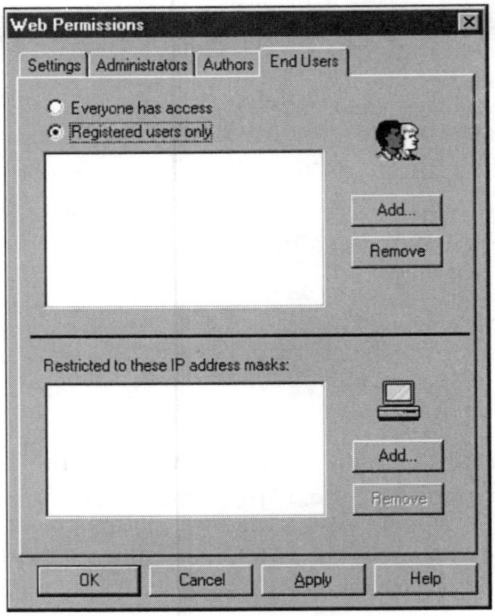

You can use the End Users tab to bring an end to some people being users!

Making a List of the In-Crowd

Click the **Add** button, and a New User dialog box pops up, needing a user name to be typed in, and the password to be typed in twice. Let the user enter this information; if he's going to be a user on your system, she'll have to do her share of the work! Click the **OK** button when done. Repeat this for all the users that you want to add. When done, click the **OK** button on the larger dialog box, and the user permission information will be sent to the web's server.

Black-Balling Users

To strike a user from your vaunted ranks and cast him out with the ordinary people, just pull up the **End User** tab on the Web Permissions dialog box again, select the user, and click the **Remove** button. Click **OK** when you finish, and the user's account will be torn from the sacred list of users on the server.

Don't Let Him In: You Don't Know Where He's Been!

In addition to limiting administrators, authors, and users based on their account names, you can also limit them based on which computer they are connecting from. That way, you can make sure that someone with a stolen password isn't connecting from outside and altering the page with your Mock Apple Pie recipe so that it includes real apples. You can also make sure that your authors are hard at work where they are supposed to be, rather than dialing in from home, drinking margaritas, and watching Gilligan's Island reruns while slowly doing their work.

Suit & Tie Required: Keeping Out Riffraff Using Address Code

The way that you specify what computers are allowed access is by using their *Internet Protocol Address*, more often called an *IP Address*. Every computer hooked to the Internet has an IP Address, which is four numbers (1 through 256) separated by periods (such as 19.177.12.233). (Sneaky computers have tried to claim Social Security benefits based on these numbers.) Computers permanently connected to the Net have permanent addresses, while someone dialing in from home is given a different address each time they call.

Setting Which Addresses Are Admitted

The address restrictions are set separately for each category of access, because you may want to let anybody connecting from anywhere have user access, but make sure that anyone trying to be an administrator is in the building. That way, sinister, vicious spy types who want to prevent the free world from having the secret to Mock Apple Pie will have to sneak by your ever-vigilant receptionist to do so.

To set these restrictions on the current web, pull up the Web Permissions dialog box by using the **Tools, Permissions** command (again! Yup, that dialog box is the center of your whole security world!). Select the tab for the category of access that you want to restrict.

In the bottom half of the tab, you'll see an area for a list of acceptable IP addresses. Click the **Add** button next to that. In the New IP Mask dialog box that appears, type the four IP address numbers into the four boxes provided; then click the **OK** button. The IP Address you typed in will now be on your list of acceptable addresses. Click the **OK** button under the address list, and this new permission information will be sent to the server.

One-Eyed Queens and Asterisks are Wild!

You can add a whole group of IP Addresses at once by using wild cards in the number fields. When you put an asterisk into one of the four fields, this tells the system that any number is okay there. For example, you could enter 135.17.*.*, and that way, any computer with an address from 135.17.1.1 through 135.17.256.256 can be used to access the web. Of course, you miss out on the keen Zen experience of entering each of those sixty-five thousand, five hundred, and thirty-six addresses by hand!

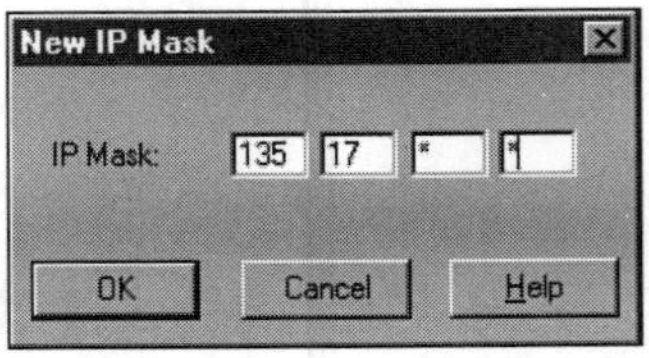

Entering the IP address, using asterisks as wild cards.

Once you put an asterisk into one of the slots, you have to put an asterisk into all of the slots after it. You can't set up an address limitation like 137.*.29.*. (That's a limitation on your limitations!)

Getting Un-Addressed

To remove an IP Address from your approved list, just bring up the Web Permissions dialog box, select the address on the proper tab, and click the **Remove** button. There's an all-wild-card address (*.*.*.*, giving all addresses permission) on the administrator list that you will want to remove like this, but only after you've added acceptable IP Addresses! If you could successfully delete it without adding an acceptable address, then no one will have permission to administer the web from anywhere—and that's a problem you can't fix, since you need to get on as an administrator to fix it!

Sometimes, There's No Stopping Those Users

The IP Address restriction on users only works if you are publishing your site on a server with FrontPage-compatible server extensions.

Physical Security

You've taken care to make sure that you are the only one with administrator or even author access, and all of the web files are residing on your own hard disk rather than some common server. Your password is a combination of Planck's Constant and the Italian word for "oxen." After a hard morning at work, you head off to the Burger Czar for a Double Bolshevik Burger and a Siberian Milk-like Shake. When you get back to your office, you find that some kind soul, in an effort to figure out FrontPage without the help of a *Complete Idiot's Guide*, has managed to delete several pages and replace the contents of another with the words to the hit song "How Can I Miss You Badly, Baby, If You Won't Ever Leave Me Alone?" What was your big mistake?

Answer: Eating all that fatty food. And forgetting to get some of those yummy Krispy KGB Fries with it.

Your real problem is that someone just walked into your office, sat down at your computer, and started using the copy of FrontPage that you left running on your machine. You can make your house a veritable fortress, but if you leave the front door open, people will still come up and try to sell you insurance.

There are several steps you can take to discourage this. The first is *don't leave FrontPage running*. Once you load up a web and enter your password, it's an open door. The computer isn't sophisticated enough to say "hey, you're not the same organic individual who was typing when the password was entered."

The second is to take advantage of your screen saver's password protection features. This way, you can walk from your computer, and after the screen saver has come up, your computer isn't usable until someone enters the password.

Of course, if you had an infinite number of monkeys banging away randomly on an infinite number of keyboards, eventually one of them will randomly type your password. The best way to avoid this is to not let an infinite number of monkeys into your office. Lock the door!

If you're working on sensitive material in a multiple-author environment, you should make sure that everyone is taking reasonable, appropriate security precautions. It does no good to bar your door against the invading hordes if, down the hallway, someone is saying "Invading hordes! I've been wondering about how you were doing! Wanna come in and mess around with our web site?"

Backups: Wrath of God Insurance

No password system can possibly protect your computer from being struck by lightning, washed away in a flood, or eaten by giant mutant bumble bees.

As such, you should make sure that backup copies of your web files are made at regular intervals. If whoever is in charge of the server is backing up the files properly (including occasionally storing copies in another building, in case the worst occurs, and not constantly reusing the same backup tape, so that you can get files of the previous backup as well as the most recent), then you can count on that. Otherwise, you can use the Copy Web feature to store a copy of your web site on some other server.

Be Careful, Not Paranoid

Take all of the security suggestions with a dose of realism. If you're building a corporate intranet site with the plans for the new top-secret missile defense system, then heavy security precautions are necessary. If you're just putting together a World Wide Web site telling everyone about your favorite roller coaster, then you can be much more relaxed about it. The invading hordes don't care much about roller coasters anyway.

The Least You Need to Know

- FrontPage lets you choose who has permission to act as administrators, authors, and users on your web.
- Administrators control the web project, including setting the permission lists.
- Authors can create, change, and delete web pages.
- Users can view the web.
- The permission list for the Root Web applies to all the webs on the site, unless you tell it differently.
- To see or change the permission list, use the Explorer's **Tools, Permissions** command.
- Restricting users only works if you're web site is on a server with FrontPage-compatible extensions.
- Don't let unauthorized people use your computer while FrontPage is running.
- Computer malfunction can ruin your web files more easily than a person can, so back up your files frequently.

Chapter 24

Using a To Do List

By the End of This Chapter You'll Be Able to...

- Make a To Do List
- Pick who has To Do the tasks
- Manage the To Do List
- Remove things that are done
- Look at the HTML version of the To Do List
- Complain about all the problems with the To Do List

Creating a big web site is a lot of work. Pages have to be created, images put in place, links checked, donuts bought and eaten. When you are dealing with a lot of tasks, particularly when you're dealing with a lot of different authors who are supposed to be doing them, it can all get very messy.

The fine folks at Microsoft (who have to work on many ungainly projects themselves, such as programming Excel or trying to find a birthday gift for the difficult-to-shop-for Bill Gates) have given you the tools to help keep all this effort organized. With FrontPage's To Do List manager, you can keep track of what has been done, what has yet to be done, and who has yet to do what has yet to be done!

Why Do That to Do Voodoo?

If you are administering a web project, you could keep track of all the assignments on a piece of paper, checking off what has been done, having people phone you when they find something else that needs to be done, and reminding folks of what they need to do.

The To Do List can save you a lot of that work, because when one of the authors finds something that needs to be done, he can add it to the list for you. Everyone working on the project can see the latest version of the list at any time, since it's stored with the web. And, when something is done, it just gets checked off. There is also an automatic history kept of what got done when, so you can see who was effective and efficient.

The best labor-saving part of the To Do List is that with a few keystrokes, you can take the assignments assigned to you and change the list so they're assigned to someone else. Properly used, this can save you a ton of effort!

All of these are excellent reasons why creating a To Do List should be at the very top of your To Do List!

Viewing the To Do List

Calling up the To Do List from the Explorer or the Editor takes just the push of a button—or actually, the push of a thumbtack, since that's the picture on the **Show To Do List** button (which is called **To Do List** on the Explorer toolbar).

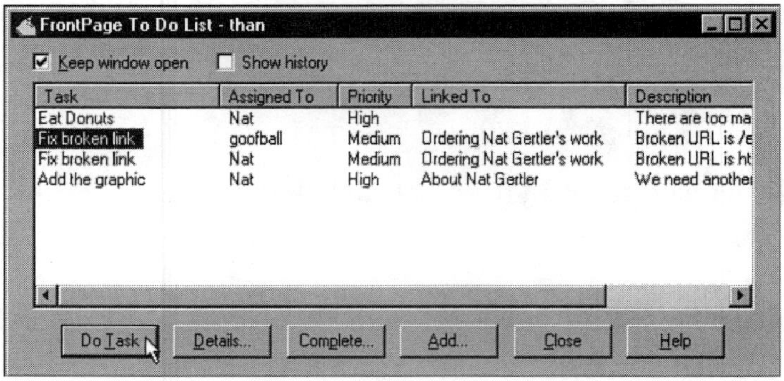

The To Do List display shows all of the waiting tasks for this web, and lets you add, remove, or alter the entries.

The To Do List display has columns for **Task** (the job that has to be done), **Assigned To** (the administrator or author stuck with doing it), **Priority** (whether it's of High, Medium, or Low urgency), **Linked To** (the name of the page that has to be fixed) and **Description** (where you can put a fuller explanation of what needs to be done, or any other information you feel is useful, such as the phone number for a good pizza place). If you check the **Show history** box, you will see there will also be a **Completed** column, listing when the tasks were finished.

There's a scroll bar across the bottom of the list that lets you scan across all the fields. If you have more than 10 items on the list, there will also be a vertical scroll bar. Keeping the window this small means that you'll never be faced with more than 10 tasks at a time; the others are out of sight, out of mind!

All Sorts of Sorts!

One of the keen features of the To Do List display is that the header for each column is also a button that you can use to sort the list. Click the **Assigned To** button, for example, and the assignments will be listed in alphabetical order, based on who they are assigned to. This way, all of the tasks assigned to each person will be grouped together. Click the **Priority** button, and the most important tasks appear at the top, which lets you get right to work on them. Click the **Description** button, and the list is sorted in alphabetical order by the description...which is absolutely useless, but you can do it if you want!

Column Compression

You can change the width of the columns on the To Do List, making individual columns narrower or wider. Why would you want to do this? Well, there's always the cheap thrill of being in control of the computer, but by now, you've likely grown blasé about that. However, if you're using long entries in the description field, you may want to make the display of that field wider, so that you can see more of it without calling up the special Detail display (described later). And, you may want to make the other fields smaller so that you don't have to use the scroll bars to see the full entry.

To change a column's width, point to the line at the right edge of the column header. Your pointer will turn into a vertical bar with arrows coming off of it from either side. Hold down the mouse button and slide the mouse to the right (to make the column bigger) or the left (to make it smaller). If you want, you can shrink all of the columns down to zero, and then when someone asks you if you completed your tasks, you can tell them that you didn't see any on the list!

Shrinkability

If you're working alone, the column you can safely shrink is the Assigned To column, since everything is assigned to you anyway. No matter how many people are working on the project, you can shrink the Priority column until just the P is showing, and you'll still see enough to identify whether it's a High, Medium, or Low priority.

Building Up the List

A list isn't really a list if there isn't anything on it. If you couldn't add To Do items to the list, you'd be utterly listless.

The most obvious way to add something to the list is to click the **Add** button on the list display. This brings up a dialog box with spaces for **Task Name**, **Assign To**, and **Description**, as well as a set of radio buttons to let you set the priority. By default, it will stick *your* name into the **Assign To**, so if you don't want to get stuck with the work, now is the time to change it!

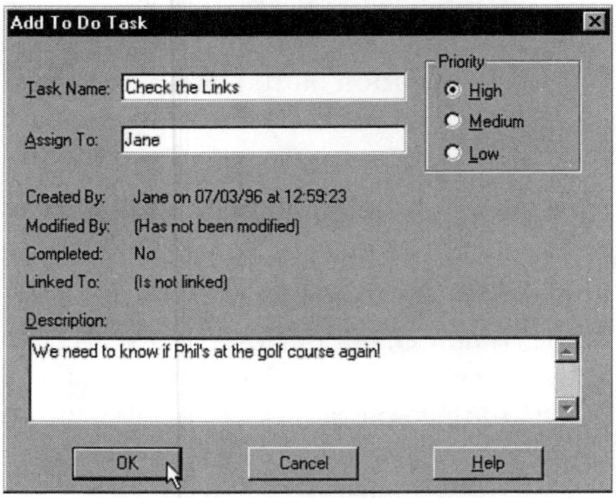

The Add To Do Task form includes information that you can't change, recording who added this item to the To Do List and when it was added.

When you're done typing in the information, click the **OK** button and the task will appear on the list.

A Better Adder in the Editor

If you're editing a page and you see something that you need to fix, but you aren't going to fix it right away, there's a better way to add it to the To Do List. Pull down the **Edit** menu and select the **Add To Do Task** command. This pops up a form that looks *almost* exactly like the other adding form, with one minor difference: the name of the file you were editing appears as one of the uneditable pieces of information.

Check This Out...

Attemptify Cleariosity

When you're adding a task, put some effort into what you write into the Description field. It's very easy to whip off a little comment such as "Fix this" or "spelling" or "check image" and think you're going to remember what you were supposed to do when it comes time to do it. However, if you're putting a task on a To Do List, it means that you aren't doing it right now, and the time that you're going to do it may be farther away than you think.

Being clear is even more important when you're setting up the task for someone else to do. You know what the problem is. It probably popped right out at you, and you may think it would be obvious to anyone, but different people see things differently. (Even not-so-different people can see thing differently at times.) If you write up a task as "fix image," the person assigned may see something wrong with a different image on that page, fix it, and take the task off of the list while the original problem is still there.

When you see this task on the To Do List, the name of this page will appear in the **Linked To** column. This not only lets you keep track of what page needs fixing, it also...no, wait, that will be telling. I can't give away all my secrets now! Keep reading!

Similar Better Adder in Explorer

On the **Edit** menu of the Explorer, there is also an **Add To Do Task** that works like the one in the Editor. It also includes a page name in the **Linked To** column. The page it lists is the one you currently have selected in the Explorer's Link View, Outline View, or Summary View.

Quick, Think "Fix Link!"

If you're using the **Verify Links** command to make sure that all of your links go somewhere, and you happen to find that you have links that need to be checked or fixed, taking care of this is easy. On the **Verify Links** list, select the entry for the broken link by clicking it.

Next, click the **Add Task** button, and a new task will automagically be added to the To Do List, without you having to fill out any form. The task name will be **Fix broken link**, and the description will list the bad URL being linked to. The page with the bad link on it will

Check This Out...

To Do? What To Do? When you use the **Add Task** button on the Verify Link page, it puts the words **To Do** in the status column of the Verify Link list. It forgets this, however, the moment you close this display. If you select **Verify Links** again, it will show you the same broken link again, with the broken status.

be listed in the **Linked To** field. All this is wonderful. The only bad thing is that your name is listed as the person responsible, but I'm about to show you how to change that.

Changing Tasks—Into Slightly Different Tasks

Sometimes, you'll need to change a task. You'll want to increase the priority, perhaps, or correct the description. And, of course, when no one's looking, you want to change it from being your responsibility to being someone else's.

To do this, click the **Show To Do List** button to bring up the list. Select the list item by clicking it; then click the **Details** button. The form that pops up looks like the task adding form, only everything is already filled in.

Edit the fields that you want to change; then click the **OK** button to save the changes.

...And Grant Me the Serenity to Accept the Things I Cannot Change...

You can't change the Task Name field of any task you added via the **Add Task** button in the Verify Links dialog box. The computer chose to name it Fix broken link, the computer knows it's right, and the computer ain't gonna let you mess with it!

Doing the Work (sigh)

No matter how you plot and scheme, eventually you will be stuck with actually doing some work. It is one of the sad truths of human existence.

If the work you have to do was added to the list using the **Edit, Add To Do Task** command or from the Verify List dialog box, then, at least, your work will be a wee bit easier. That's because, in these cases, the To Do List has the name of a page in its Linked To field. Pull up the To Do List, and select the task in question. The **Do Task** button, which was grayed out before, now becomes solid and clickable. All you have to do is click this button and...

No, no, don't get your hopes too high. The computer won't actually *do* the task for you. However, when you click this button, the computer *will* automatically load the linked-to page into the Editor, so you can go right to work on it! This feature is so amazingly useful that, every time you use it, you should immediately celebrate its existence by taking a coffee break!

Techno Talk

Other Link-to-ers

If you create a link to a page that doesn't exist yet, FrontPage lets you put creating that page on the To Do list. There are also a number of wizards and templates that you can use with FrontPage, add-ons that give FrontPage additional features to make it easier to use or more powerful. Many of these can add items to the To Do List and will usually fill in the Linked To field.

"Do Task" Didn't Do Its Task!

Occasionally, you will click the **Do Task** button and get an error message. This usually happens because a page has been deleted or renamed. If it has been deleted, you're off the hook! After all, there's no need to fix a deleted page, so just delete that task from the list. If it has just been renamed, however, you might have to hunt it down.

I Did My Work! What Now?

After you complete your assigned task, it's time to let the To Do List know what you accomplished (unless, of course, you want to make it look like you have a lot of work left to do, so no one will stick you with any more).

To do this, pull up the To Do List. Select the task you just finished by clicking it (the **Task** field becomes highlighted). Click the **Complete** button, and a Complete Task dialog box appears, with two radio buttons. The **Mark this task as completed** radio button is selected already. Since that's what you want to do, click the **OK** button.

FrontPage will mark this task as completed, recording the time and date at which it was finished. It will still be in the Web's To Do file but will only show up when someone lists the history.

Nobody's Going to Do the Work! Hah!

If there's a task that it turns out doesn't need to be done (either it was put on incorrectly, or something else was changed that makes it unnecessary), you can delete it from the list. (You can also do this if it's a task that you just don't want to do, but that's not very nice.)

To delete a task from the list, first select the task. Click the **Complete** button, and the dialog box with two radio buttons appears. Click the lower button, marked **Delete this task (do not save in the To Do List history)**; then click the **OK** button. The task will be completely eliminated from the To Do List—never to be seen again!

The History of To Do

The To Do List keeps a record of completed tasks. By default, it doesn't show these tasks on the list. However, if you want a record of the project, or simply would rather spend your time glorying in the work you've already completed rather than worrying about the work to come, click the box marked **Show history**. A check mark appears in the box, and all of the finished tasks reappear on the list.

In this To Do list, everything to be done has been done, so it's time to go home and play air hockey!

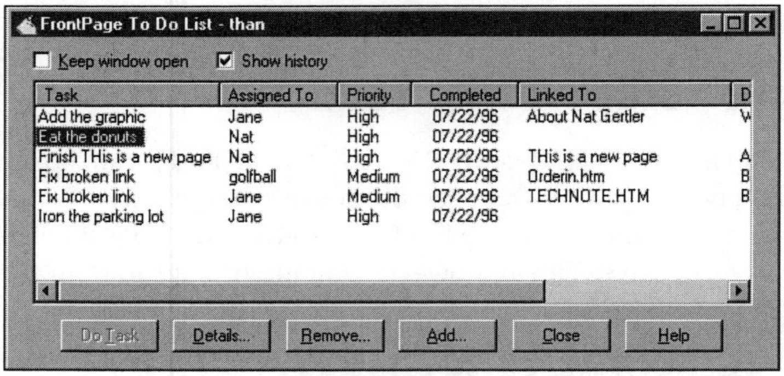

When you display the history, a new column appears in the list. This is the **Completed** column, and it lists the date that the project was completed. If you click this column header, the list will be sorted so that the incomplete tasks appear at the top. Beneath them, the tasks will be listed in the order completed, from the most recent on back. The list even has the exact time that the task was marked as completed, down to the second. Why you'd want to know the second is beyond me.

I Did It at Thirteen O'Clock?

If the times listed in the Details of the To Do List section look a little odd, don't worry. The system is just using a 24-hour clock. If the hour is below 12, it's AM. If the hour is above 12, subtract twelve, and consider it to be PM (for example, 14 o'clock equals 2 PM)).

The Dangers of To Do

The To Do system is not perfect. As noted before, it's not smart enough to recognize that a page slated for repair has been deleted. That's just an irritation. There are a couple of problems that, in the wrong conditions, could be more, uh, problematic.

Who Changed It?

Despite all the joking about shoving your work off on others, this is not something that most people are going to do. However, if someone *does* happen to do it in some large, multi-author environment, there's no way to know who made the change.

If you select an incomplete project and click the **Details** button, you will see a noneditable field marked **Modified by**. This field is *supposed* to hold the name of the person who last changed this task's entry, as well as the time when the change was made. However, at least as of the initial release, this doesn't work. The field always reads (Has not been modified), even if it has been changed. There is no visible way to find if a task has been changed, much less who changed it.

Because of this, anyone with Author permissions on this web can cause problems for the project just by messing with the To Do List. On the other hand, you shouldn't give author permission to anyone you don't trust, since that power also gives them the ability to delete pages and perform other hijinx.

The Nonexistent Author

The To Do List never refers to a list of people with Author permission for that web. On one level, it would be quite nice to pull down a menu of all the people authorized to work on the web, and pick which one of them to stick with this project. That, however, is just a matter of convenience.

The potential problem pops up because you may, inadvertently, assign a task to someone who doesn't have author privileges on that web. This is probably not a problem if you are dealing in a small environment with only two or three authors. However, if you are dealing in a large development environment, with a lot of people who have different permissions on different webs, the odds of such a mistake are much higher.

To make matters just a little worse, the person who was wrongly assigned the task won't find out and call it to your attention, because she can't see the To Do List for that web; she can only see the To Do Lists on webs she is an author for.

Put Worrying on Your "To Don't" List

None of these problems are too large, or worth fretting about (especially if you only have a handful of authors). As long as you're aware of the potential for them, everything should be fine.

The Other To Do List Display

The To Do List display you've been looking at is part of the FrontPage product. You need to be running FrontPage in order to look at it. But, what if you're a properly authorized user, with all the access to the hidden and private files of the web, and you dialed in from a friend's machine? Can you check the status of the list from a machine without FrontPage?

Of course! If the answer was "no," do you think I would have brought it up? Actually, you can check the current To Do List and the history list using a standard Web browser. You just have to know where to look!

In the directory your web is stored in a subdirectory called **_vti_pvt**. In that subdirectory is a file called **_x_todo.htm**. Use a standard Web browser to take a look at this file (if your browser is old enough that it doesn't support tables, you'll need a newer one).

This file has all of the active To Do tasks, listed as a table. This display contains the same information as the standard To Do display, but it has things arranged a bit differently (just to keep you on your toes). For example, the priorities are listed as 1, 2, and 3 rather than High, Medium, and Low. (And, if it makes sense to you that a *low* number means *high* priority and vice versa, then you've been spending too much time with your computer!)

The To Do HTML file has basically the same information as the usual view of the list.

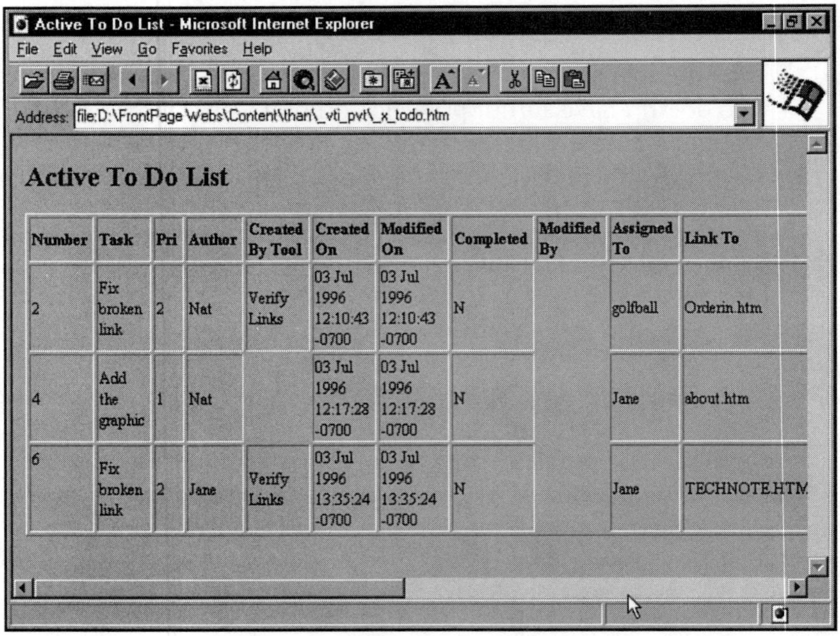

While this HTML page only has the current To Do List, there is another file in the same directory with the list of completed tasks. The file name for the complete list is **_x_todoh.htm**, and it has the same columns. The history page uses the Modified On and Modified By columns to record who completed the task and when. The current tasks page has those columns, but doesn't really use them at all.

Both HTML pages have one column of information that you won't find on the standard display. This column is called **Magic**, and it's used by wizards and templates that put things on the To Do List for you. This is where they store information they feel the need to keep track of. For example, when you use the **Add Task** button on the Verify Links display, the program stores the address of the bad link in the **Magic** column.

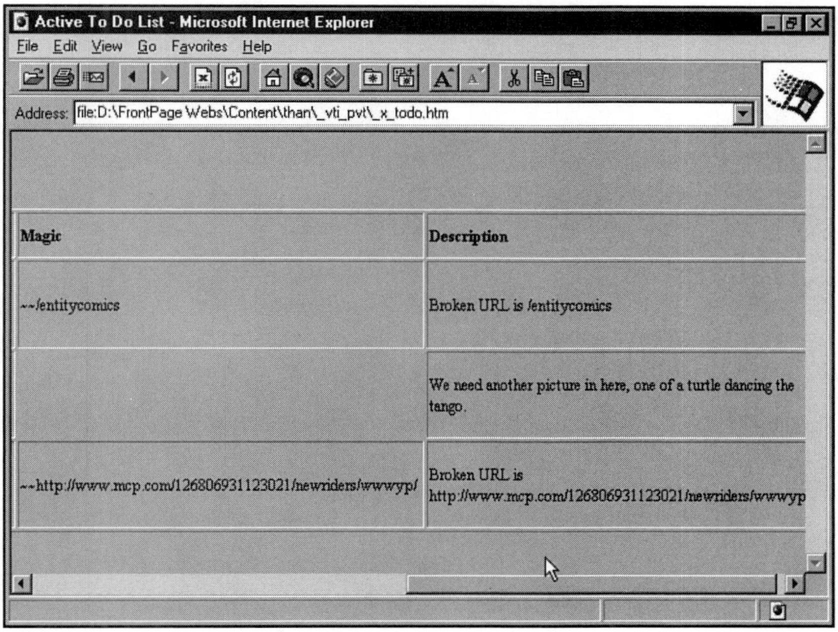

Because this table has a lot of columns and some big data, you'll probably have to scroll sideways to see the whole thing.

I guess it's just another sign that the World Wide Web has truly taken over; even magic is being used just to point to URLs!

The Least You Need to Know

- The To Do List is a built-in feature that helps you keep track of what needs to be done on the web.
- For each task listed in the To Do List, there's information about what the task is, who is assigned to do it, and how urgent it is.

- Anyone with author permission or administrator permission can add tasks to the To Do List, change tasks, or delete tasks.
- The To Do List includes a history of completed tasks and who completed them. These tasks are only listed by request.
- Some To Do List entries include the name of the page that needs working on. Selecting that task and clicking the **Do Task** button loads that page into the editor.
- There are HTML versions of the current To Do List and a list of completed tasks.

Speak Like a Geek: The Complete Archive

anchor The destination of a link. See *links*.

article A *message* that a user posts to a discussion group.

associate To establish a connection between a given file type and the application needed to view or play that file type. When a user clicks a link to a particular file, it is through association that the Web browser knows which application to turn the file over to, so that it can be viewed or listened to.

attribute A variable that further defines an HTML command. For example, the ALIGN=CENTER attribute can be used to further define the <p> (paragraph) tag to tell the user's Web browser to center the text in the paragraph between the margins. See *HTML* and *tag*.

background The web page provides the background for your text. You can change the color of this background or insert a background image.

bookmark A mark set in a web page, which allows you to create a link to some place other than the top of the page. See *links*.

Boolean operators Conjunctions including "and" and "or" that are used to separate search terms. For example, if you search for "Clinton and Whitewater," you get a list of all resources that relate to both "Clinton" and "Whitewater." If you use "or," the search is much broader, finding anything that relates to either "Clinton" or "Whitewater."

bot See *WebBot*.

bps Short for *bits per second*, this is a unit used to measure the speed of data being transferred between two computers. Most transfers on the Web take place at 14,400 bps or higher.

browser See *Web browser.*

bullet A small graphic used to highlight each item within a list.

bulleted list An unordered list of items preceded by a small bullet.

CGI A programming language that allows a web page designer to automate certain functions, such as the retrieval of data from a form.

client Of two computers, the computer that's being served. Whenever a user connects to your web site, the computer at that site is the *host server,* and his computer is the *client* or customer.

compressed file A file that has been condensed so that it takes up less disk space and travels faster through network and modem connections. Before you can use a compressed file, you must *decompress* (or expand) it using a special program. Popular decompression programs include PKZIP (for DOS) and WinZip (for Windows).

decompress To expand a compressed file and make it usable.

definition list A listing of definitions such as a glossary.

Dial-Up Networking A program that comes with Windows 95 that establishes the Internet connection.

directory list A list in a web page that is formatted similar to a directory list on your hard disk. However, most Web browsers do not display directory lists any differently than bulleted lists.

discussion group Similar to a newsgroup, a FrontPage discussion group provides a means for your users to ask questions and exchange information with each other. See *newsgroup, article, forum, thread,* and *post.*

document source The coded document that controls the way web pages look. See *HTML.*

domain name A unique identification for an Internet site; also known as *host name.* Each computer on the Internet has a domain name that distinguishes it from other computers on the Internet. Domain names usually provide some vague indication of the establishment that runs the server. For example, the domain name of the White House server is www.whitehouse.gov.

download To copy a file from another computer (usually an FTP server) to your computer. See *upload.*

e-mail A system by which people can send and receive messages through their computers, either on a network or by using modems.

FAQ *(frequently asked questions)* Pronounced "fak," this is a list of answers to the most often-asked questions at a particular Internet site. You might consider adding a FAQ page to your web site to answer your users' most common questions.

form Basically, a form is a dialog box pasted onto a web page. You might use a form on one of your web pages to take credit card orders, register users, or obtain feedback.

forum An area of an online service such as CompuServe or America Online that is devoted to a particular topic.

frame Frames divide a browser window so that several web pages can be viewed at the same time. You create frames in your web pages with the Frames Wizard.

frame set A web page that contains the instructions needed to create a framed web page within a Web browser's window.

FrontPage Editor The program within the FrontPage suite with which you create and edit your web pages.

FrontPage Explorer The program within the FrontPage suite with which you create and edit your web.

FTP (*File Transfer Protocol*) A set of rules that govern the transfer of files between computers. When a user downloads a file from your web site, she is using FTP protocol.

GIF file (*Graphic Interchange Format)* Pronounced "giff file" or "jiff file, "this is a picture file that's often a photograph or painting. A format developed by CompuServe for transferring graphics files, this format is good for storing lots of graphics information in very little space.

hexadecimal The notation for a base-16 numeral, which uses the letters A–F as replacements for the numbers 10, 11, 12, and so on. Hexadecimal notation is used in the designation of color values in HTML.

hits In a search, the number of times a search word was found within your web pages. The higher the number, the more likely it is that a particular web page contains the information the user is looking for. See *score*.

home page The main page in your web site. This is the page that greets when a user first connects to your web site.

hotspot An area of a graphic, which when clicked, links the user to another web page, a file, or a graphics image.

host name See *domain name*.

host server The host server is the computer that has the information. The user's computer is the client, requesting information from the host computer, which is the computer that contains your web site.

HTML (*HyperText Markup Language*) HTML codes tell the user's Web browser how to display the elements in your web pages, such as your text, headings, lists, links, graphics images, and frames. As you create your web page, FrontPage converts your selections to the proper HTML codes.

HTTP (*HyperText Transfer Protocol*) A set of rules that govern the exchange of data between a Web host server and a client (the user's computer). The address for every host server on the Web starts with **http**. However, there are other types of servers on the Internet, whose addresses start with other letters. Gopher addresses start with **gopher**, FTP with **ftp**, WAIS with **wais**, USENET with **news**, and Telnet with **telnet**.

hyperdocument A web page that contains links connecting it to other pages. On the Web, a hyperdocument might contain links to other text, graphics, sounds, or movies.

hyperlinks Icons, pictures, or highlighted chunks of text that connect two documents. When a user clicks a hyperlink (usually simply called a link), he's connected to a related web page.

import The process of making a file available for use in your web.

in-line image A graphic that appears inside a web page.

Internet The world's largest system of interconnected networks. The Internet was originally named ARPAnet after the Advanced Research Projects Agency in the Defense Department. The agency developed the ARPAnet in the mid-1970s as an experimental project that would allow various university and military sources to continue to communicate in a state of national emergency. Now, the Internet is used mostly by private citizens for connecting to databases, exchanging electronic mail, and finding information.

Internet Explorer Popular Web browser from Microsoft. See *Web browser* and *Netscape Navigator.*

Java A technology that enables a web page designer to create animations and other moving video clips and embed them in their web pages. FrontPage does not offer any direct support for Java; however, you can start a Java program in a web page using the HTML Markup bot.

JavaScript A variation of pure Java, developed by Netscape, in which Java code is embedded directly within an HTML document. By contrast, a programmer using only Java creates and saves his program as a separate file. That program is then launched from the HTML page by a single command. You can insert small JavaScripts into a FrontPage web page using the HTML Markup bot.

JPEG (*Joint Photographic Experts Group*) A file-compression format used for storing graphics files. Typically, JPEG files offers higher quality than GIF files, but they are much larger. However, you can adjust the compression ratio of JPEG files in order to find a nice balance between file size and graphics quality.

links (*hyperlinks*) These are icons, pictures, or highlighted chunks of text that connect the current page to other pages in your web, pages out on the WWW, graphics, movies, or sounds.

logical codes In a web document, codes that provide general directions on how to display text. For example, **<em>** stands for emphasis, which might mean bold or italic. Physical codes give more precise instructions. For example, **<b>** means bold. See *tags*.

login To connect to another computer on the Internet so that its resources can be used. For example, you can restrict access to your web so that your users must enter a user name and a password in order to obtain access to it.

logout To disconnect from another computer on the Internet.

menu list A list on a web page that is formatted like a list of menu choices. However, most Web browsers display menu lists as they might a bulleted list.

MIME (*Multi-purpose Internet Mail Extensions*) A protocol that controls all file transfers on the Web. A Web browser such as Netscape Navigator uses MIME to recognize different file types. If an HTML document arrives, Navigator "knows" to play that file. If an MPG file arrives, Navigator calls the associated helper application. MIME was originally developed to attach different types of files (usually multimedia files) to e-mail messages.

modem (modulator-demodulator) A modem is a device that translates computer information into sound and transmits those sounds over conventional telephone lines that receive such sounds and translate them into computer data.

monospace In typesetting, a typeface in which all characters have the same width. When you select the Formatted style, text appears in a monospace font.

MPEG (*Moving Pictures Expert Group*) A video-compression and movie presentation standard used for most video clips stored on the Web. If you provide a link to an MPEG file, the user must have an MPG or MPEG player to watch it.

Netscape Navigator Popular Web browser from Netscape.

newbie Term for a new user on the Internet.

newsgroup An Internet bulletin board for users who share common interests. There are thousands of newsgroups ranging from art to pets (to pet art). Newsgroups let users post messages and read messages from other users. In FrontPage, you can create discussion groups, which are very similar in nature to newsgroups.

numbered list A list of items presented in a particular order, such as the steps for a procedure.

ordered list See *numbered list.*

Personal Web Server The program within the FrontPage suite that allows you to test your web without connecting to the Internet.

physical codes In a web document, codes that provide specific directions on how to display text. For example, **<bold>** stands for bold. *Logical codes* give less precise instructions. For example, **<em>** means emphasis, which might mean bold or italic.

post To send a message to a newsgroup or a discussion group for all to see.

protocol A set of rules that governs the transfer of data between two computers.

relative reference In a web document, a link that refers to the location of another page or file in relation to the address of the current page. For example, if the page is in the /PUB directory, and a linked page is in /PUB/HOME, a relative reference might specify /HOME. An absolute reference would have to give the complete path (/PUB/HOME).

score In a search, a number that indicates the relative likelihood that a particular web page contains the information the user needs.

search tool A searchable index of Web pages. Popular Web search tools include Yahoo, WebCrawler, and Lycos. You can include your own search form in your web, so a user can search its pages for information.

service provider The company that you pay in order to connect to their computer so you can get on the Internet. Typically, you'll publish your FrontPage web to your service provider, although you can certainly choose a different provider if you want.

shareware Computer programs you can use for free and then pay for if you decide to continue using them. Many programmers use the Internet to distribute their programs, relying on the honesty and goodwill of Internet users for their income.

table Use a table to organize columnar data. A table consists of horizontal rows and vertical columns. The intersection of a row and a column creates a *cell.*

table of contents A listing that includes links to the pages in your web. You create a TOC using the Table of Contents bot.

tags HTML codes that work behind the scenes to tell a Web browser how to display a document and how to open other linked documents. Tags control the look of text, links, graphics, frames, and other page elements. An HTML tag is always surrounded by the < and > characters. See *HTML.*

template A fill-in-the-blanks web page, or a preconstructed web site.

thread In a FrontPage discussion group or a USENET newsgroup, threading is a way of grouping messages so the user can quickly see the order of a particular conversation.

tiled Repeating a graphic on a web page both horizontally and vertically.

To Do List The program within the FrontPage suite with which you can track tasks.

unordered list See *bulleted list.*

upload To copy a file from your computer to another computer. You usually upload files to share them with other users. See *download.*

URL (*Uniform Resource Locator*) An address for an Internet site. The Web uses URLs to specify the addresses of the various servers on the Internet and the documents on each server. For example, the URL for the White House server is **http://www.whitehouse.gov**. The **http** stands for HyperText Transfer Protocol, which means this is a Web document. **www** stands for World Wide Web; **whitehouse** stands for White House; **gov** stands for Government.

USENET (*user's network*) USENET sets the standards by which the various newsgroups swap information. See *newsgroup*.

VRML (*Virtual Reality Modeling Language*) VRML is a method that enables a Web browser to bring a seemingly three-dimensional world to life on a PC's two-dimensional screen. If you include a link to a VRML file on a Web page, the user must have a Web browser or a separate helper program that can play VRML files in order to view it.

WebBot A tool that automates certain web page functions.

Web browser Any of several programs you can use to navigate the World Wide Web. The Web browser reads the HTML codes in a web page in order to display it properly on the user's screen. Netscape Navigator and Internet Explorer are popular Web browsers.

web page A document that is viewed with a Web browser.

Web master The person who created and maintains a web document. (This is *you*.)

Web server A specialized computer on the Internet that's devoted to storing and serving up web documents. To publish your FrontPage web, you'll select a Web server (host server).

wizard A web site or web page creation guide.

World Wide Web A collection of interconnected documents stored on computers all over the world. These documents can contain text, pictures, movie clips, sounds, and links to other documents. You move from one document to another by clicking links.

WWW See *World Wide Web*.

WYSIWYG (*What-you-see-is-what-you-get*) When a document is presented on-screen in WYSIWYG mode, it is displayed as it will appear when printed.

zip To compress a file so that it takes up less space and transfers more quickly. If you provide a link to a zipped file, the user must unzip it before she can use it.

Index

Symbols

A

B

C

D

E

F

G

H

I

J

K

L

M

N

O

P

T

Installing FrontPage

Installing FrontPage is not difficult; if you've installed one Windows program, you've installed them all. However, when installing FrontPage, you might encounter a few bumps along the way. Just follow these steps:

Whoa, Nellie!

Before you can install FrontPage, you have to buy a copy first or download it off of the Microsoft Web site, located at http://www.microsoft.com. Of course, like everything Microsoft, FrontPage is not free. Make sure that you pay the proper fee for using FrontPage before you start using it to build your Web site.

1. Open **Explorer** or **File Manager** and double-click the **FrontPage file**. The files it contains will unzip and appear in the current directory.
2. After the WinZip utility stops doing its thing (unzipping or expanding the files), close the DOS window to get it out of the way.
3. Switch back to **Explorer** or **File Manager**, and double-click the newly unzipped **SETUP.EXE** file that you'll find there.
4. You'll see a warning telling you to close your other programs (in case the installation program whigs out and locks up your PC). Do so and then click **Next>**.
5. If you want, you can change the directory in which FrontPage will be placed. Most people don't bother with this, since it's easier to choose the default directory, but if you have a unique system for structuring the data on your PC, then it's worth the time to select the exact place where you want FrontPage installed. Just click **Browse**, select a directory, and then click **OK**. Click **Next>**.
6. Select the **Typical** installation option and click **Next>**.
7. Again, if you want, you can change the default directory. This time, you're selecting the directory where you want the Personal Web Server to appear. To do that, click **Browse**, select the directory you want, and then click **OK**. Then, click **Next>**.
8. You can select the folder in which to place the FrontPage icons. Click **Next>**.
9. Verify your selections and then click **Next>** to start the installation.

10. Enter the login name and password you want to use while working with your FrontPage web. The password prevents uglies from changing your web pages without your knowledge. Your login name and password *cannot* contain any spaces. Type your password again, just to see if you can. Then click **OK**.

Two's a Crowd

If you plan on distributing the workload and allowing some of your co-workers to participate in the "fun" of maintaining your web site, you can assign them separate login names and passwords. See Chapter 23 for help.

Locked Out

If you forget your password, you're locked out—in other words, you won't be able to open your web and make changes to it. So write your password down and store it in a safe place. If you forget your password, you'll have no choice but to reinstall FrontPage and start over.

11. Click **Finish**. If you want to go home and you don't feel like playing now, deselect the **Start the FrontPage Explorer now** option before you click **Finish**.
12. FrontPage will wave its magic wand and search your system for the name of your Internet server (host name). Click **OK** to begin.
13. That's all there is to the FrontPage installation! Click **OK**.

GET CONNECTED
to the ultimate source of computer information!

The MCP Forum on CompuServe

Go online with the world's leading computer book publisher! Macmillan Computer Publishing offers everything you need for computer success!

Find the books that are right for you!

A complete online catalog, plus sample chapters and tables of contents give you an in-depth look at all our books. The best way to shop or browse!

- Get fast answers and technical support for MCP books and software
- Join discussion groups on major computer subjects
- Interact with our expert authors via e-mail and conferences
- Download software from our immense library:
  - Source code from books
  - Demos of hot software
  - The best shareware and freeware
  - Graphics files

Join now and get a free CompuServe Starter Kit!

To receive your free CompuServe Introductory Membership, call **1-800-848-8199** and ask for representative #597.

The Starter Kit includes:

- Personal ID number and password
- $15 credit on the system
- Subscription to *CompuServe Magazine*

Once on the CompuServe System, type:

GO MACMILLAN

for the most computer information anywhere!

MACMILLAN COMPUTER PUBLISHING

CompuServe

A VIACOM SERVICE

The Information SuperLibrary™

CHECK OUT THE BOOKS IN THIS LIBRARY.

You'll find thousands of shareware files and over 1600 computer books designed for both technowizards and technophobes. You can browse through 700 sample chapters, get the latest news on the Net, and find just about anything using our massive search directories.

All Macmillan Computer Publishing books are available at your local bookstore.

We're open 24-hours a day, 365 days a year.

You don't need a card.

We don't charge fines.

And you can be as **LOUD** as you want.

The Information SuperLibrary

http://www.mcp.com/mcp/ ftp.mcp.com

Copyright © 1996, Macmillan Computer Publishing USA A Simon & Schuster Company

Complete and Return this Card for a *FREE* Computer Book Catalog

Thank you for purchasing this book! You have purchased a superior computer book written expressly for your needs. To continue to provide the kind of up-to-date, pertinent coverage you've come to expect from us, we need to hear from you. Please take a minute to complete and return this self-addressed, postage-paid form. In return, we'll send you a free catalog of all our computer books on topics ranging from word processing to programming and the internet.

r. ☐ Mrs. ☐ Ms. ☐ Dr. ☐

ame (first) ☐☐☐☐☐☐☐☐☐☐☐ (M.I.) ☐ (last) ☐☐☐☐☐☐☐☐☐☐☐☐☐☐☐

ddress ☐☐☐☐☐☐☐☐☐☐☐☐☐☐☐☐☐☐☐☐☐☐☐☐☐☐☐☐☐☐☐☐☐☐☐

☐☐☐☐☐☐☐☐☐☐☐☐☐☐☐☐☐☐☐☐☐☐☐☐☐☐☐☐☐☐☐☐☐☐☐

ty ☐☐☐☐☐☐☐☐☐☐☐☐☐☐☐ State ☐☐ Zip ☐☐☐☐☐ ☐☐☐☐

ıone ☐☐☐ ☐☐☐ ☐☐☐☐ Fax ☐☐☐ ☐☐☐ ☐☐☐☐

ɔmpany Name ☐☐☐☐☐☐☐☐☐☐☐☐☐☐☐☐☐☐☐☐☐☐☐☐☐☐☐☐☐☐☐☐☐

mail address ☐☐☐☐☐☐☐☐☐☐☐☐☐☐☐☐☐☐☐☐☐☐☐☐☐☐☐☐☐☐☐☐☐

Please check at least (3) influencing factors for purchasing this book.

- ont or back cover information on book ☐
- ecial approach to the content ☐
- ɔmpleteness of content ☐
- ıthor's reputation ☐
- blisher's reputation ☐
- ɔok cover design or layout ☐
- dex or table of contents of book ☐
- ice of book ☐
- ecial effects, graphics, illustrations ☐
- her (Please specify): ______________ ☐

How did you first learn about this book?

- w in Macmillan Computer Publishing catalog ☐
- commended by store personnel ☐
- w the book on bookshelf at store ☐
- commended by a friend ☐
- ceived advertisement in the mail ☐
- w an advertisement in: ______________ ☐
- ad book review in: ______________ ☐
- her (Please specify): ______________ ☐

How many computer books have you purchased in the last six months?

- is book only ☐
- ɔoks ☐
- 3 to 5 books ☐
- More than 5 ☐

4. Where did you purchase this book?

- Bookstore ☐
- Computer Store ☐
- Consumer Electronics Store ☐
- Department Store ☐
- Office Club ☐
- Warehouse Club ☐
- Mail Order ☐
- Direct from Publisher ☐
- Internet site ☐
- Other (Please specify): ______________ ☐

5. How long have you been using a computer?

- ☐ Less than 6 months
- ☐ 6 months to a year
- ☐ 1 to 3 years
- ☐ More than 3 years

6. What is your level of experience with personal computers and with the subject of this book?

	With PCs	With subject of book
New	☐	☐
Casual	☐	☐
Accomplished	☐	☐
Expert	☐	☐

Source Code ISBN: 0-7897-0928-7

7. Which of the following best describes your job title?

- Administrative Assistant ☐
- Coordinator ☐
- Manager/Supervisor ☐
- Director ☐
- Vice President ☐
- President/CEO/COO ☐
- Lawyer/Doctor/Medical Professional ☐
- Teacher/Educator/Trainer ☐
- Engineer/Technician ☐
- Consultant ☐
- Not employed/Student/Retired ☐
- Other (Please specify): ____________ ☐

8. Which of the following best describes the area of the company your job title falls under?

- Accounting ☐
- Engineering ☐
- Manufacturing ☐
- Operations ☐
- Marketing ☐
- Sales ☐
- Other (Please specify): ____________ ☐

9. What is your age?

- Under 20
- 21-29
- 30-39
- 40-49
- 50-59
- 60-over

10. Are you:

- Male
- Female

11. Which computer publications do you read regularly? (Please list)

____

Comments: ____________________

Fold here and scotch-tape to m

NO POSTAGE NECESSARY IF MAILED IN THE UNITED STATES

BUSINESS REPLY MAIL

FIRST-CLASS MAIL PERMIT NO. 9918 INDIANAPOLIS IN

POSTAGE WILL BE PAID BY THE ADDRESSEE

ATTN MARKETING
MACMILLAN COMPUTER PUBLISHING
MACMILLAN PUBLISHING USA
201 W 103RD ST
INDIANAPOLIS IN 46290-9042